Palgrave Studies in the Enlightenment, Romanticism and Cultures of Print
General Editors: **Professor Anne K. Mellor** and **Professor Clifford Siskin**
Editorial Board: **Isobel Armstrong**, Birkbeck & IES; **John Bender**, Stanford; **Alan Bewell**, Toronto; **Peter de Bolla**, Cambridge; **Robert Miles**, Victoria; **Claudia L. Johnson**, Princeton; **Saree Makdisi**, UCLA; **Felicity Nussbaum**, UCLA; **Mary Poovey**, NYU; **Janet Todd**, Cambridge

Palgrave Studies in the Enlightenment, Romanticism and Cultures of Print will feature work that does not fit comfortably within established boundaries—whether between periods or between disciplines. Uniquely, it will combine efforts to engage the power and materiality of print with explorations of gender, race, and class. By attending as well to intersections of literature with the visual arts, medicine, law, and science, the series will enable a large-scale rethinking of the origins of modernity.

Titles include:

Scott Black
OF ESSAYS AND READING IN EARLY MODERN BRITAIN

Claire Brock
THE FEMINIZATION OF FAME, 1750–1830

Brycchan Carey
BRITISH ABOLITIONISM AND THE RHETORIC OF SENSIBILITY
Writing, Sentiment, and Slavery, 1760–1807

E. J. Clery
THE FEMINIZATION DEBATE IN 18TH-CENTURY ENGLAND
Literature, Commerce and Luxury

Adriana Craciun
BRITISH WOMEN WRITERS AND THE FRENCH REVOLUTION
Citizens of the World

Peter de Bolla, Nigel Leask and David Simpson (*editors*)
LAND, NATION AND CULTURE, 1740–1840
Thinking the Republic of Taste

Elizabeth Eger
BLUESTOCKINGS
Women of Reason from Enlightenment to Romanticism

Ina Ferris and Paul Keen (*editors*)
BOOKISH HISTORIES
Books, Literature, and Commercial Modernity, 1700–1900

George C. Grinnell
THE AGE OF HYPOCHONDRIA
Interpreting Romantic Health and Illness

Ian Haywood
BLOODY ROMANTICISM
Spectacular Violence and the Politics of Representation, 1776–1832

Anthony S. Jarrells
BRITAIN'S BLOODLESS REVOLUTIONS
1688 and the Romantic Reform of Literature

Michelle Levy
FAMILY AUTHORSHIP AND ROMANTIC PRINT CULTURE

April London
LITERARY HISTORY WRITING, 1770–1820

Robert Miles
ROMANTIC MISFITS

Tom Mole
BYRON'S ROMANTIC CELEBRITY
Industrial Culture and the Hermeneutic of Intimacy

Nicola Parsons
READING GOSSIP IN EARLY EIGHTEENTH-CENTURY ENGLAND

Andrew Rudd
SYMPATHY AND INDIA IN BRITISH LITERATURE, 1770–1830

Erik Simpson
LITERARY MINSTRELSY, 1770–1830
Minstrels and Improvisers in British, Irish and American Literature

Anne H. Stevens
BRITISH HISTORICAL FICTION BEFORE SCOTT

David Stewart
ROMANTIC MAGAZINES AND METROPOLITAN LITERARY CULTURE

Mary Waters
BRITISH WOMEN WRITERS AND THE PROFESSION OF LITERARY CRITICISM, 1789–1832

Esther Wohlgemut
ROMANTIC COSMOPOLITANISM

David Worrall
THE POLITICS OF ROMANTIC THEATRICALITY, 1787–1832
The Road to the Stage

**Palgrave Studies in the Enlightenment, Romanticism and Cultures of Print
Series Standing Order ISBN 978–1–4039–3408–6 hardback
978–1–4039–3409–3 paperback**
(*outside North America only*)

You can receive future titles in this series as they are published by placing a standing order. Please contact your bookseller or, in case of difficulty, write to us at the address below with your name and address, the title of the series and the ISBN quoted above.

Customer Services Department, Macmillan Distribution Ltd, Houndmills, Basingstoke, Hampshire RG21 6XS, England

Sympathy and India in British Literature, 1770–1830

Andrew Rudd

© Andrew Rudd 2011

All rights reserved. No reproduction, copy or transmission of this publication may be made without written permission.

No portion of this publication may be reproduced, copied or transmitted save with written permission or in accordance with the provisions of the Copyright, Designs and Patents Act 1988, or under the terms of any licence permitting limited copying issued by the Copyright Licensing Agency, Saffron House, 6–10 Kirby Street, London EC1N 8TS.

Any person who does any unauthorized act in relation to this publication may be liable to criminal prosecution and civil claims for damages.

The author has asserted his right to be identified as the author of this work in accordance with the Copyright, Designs and Patents Act 1988.

First published 2010 by
PALGRAVE MACMILLAN

Palgrave Macmillan in the UK is an imprint of Macmillan Publishers Limited, registered in England, company number 785998, of Houndmills, Basingstoke, Hampshire RG21 6XS.

Palgrave Macmillan in the US is a division of St Martin's Press LLC,
175 Fifth Avenue, New York, NY 10010.

Palgrave Macmillan is the global academic imprint of the above companies and has companies and representatives throughout the world.

Palgrave® and Macmillan® are registered trademarks in the United States, the United Kingdom, Europe and other countries.

ISBN 978–0–230–23339–3   hardback

This book is printed on paper suitable for recycling and made from fully managed and sustained forest sources. Logging, pulping and manufacturing processes are expected to conform to the environmental regulations of the country of origin.

A catalogue record for this book is available from the British Library.

Library of Congress Cataloging-in-Publication Data
Rudd, Andrew, 1979–
Sympathy and India in British literature, 1770–1830 / Andrew Rudd.
  p. cm.
Includes index.
ISBN 978–0–230–23339–3 (hardback)
 1. English literature—18th century—History and criticism. 2. English literature—19th century—History and criticism. 3. India—In literature. 4. Orientalism in literature. I. Title.
PR448.I534R83 2011
820.935854—dc22   2011004367

10 9 8 7 6 5 4 3 2 1
20 19 18 17 16 15 14 13 12 11

Printed and bound in Great Britain by
CPI Antony Rowe, Chippenham and Eastbourne

For my parents

Contents

List of Figures	viii
Acknowledgements	ix
Introduction	1
1 Edmund Burke and the Trial of Warren Hastings	26
2 'No Less Pious than Sublime': The Sympathetic Vision of Sir William Jones	56
3 Sympathy in a Hot Climate: British and Indian Subjects at the Turn of the Century	87
4 Gothic Sympathy and Missionary Writing	117
5 Reorientating the Orient: Sympathy, the East and Romantic Period Literary Criticism	140
Epilogue: Orientalism under Pressure	165
Notes	169
Sources	195
Index	213

List of Figures

1.1 James Sayers, *Galante Show 'Redeunt Spectacula Mane'* (1788)
     Courtesy of the Lewis Walpole Library, Yale University   44
1.2 James Gillray, *Camera-Obscura* (1788)
     Courtesy of the British Museum   45
1.3 James Sayers, *Last Scene of the Managers Farce* (1795)
     Courtesy of the Lewis Walpole Library, Yale University   53
2.1 Arthur William Devis, *Sir William Jones* (1793)
     Courtesy of the British Library   71
3.1 Thomas Daniell, *View of Calcutta* (1786–8)
     Courtesy of the British Library   94

Acknowledgements

The book began as a doctoral thesis at the University of Cambridge. My first debt is to my supervisor, Nigel Leask, whose work on Romanticism and the East was the inspiration for my own project. Sincere thanks are due to Trinity College, Cambridge, for providing an exemplary research environment and support, including funding for a research visit to India through the Cambridge Commonwealth Trust and Eddington Fund. The project could not have been completed without financial support from the AHRB (now the AHRC) who funded my postgraduate studies in their entirety. I would also like to thank Maggie K. Powell and the staff of the Lewis Walpole Library, Yale University, for a fruitful pre-doctoral fellowship in 2004. To my hosts in India, Sriram Kilambi and Cherry Verghese, I am under enormous obligation for their unfailingly generous hospitality. The expertise of librarians at the British Library, Cambridge University Library's Rare Books department, the Bodleian Library (Rhodes House) and the Beinecke Rare Books and Manuscripts Library has been instrumental to my research.

Many friends and colleagues have given advice, guidance and moral support along the way. Among them are Nigel Aston, Piers Baker-Bates, C.A. Bayly, Timothy Brittain-Catlin, Peter Cochran, Joanna de Groot, Georgina Evans, Michael J. Franklin, Katie Halsey, Howard Erskine-Hill, Mary Jacobus, Sarah Johnson, Louise Joy, Howard Leithead, P.J. Marshall, Jenny McAuley, Philip O'Connell, Jane Partner, Adrian Poole, Stephen Parkes, Lynda Pratt, Sophie Read, Rosane Rocher, Andrew Sanders, Alison Shell, Jane Slinn, A.J. Stockwell, Kate Teltscher, Shafquat Towheed, Andy Tucker and Angus Vine.

Profound thanks are due to Jonathan Sanders, Alison Shell and Arnold Hunt for reading the manuscript in the final stages. Any remaining errors are, of course, my own. At Palgrave Macmillan I wish to thank Paula Kennedy for her help in bringing this book to fruition.

Chapter 4 was previously published in a chapter of *New Readings in the Literature of British India* (Stuttgart: ibidem-Verlag, 2007), ISBN 978 3 89821 673 9, ed. Shafquat Towheed, and is republished with the kind permission of ibidem-Verlag. Chapter 5 was previously published in *Romanticism* 13.1 (2007) and reappears courtesy of Edinburgh University Press (the original can be consulted at http://www.eupjournals.com/journal/com).

Finally, thanks to my parents and my sister Catherine. I owe more than words can express to Paul Burditt for his love and encouragement.

Introduction

> Facts coming from afar made little impression: their novelty could not rouse, nor their variety amuse the mind. With a self-denial uncommon in a spirited nation, we heard, without emotion, of the great actions of some of our countrymen; and, if we listened to any detail of oppressions committed by others, it was with a phlegmatic indifference, unworthy of our boasted humanity.
>
> Alexander Dow, *The History of Hindostan* (1768)[1]

It may at first sight seem perverse to write of sympathy and India in a study of late eighteenth- and early nineteenth-century British literature. This, after all, was a time when the East India Company, following the Mughal Emperor Shah Alam II's bestowal of *diwani* in 1765, was transformed from a trading body into a significant regional military and political power. A chartered company of merchants with a minimum of supervision suddenly found itself lord and master of a vast and populous tranche of the subcontinent. Questions were raised, in Britain and around the world, about the moral propriety of a commercial organisation presiding over the welfare of tens of millions of people. Public outrage galvanised around the famine of 1769–70, in which over 10 million Bengalis died of starvation, and the alleged despotic rule of the Governor-General, Warren Hastings, who stood trial for 'high crimes and misdemeanours' before the House of Lords between 1788 and 1795. The Company was accused of the economic exploitation of India through its trading monopoly and depredations and annexations through the force of arms. In terms of conventional postcolonial analysis, dealings between Britain and India in this period would appear to leave little room for benevolent fellow-feeling.

One of the arguments of this book is that it was precisely because of India's status as an object of humanitarian concern that sympathy is visible in British literature on the subject. This study explores the uses of sympathy in relation to colonisation in India as it appears in the literature of the late eighteenth century and Romantic period. It examines changing representations of India as a literary topic and the aesthetic underpinnings of British Orientalist literature, which, as a result of Britain's deepening involvement there, centred on India and the surrounding region. At the outset, it is worth clarifying the sense in which the term 'sympathy' will be employed and discussed over the course of this book. There has been a great deal of recent critical interest in imaginative sympathy, which may be briefly described as the faculty of mind whereby a person can enter into the thoughts and feelings of another through the exercise of imagination. It is distinct from sensibility, the underlying capacity to feel, and the moral sentiment, the currency in which emotional ideas are transferred. The roots of this formulation of sympathy are generally traced to the moral philosophy of the mid eighteenth century, notably the writings of Scottish Enlightenment thinkers such as Francis Hutcheson, David Hume and Adam Smith. These figures analysed for the first time how the passions were stirred and directed by objects of contemplation, notably by spectacles of suffering and distress, to which the human mind was naturally drawn in accordance (it could be argued) with the will of a beneficent creator. Sympathy depended first and foremost on the awakening of 'interest' in an object; consequently the objects most powerfully generative of sympathy were those that struck at the vitals of the sense of self.

These early treatises on sympathy shared a distinctively sceptical view of the outward limits of the mind that the book will argue problematised Britain's imaginative encounter with India at a fundamental level. Eighteenth-century moral philosophers remarked upon two qualities of sympathy which, if followed to their logical conclusions, placed any attempt to conceive of a remote and culturally different nation such as India in doubt. The first concerned spatial difference: the strength of an idea was held to be in proportion to its physical proximity to the self, so that a person sympathises more readily with someone or something that is close at hand (hence the discourse of sympathy privileged the immediacy of eyewitness accounts). As the extract from Alexander Dow's *The History of Hindostan* (1773) shows, the diminished force of ideas 'coming from afar' was a recognised facet of imaginative engagement with India from the beginning and India's seeming inability to stir the passions disturbingly exposed how tightly the culture of sensibility could be circumscribed. Hume argued that the outermost boundary of imaginative sympathy was the nation state, and believed that the transfer of ideas within the polity was constitutive of national character but could travel no further. The second was the imagination's selectiveness in gravitating towards certain objects, creating what might be termed a hierarchy of affect. The sociable transfer of ideas teaches us to sympathise with what is most recognisable to us, hence the imagination cannot easily access what is culturally unfamiliar. Postcolonial criticism schematises this as a dichotomy of self and other and this book likewise seeks to uncover many contradictions and pressures in the ambiguous space of the colonial contact zone.[2]

As Jonathan Lamb has shown in his seminal study *The Evolution of Sympathy in the Long Eighteenth Century* (2009), the conception of sympathy was never static, nor was there consensus about its nature and operations. The imaginative framework sketched out above refers to what Lamb categorises as 'mechanical' sympathy, the more rigid delineations found in the works of moral philosophers.[3] Over the successive decades, manifold branches and gradations of sympathy developed in dialogue with cultural, social, and political developments, notably the French Revolution, whose excesses in the eyes of many in Britain were steeped in a suspect form of false sensibility. Authors of the Romantic period evolved their own concepts of sympathy, which were sometimes habituated to the point of invisibility, one reason for their only relatively recent scholarly excavation. These changes coincided with dramatic developments in the colonial sphere that provide a chronological logic for this book, and are intended to help draw parallels between literary culture in Britain and colonial activity in India. One fascinating paradox of British writing on India is that, while the 'exotic East' was deemed to be highly modish subject matter (as numerous studies of Orientalist writing attest), the hard imaginative labour required to depict it often confounded reading audiences and thwarted many an aspiring Orientalist author. This book will seek to demonstrate the nature and range of problems engendered by imaginative engagement with India in colonial writing of the period as well as the aesthetic strategies that were evolved to surmount them.[4]

Thomas Campbell's popular and critically acclaimed poem of 1799, *The Pleasures of Hope*, offers a clear and indeed typical illustration of the thematic convergence of sympathy and India that occurred during the period in question. The poem was a carefully crafted blend of sentimentalism, moderate Whig politics and Orientalism. In the words of Geoffrey Carnall it was 'peculiarly welcome to those in sympathy with political reform who were at their most despondent over the bloodshed of the French Revolution'.[5] The formula was evidently to the public taste, for 17,000 copies were sold between 1799 and 1826.[6] The poem consists of a sequence of scenes in which individuals are sustained through their misery by Hope, personified as a goddess. In the first scene, a mother anxiously watches over the 'couch where infant beauty sleeps', hoping that her son will enjoy better prospects than his absent father; the next features a madwoman who continually scans the horizon for her dead sailor husband's return; in the third, we glimpse an itinerant beggar who passes a rustic cottage and wishes that 'for me some home like this would smile, / Some hamlet shade, to yield my sickly form'.[7] Such tropes were commonplace in sentimental literature and do little more than account for the poem's popular appeal. More remarkable, and by way of introduction to the subject of this book, is the extension of Campbell's compassionate conspectus to India. Like ripples on the water, the poem steadily expands its horizons from the personal to the domestic and finally to the international as the poet considers 'the wrongs of fate, the woes of human kind', which are transmuted by Hope into 'blissful omens' and 'boundless fields of rapture yet to be' (p. 25). Campbell embarks on a panoramic sweep across the deserts of Libya, the salt mines of Siberia and the African slave coast by way of Poland, then embroiled in its struggle for independence (a cause to which Campbell was particularly devoted). He denounces 'tyrants' who 'in vain trace ... the wizard ring' and 'limit mind's unwearied spring', which leads him to the topic of India, whose Mughal rulers were synonymous with Oriental despotism in the contemporary British imagination (p. 33).

Campbell recounts India's history of oppression beneath 'Timur's iron sceptre' before posing an elaborate rhetorical question to its Hindu population:

> When Europe fought your subject realms to gain,
> And stretch'd her giant sceptre o'er the main,
> Taught her proud barks their winding way to shape,
> And brav'd the stormy spirit of the Cape;
> Children of Brama! then was mercy nigh
> To wash the stain of blood's eternal dye?
> Did Peace descend, to triumph and to save,
> When free-born Britons cross'd the Indian wave?

> Ah, no! to more than Rome's ambition true,
> The Nurse of Freedom gave it not to you!
> She the bold route of Europe's guilt began,
> And, in the march of nations, led the van! (p. 42)

The bold and adventuring language of the earlier lines gives way to the more emotive image of the Hindus as 'children' stained with blood from centuries of oppression. Britain has acted towards them not as a nursemaid relieving the horrors of tyranny but as a Roman conqueror. The play of emotions here aims to expose the manifest inconsistency of Britons who boast of liberty but do not grant it to their Indian subjects, a recurring claim levelled against the colonial enterprise through the era under discussion. The sentimental tone predicates a common humanity between Britons and Indians that challenges the hypocrisy of the colonial encounter.

The Indian section of Campbell's poem contains a mixture of references to the contemporary East India Company and borrowings from the Orientalist scholarship associated with Sir William Jones and his followers. In the former category, Campbell indicts the Company's response to the Bengal famine. Company officials were accused of exacerbating the disaster through their apparent reluctance to distribute stockpiled crops to the population.[8] The anger that Campbell directs against the Company's servants, 'rich in the gems of India's gaudy zone, / And plunder pil'd from kingdoms not their own', suggests that the famine had lost none of its moral piquancy over the two decades prior to the appearance of the poem (p. 43). He decries the iniquities of colonial trade in a series of detailed references to the disaster:

> Degenerate Trade! thy minions could despise
> The heart-felt anguish of a thousand cries;
> Could lock, with impious hands, their teeming store,
> While famish'd nations died along the shore;
> Could mock the groans of fellow-men, and bear,
> The curse of kingdoms peopled with despair;
> Could stamp disgrace on Nature's hollow name,
> And barter, with their gold, eternal shame! (p. 43)

The register of the poem then switches to one of Orientalist esotericism. Amidst a portentous storm, Brahma appears, 'with murmuring wrath, and thunders from on high' to 'pour redress on India's injur'd realm / The oppressor to dethrone, the proud to whelm' (pp. 44–5).

Campbell confuses Brahma with the tenth avatar of Vishnu, Kalki, as he vanquishes the Company and its lackeys and restores 'primeval peace' to India (p. 46). Brahma's singular intervention in the affairs of a modern joint-stock company of merchants unwittingly evokes the Hindu Puranas, in which past and present intermingle and gods and mortals walk the earth together. Campbell explains in an endnote that the Hindu gods 'Ganesa' and 'Seraswatee' correspond to 'the Pagan deities, Janus and Minerva', which suggests that Campbell was familiar with Jones's essay 'On the Gods of Greece, Italy and India' (published in 1788), where parallels between the Hindu and the classical pantheons were adumbrated (p. 89).[9] Yet despite the exoticism these names lend to the poem, they also serve as reminders that spontaneous fellow-feeling towards India and Hinduism did not come naturally to British readers. Writers who offered Eastern fare to the reading public were frequently obliged to insert signposts to more familiar frames of reference.

The Pleasures of Hope is typical in several respects of the Orientalist genre of writing not least in combining the exoticism of Indian mythology with the more mundane reportage of topical colonial events. India is presented paradoxically as a land of infinite wealth and a site of immeasurable suffering, the twin legacies of Oriental despotism. Additionally, the poem is situated within a nexus of Orientalist texts that continuously cross-fertilised each other, witnessed in the extensive explanatory notes to other publications found within and at the margins of the poem. On the subject of despotism Campbell cites the pro-Hindu prefatory essay from Elizabeth Hamilton's *Translation of the Letters of a Hindoo Rajah* (1789), whilst on the depredations of the East India Company he quotes an extract from the anonymous *Short History of the English Transactions in the East Indies* (1776), a work also used as an authority on India in Samuel Johnson's *Lives* (1779–81). In other ways the poem belongs to the unique corpus of imaginative writing on India that constitutes the particular focus of this study. The more amorphous notion of the 'fabulous Orient' that Ros Ballaster has delineated runs counter to the economic, military and political specificity of the Indian experience in Britain at the end of the eighteenth century.[10] Many of Campbell's readers would have been personally acquainted with individuals who lived, worked or had a financial stake in the East Indies and all would have been familiar with the controversies and debates surrounding the East India Company's activities there. Some writers of the time had a direct financial take in the Company, notably Thomas Love Peacock, who rose to become Examiner of Correspondence (preceded by James Mill and succeeded by John Stuart Mill) at the Company's headquarters in Leadenhall Street; others, such as Shelley and Robert Southey, enquired about the possibility of obtaining posts there.[11] The exotic tropes of Orientalism could not in fact be applied to British India without reference to its more mundane status as a dominion of the Company. Such tropes certainly could be and regularly were subverted for personal or political purposes, but India called forth a host of topical associations in ways that other 'Orientalisms' did not.[12]

The overt sentimentalism of *The Pleasures of Hope* seems far removed from the pioneering *Lyrical Ballads* of Wordsworth and Coleridge published in the previous year. Yet the sentimental mode was uniquely suited to writing on India for several reasons. In the first place, its accent on emotionality and affect lent itself to sympathetic engagement with contemporary rather than historical subject matter. Sentimental literature was addressed to a modern readership and, in portraying scenarios that were rooted in modern life, aspired to be an instrument of moral edification. This offered rich potential for authors who wished to incite indignation against the East India Company and alert readers to what was being done in Britain's name on the subcontinent. The habitual gendering of India as female also reinforced the sympathetic drama of Bengal as the virtuous maid in distress, nabobs the circling rakes. It is highly significant that in *The Pleasures of Hope* Campbell 'mourns' the world's sufferings with a 'sympathizing mind' for in doing so he invokes a set of aesthetic conventions with a defined ethical function that was integral to the culture of sentimentalism overall as it was formulated in the period (p. 25). The brand of sentimentalism that underpinned the original notion of sympathy has traditionally been regarded as having been replaced with the more solipsistic ideologies of Romanticism by the latter years of the eighteenth century. However, several tenets of sentimental literature and imaginative sympathy in particular remained fundamental to theories of literature around the turn of the nineteenth century and beyond.[13] This, coupled with the undeniable fact that writing on India was not amongst the most innovative being produced during these years, meant that sentimental conceptualisations of sympathy survived as vital parts of Romantic literary culture, most strikingly in the context of colonial exile where they flourished with a hybrid vigour.

The changes in Britain's relations with India over the course of the eighteenth century were so momentous that some contemporaries had difficulty grasping the scale of responsibility involved whilst others were cowed with awe.[14] The Mughal Emperor Shah Alam II's grant in 1765 of *diwani* (the right to raise revenues) over the so-called 'triple presidency' of Bengal, Bihar and Orissa effectively handed the

Company a licence to govern. But according to whose traditions should British India, that perplexing grafting together of divergent traditions, be governed? Worryingly for some in Britain, under the governorship of Warren Hastings (Governor-General of Bengal in 1772–73 and Governor-General of India in 1773–85), the colonial administration upheld Mughal customs such as the ritual exchange of gifts and titles and the sponsorship of local religious festivals.[15] Simultaneously, the alleged corruption of Company servants, dubbed 'nabobs' (after the Persian word *nawab*, meaning a deputy of the Mughal Emperor), who earned vast fortunes from illegal private trade, led to accusations that some Britons were 'going native' and taking on the aspect of Oriental despots whom they had supposedly supplanted for the better. Successive measures were enacted by the government in London to bind the Company to centralised control. Lord North's Regulating Act of 1777 established a Supreme Council, based in India, to supervise the affairs of Calcutta, Madras and Bombay; William Pitt's more substantial East India Act of 1784 created a parliamentary Board of Control to scrutinise the Company's own Board of Directors; and Lord Cornwallis's Permanent Settlement of 1793 introduced British-style laws of land tenure to Bengal that have been described by C.A. Bayly as precipitating a 'virtual revolution in the concept of property' in Asia.[16] Some in Britain (labelled 'Orientalists' by Eric Stokes, one of the many diffuse applications of the term) continued to favour a form of government that preserved ancient Indian laws, usages and customs; others ('Anglicists') held that it was more just for India to be governed according to British principles.[17] Military victories over the Sultanate of Mysore in 1799 and the Maratha Confederacy in 1808 contributed to a mounting sense that Providence favoured the British cause. The growing evangelical movement in Britain around the turn of the nineteenth century seized upon Britain's military successes in India as evidence that colonial occupation of India was divinely inspired.

The exponential growth in published titles relating to India appeared to shadow the expansion of Britain's territorial possessions there. Indeed, many works of scholarship were directly dependent on the physical access that colonial expansion in the Indian regions afforded. Mark Wilks's *Historical Sketches of the South of India, in an Attempt to Trace the History of Mysoor* (1810–17) was regarded by its author as an attempt to fill in an 'absolute blank' of local history, made possible only after the pacification of Mysore.[18] Similarly, towards the end of the years covered by this book, James Tod's *Annals and Antiquities of Rajast'han or the Central and Western Rajput States of India* (1829–32) was the product of years of primary research conducted whilst the author was political agent for the states of western Rajputana.[19] There was a great amassing of information on India following Sir William Jones's inauguration in Calcutta in 1784 of a 'society, for inquiring into the history, civil and natural, the antiquities, sciences and literature of Asia', the celebrated Asiatic Society of Bengal.[20] The Society's journal, *Asiatic(k) Researches* (published between 1788 and 1833), published a cornucopia of amateur scholarship on topics as diverse as Indian astronomy, ornithology, geography, a cure for elephantiasis, cave measurement and 'the spikenard of the ancients'. Key translations of Indian legal and religious texts, including Nathaniel Brassey Halhed's *A Code of Gentoo Laws* (1776), Charles Hamilton's *Hedàya; or, Guide: A Commentary on the Musselman Laws* (1791) and Jones's *Institutes of Hindu Law; or The Ordinances of Menu* (1794) have with some justification been interpreted as attempts by the colonial state to prise indigenous fingers, especially Brahmin ones, from the levers of knowledge and power.[21]

Despite this it would be a simplification straightforwardly to equate imaginative literature written about India with colonial power dynamics. The critical paradigm with which any study on this topic must engage is of course Edward W. Said's *Orientalism* (1978), which argued that from the late eighteenth century onwards 'Orientalism' was 'a Western style for dominating, restructuring, and having authority over the Orient'.[22] Notwithstanding the multiple revisions, refinements and outright refutations to which Said's work has been subjected over the past few decades, its abiding achievement that must be given due weight was to immerse texts that had previously been viewed uncritically, even indulgently, in isolation from their context in the energising stream of postcolonial politics. Since the inception of postcolonial literary criticism, it has become an ironic commonplace to describe Said's own view as monolithic and lacking in nuance, and indeed literature (as opposed to anthropology, history, legal studies, or other disciplines that could be said to 'fix' an object of study) through its inherent slipperiness remains uniquely difficult to yoke to the theory of Orientalism.[23] It would be problematic in the extreme to cast individual literary authors as mere agents of the colonial state given that many of the authors covered in this book, among them Burke, Jones, Robert Southey and Thomas Moore, sought to compromise, counteract or in some way reform existing colonial practices. The sentimental premises of sympathy moreover encouraged them to engage with colonised peoples as fellow subjects and equals, however naive or misguided such efforts may appear from a postcolonial perspective today. Like Christian missionaries, who frequently thwarted and acted at cross purposes to colonial officialdom, sentimental writers on India radically skewed prevailing systems by sympathising with colonised subjects on an individual level.[24]

The Enlightenment systems of thought from which sympathy emerged have in themselves been regarded as capable of subverting the very notion of imperialism.[25] In certain cases, sympathetic engagement with India complicated the activities of officials whose professions committed them to the enforcement of colonial power. For example, Jones and Hastings are often grouped together as cosmopolitan figures despite their status as colonial officials (Jones as a judge in the Bengal Supreme Court and Hastings as Governor-General). In his dedicatory epistle to Charles Wilkins's translation of *The Bhăgvăt-Gēētā* (1785), Hastings wrote that Hinduism's holy texts will survive 'when the British dominion in India shall have long ceased to exist, and when the sources which it once yielded of wealth and power are lost to remembrance', words that could be said to display a salutary cultural deference despite their author's expansionist policies.[26] Jones's description of the Gupta playwright Kalidasa in the preface to his translation of *Sacontalá; or, The Fatal Ring* (1789) as the 'Shakespeare of India' can similarly be seen as an attempt to elide cultural differences between Indian literature and the English canon.

Sympathy in India could be directed towards colonial actors suffering on Britain's behalf, as Linda Colley has shown in *Captives* (2002), which describes how atrocities such as the 'Black Hole of Calcutta' in 1756 and the military reversals of the Seven Years War (1756–63) produced myriad images of British suffering for sympathetic consumption by sentimentally inclined readers.[27] Yet the sympathetic gaze was overwhelmingly directed towards the indigenous victims of European colonialism, most compellingly African victims of transatlantic slave trade. The recent bicentenary of the Abolition of the Slave Trade Act in 1807 restored to public prominence Josiah Wedgwood's medal with its celebrated motto, 'AM I NOT A MAN AND A BROTHER?', an icon of sympathetic fellow-feeling in the face of suffering.[28] If the very figure of the slave was pitiful, his plight was painful for Europeans to contemplate, as Coleridge appreciated when he remarked in a lecture given in Bristol in 1795 that 'it would lacerate the feelings too much to detail the dreadful cruelties exercised upon the negro slaves. The diminution of the human species by this infernal trade mocks calculation'.[29] It may well be argued that the application of sympathy to scenarios of genuine suffering, as opposed to those found in works of fiction, fostered a cult of morbid voyeurism in which emotion was awakened at the expense of actual action. Peter Hulme has interpreted this process as another type of consumerism, writing that as the eighteenth century wore on 'sentimental sympathy began to flow out along the arteries of European commerce in search of its victims'.[30] In fairness sympathy was employed in the late eighteenth and early nineteenth centuries much as some charitable publicity material is today: to elicit compassion for suffering individuals as part of an emotional call to arms. Then as now it is a mode of representation open to the charge of moral exploitation.

Advocates of free trade opposed slavery and mercantilism alike on economic grounds, but it fell to dissenting and evangelical groups, prominent among them the so-called Clapham Sect associated with William Wilberforce, Charles Grant and Lord Teignmouth, to focus moral outrage on colonial misdemeanours committed overseas. Adapting Vincent Harlow's phrase, P.J. Marshall has introduced the concept of a 'moral swing to the East' taking place in the decades either side of 1800.[31] As concern mounted in Britain about the East India Company's conduct in India, the subcontinent increasingly became a pole for sympathetic concern. Unsurprisingly, the same people who campaigned for the abolition of slavery also enquired into the moral state of British East India. The poem *Tea and Sugar; or, The Nabob and the Creole* (1792) by 'Timothy Touchstone' neatly illustrates the imaginative links that could be forged between India and slavery. The poem, consisting of two cantos, employs the staple products commonly associated with India and the West Indies as metonyms for the unthinking consumption by the coloniser of the colonised. In the 'nabob' canto, the poet confronts readers with the violent origins of the Indian products they enjoy day-to-day:

> Thus Britons, are procur'd the Eastern wares,
> Your Iv'ry Cabinets, and your Iv'ry Chairs;
> Your Silks, your costly Gems, and baneful TEA,
> Pernicious DRUG! – to health an enemy!
>
> Which for to gain, thousands of Indians bleed,
> And base Corruption's ready-growing seed,
> Is largely strewn, o'er *Britain's* famous land,
> By an unprincipled, a savage band.[32]

The 'unprincipled, savage band' of the final line indicates nabobs who 'for the love of gold, have famine caus'd' in the territories they govern. The villain is one John Snare, who, having fought, schemed and bribed his way to riches in India, falls into dissolution and eventually commits suicide with a razor blade, a clear reference to the arch-nabob Robert Clive, who was rumoured to have died by his own hand in 1774.

As evidenced by Campbell's *The Pleasures of Hope*, the Bengal famine became the *cause célèbre* for sympathetic writers on India. Most emotive of all the depictions of the famine was that contained in Abbé Guillaume Thomas François Raynal's proscribed *Philosophical and Political History of the Settlements and Trade of the Europeans in the East and West Indies* (1772–80), which was translated into English in 1776 and 1788, and which incorporated passages by Denis Diderot. The author (possibly Diderot) at one point challenges the reader to conjure a 'horrible spectacle' of abject misery at the height of the starvation:

> The unhappy Indians were every day perishing by thousands in this famine, without any means of help and without any resource, not being able to procure themselves the least nourishment. They were always to be seen in their villages, along the public ways, in the midst of our European colonies, pale, meagre, fainting, emaciated, consumed by famine; some stretched on the ground in expectation of dying, others scarcely able to drag themselves on to seek for food, and throwing themselves at the feet of the Europeans, intreating [sic] them to take them in as their slaves.
>
> To this description, which makes humanity shudder, let us add other objects equally striking; let imagination enlarge upon them, if possible; Let us represent to ourselves infants deserted, some expiring on the breasts of their mothers; every where [sic] the dying and the dead mingled together; on all sides the groans of sorrow, and the tears of despair; and we shall have some faint idea of the horrible spectacle Bengal presented for the space of six weeks.[33]

The twin emotions the author sought to arouse were pity towards the starving and indignation over the colonial government's negligence. Both were channelled through the medium of imaginative sympathy, which gravitated towards pain and suffering as affective spectacles.

Defenders of the East India Company could also lay claim to sympathy. Colonial officials often complained of being harried by untravelled critics in Britain who knew little of the situation on the ground. William Hickey, the ebullient diarist of late eighteenth-century London and Calcutta, who, writing of a later famine in 1788, took pains to dispel the impression of callousness on the part of the colonial officials. He wrote of their 'accustomed benevolence', adding that famine is unavoidable in a country subject to extremes of weather. He emphasises the keen sensibilities of his countrymen as 'with that gentle resignation so peculiar to the natives of India', the inhabitants of Bengal

> submit[ted] to their fate and la[id] themselves down to die. Everything in the power of liberal individuals was done for their relief; indeed, one must have been less than man, absolute Buonapartes, to have witnessed such horrible scenes of misery without feeling the bitterest pangs and exerting every nerve to alleviate them.[34]

Hickey forms a double contrast of national characters: first, between the active, sensitive British and the passive, indifferent Bengalis; secondly, between the British and the hard-hearted French ruled by the tyrant Napoleon Bonaparte. Napoleon may be dynamic but as one devoid of sensibility or moral scruples is 'less than man', sentiments that find their counterpart in James Beattie's *Elements of Moral Science* (1790–93), which asserted that 'sympathy with distress is thought so essential to human nature, that the want of it has been called *inhumanity*'.[35] Hickey was also reversing the commonly expressed notion that Britons at home were conscientious while their counterparts in India were vicious. Lord Cornwallis anticipated his masters in London by abolishing slavery in Bengal in 1789, with the presidency of Bombay following suit in 1805.[36] Moreover, in a land beset by problems of an epic nature long vanished from Britain, individuals were afforded greater scope for humanitarian endeavour to the point where British India could become the springboard for a revived and specially adapted culture of sensibility.

The study of what has been termed 'Romantic Orientalism' has tended to finesse the view of power relations between European colonising nations and the East. This subgenre of Romanticism was arguably initiated with the publication of Raymond Schwab's *Oriental Renaissance* (translated into English in 1950), to whose 1984 edition Said provided a preface praising the author's expansive humanism. Schwab credited British, French and German writers on the East with having 'created the present that propels us forward', raising the possibility that Romantic authors, far from trying to subdue or codify the Orient, saw in it a liberating force that could transcend the most entrenched ideas of self, identity and nationhood.[37] Eleanor Shaffer in *'Kubla Khan' and* The Fall of Jerusalem*: The Mythological School in Biblical Criticism and Secular Literature* (1975) connected writers such as Coleridge and Heinrich Heine and the East with the wider stream of higher or biblical criticism, whose purpose was to trace the Asian origins of European culture and specifically locate the biblical Garden of Eden.[38] More recent works have taken a more historical tack, showing that literature of the Romantic period was steeped in the collective experience of empire. In the words of Alan Richardson and Sonia Hofkosh in their introduction to *Romanticism, Race, and Imperial Culture, 1780–1834* (1996), 'the sublime, the exotic, and the "primitive" themselves may be interpreted as a response to the ideological requirements, and deforming effects of colonialism'.[39] These 'deforming effects' were as likely to produce existential anxiety as much as any sense of European superiority, as Nigel Leask demonstrated in his important *British Romantic Writers and the East: Anxieties of Empire* (1992), where he argues that power relations between East and West could be 'grotesquely reversed' in the Romantic imagination.[40] Leask's conclusion reminds us that Britons in the late eighteenth century drew foreboding parallels between their own country and the Roman Empire, which Edward Gibbon argued was corrupted from within as a result of over-exposure to Eastern decadence.[41]

The roots of imaginative sympathy lie in the writings of Scottish Enlightenment thinkers such as Francis Hutcheson, David Hume, Adam Smith and Henry Home, Lord Kames, who all sought to delineate and comprehend the economy of the passions that underpinned notions of compassion, morality and the charitable instincts.[42] These were understood to bind together both groups of individuals, creating the conditions for sociability, and political entities such as the nation state. The expansion of Britain's empire in India, whose population crucially were subjects and so under the protection of the monarch and parliament, tested the furthest bounds of imaginative sympathy and the interest the British public (including reading publics) took in a distant land. It required a considerable imaginative leap to conceive of India at all, and all too often domestic concerns usurped India's claims on the attention. This would forestall advocates of Indian culture, and politicians who sought to bring the situation in India home to Britain. If the growth in Oriental literature can be read as a metaphor for the expansion of the colonial state, so too do flaws in sentimental depictions of India resemble idiosyncrasies in the structure of empire. This tension between the centrifugal and centripetal dynamics of British India was reflected in the very attempts to depict it.

India's remoteness from Britain was a recurring feature of references to colonial activity among contemporary authors. Horace Walpole, writing in his commonplace book in 1786, complained of a military blunder occasioned by the length of time it took to communicate between the centre and margin:

> One of the great mischiefs of our possessions in India is the vast Distance. At the End of the Last War with France, two naval

Engagements by Land, one by Sea, for which fourscore Officers & 2000 Soldiers were slain happened, before an account of the peace could reach India.[43]

Nine thousand miles and a six-month sea voyage away, British India was considerably desynchronised from its overseers in London. Contemporary accounts tell of letters and instructions reaching Calcutta after the intended recipient had died (which was an all too regular occurrence given the climate and the unhealthy lifestyle of most Company servants). The East India Company demanded meticulous book-keeping among its employees, partly in an attempt to preserve information over the gulf of distance and time. Yet officials on the ground were inevitably forced to rely on their own initiative when the vicissitudes of war and politics threatened Britain's interests. For all practical purposes, the structure of empire resembled a dull elephantine nervous system: a network was in place but impulses passed around it with extreme sluggishness.[44] The physical distance of India from Britain impacted not only on material communications but also on the emotional response to reportage of deeds of valour or humanitarian atrocities, as Alexander Dow warned.

One of the themes of this book is therefore the difficulty of emotional transfer between Britain and India in both the political and the cultural sphere, a phenomenon that challenges the notion of sentimentalism as an effective binding agent of empire. The problem of physical distance, the most conspicuous barrier to imaginative sympathy, was acknowledged in the moral philosophy of the Scottish Enlightenment, whose centrality to the formation of sentimentalism has been subject to much critical discussion in recent years. The language of sentiment permeated late eighteenth-century literature to such a degree that its use can appear entirely casual, but in fact all was underpinned by a habituated knowledge of the mechanics of imaginative sympathy, as theorised by Scottish Enlightenment moral philosophers earlier in the century. Francis Hutcheson, who referred to sympathy as the 'public sense' (*sensus communis*) in his *Essay on the Nature and Conduct of the Passions* (1728), held that sympathy was a fundamental tenet of social formation that enabled the individual to project his or her concern beyond the narrow compass of domestic considerations.[45] Most theories of imaginative sympathy, however, insisted that the centripetal forces of sympathy were compromised at various levels by the twin problems of geographical remoteness and cultural difference.[46] David Armitage, in *The Ideological Origins of the British Empire* (2000), cites an example from

David Hume's *Treatise of Human Nature* (1739–40) as the earliest attempt to fabricate an 'epistemology of empire', that is, to show how 'action at a distance – specifically, action at an *imperial distance* – could excite the passions and create intellectual connections'.[47] Yet the example Hume mentions, that of a West India merchant contemplating his plantations across the Atlantic and his personal stake in their welfare, is part of a wider and more sceptical discussion of how moral sentiments are diminished across time and space. In the section entitled 'Of contiguity, and distance in space and time', part of Book II, 'On the Passions', Hume reasons that 'contiguous objects must have an influence [on the passions] much superior than the distant and remote ... The breaking of a mirror gives us more concern when at home, than the burning of a house, when abroad, and some hundred miles distant'.[48] It is possible for the mind to make present to us objects that are situated geographically beyond the self, but the imagination must first traverse each intervening object and moreover is constantly recalled to the present; this state of affairs weakens our idea of the distant object. However, Hume does go on to concede that 'the consequences of a removal in *space* are very much inferior to those of a removal in *time*' (p. 429). This is because it is possible for us to imagine objects placed far apart in space but not to imagine an object at more than one point in time.

The example of the West India merchant occurs as part of this discussion. Hume states 'a *West-India* merchant will tell you, that he is not without concern about what passes in *Jamaica*; tho' few extend their views so far into futurity, as to dread very remote accidents' (p. 429). The *relative* diminution of ideas over space as opposed to time can hardly be taken as a positive endorsement of an imperial epistemology. One paradox that Hume observes is that we admire the exertion of the mind's efforts, what he calls 'this aspiring progress of the imagination', however fruitless it may be (p. 435). It takes a greater act of mind to project the imagination into the future or the past, and as a result we hold the past in higher esteem than that which is merely remote from us. Again, Hume produces an example that holds negative implications for an imperial community based upon the flow of sentiment:

> But tho' every great distance produces an admiration for the distant object, a distance in time has a more considerable effect than that in space. Antient [sic] busts and inscriptions are more valu'd than *Japan* tables: And not to mention the *Greeks* and *Romans*, 'tis certain we regard with more veneration the old *Chaldeans* and *Egyptians*, than the modern *Chinese* and *Persians*, and bestow more fruitless praise

to clear up the history and chronology of the former, than it would cost us to make a voyage, and be certainly inform'd of the character, learning and government of the latter ... this is the reason why all the relics of antiquity are so precious in our eyes, and appear more valuable than what is brought even from the remotest parts of the world. (pp. 433, 436)

Mark Salber Phillips has argued that the Scottish Enlightenment formulations of imaginative sympathy, including those of Hume and his compatriot Adam Smith, constituted a preliminary exploration of why the mind settles on the near-at-hand at the expense of other, more distant, objects followed by a secondary 'corrective' account of how the judgement works to overcome these shortcomings.[49] I want to suggest that the problem of distance was never comprehensively banished from the writings of Hume and Smith, but for both men, and additionally for Burke (who read and contributed to Enlightenment notions of sympathy), the sympathetic imagination was cast in the role of tragic hero: doomed to fail but compelled to strive for connection regardless.

In the context of colonial India, sympathetic engagement with subject peoples was an aspiration that could never be meaningfully realised, a dilemma to which contemporary literature on the subject repeatedly returned. For Smith, the attainment of sympathy with a suffering individual represented the perfection of humanity. Smith's *Theory of Moral Sentiments* (1759) had a profound influence on Burke's humanitarian campaigns but if anything its model of imaginative sympathy was even more circumspect than Hume's. Smith posits that as individuals, we can have no direct experience of what others feel but may imagine what we would feel in the same situation, summarised in the celebrated words 'though our brother is on the rack, as long as we ourselves are at ease, our senses will never inform us of what he suffers'.[50] Smith's emphasis on bodily torment demonstrates the relevance of his philosophy to representations and critiques of colonial misdemeanours, as the extract from Raynal forcefully illustrates. Nonetheless Smith posed several seemingly insurmountable problems for sentimental depictions of empire. First he argued that the affections of the sufferer and the spectator can never be wholly in tune with one another, simply because the sufferer experiences pain but the spectator does not (p. 29). The sufferer longs for the spectator to enter into 'true' sympathy (that is, literally to share his or her pain) and so assumes the position of the spectator in a reciprocal imaginative action. Because of the fundamental disjunction that exists between the two individuals, such a harmonisation cannot in reality occur.[51] Instead (and here Smith draws on his favoured doctrine of neo-Stoicism) the sufferer must lower the pitch of his or her passions to bring them more closely into line with those of the spectator (p. 34). This would suggest that highly emotive images of empire were likely to misfire, for a spectator (or reader in the literary context) can only participate in another's feelings once they have been appropriately moderated downwards.

The tragic-heroic strain of sympathy reoccurs in Smith's insistence that no matter how unlikely we are to succeed, the attempt to fulfil the biblical injunction 'love thy neighbour' remains the highest duty of mankind. He distinguishes between our effective good offices, which were ordinarily confined to 'the state or sovereignty in which we have been born or educated' and our instinctive goodwill, which 'may embrace the immensity of the universe' (pp. 235, 227). The disposition to universal beneficence Smith ascribes to the presence of the impartial spectator, the 'vicegerent of God within us', who corrects the human fault of solipsism (p. 166). Smith gives a brutally frank example of the hypothetical destruction of the Chinese empire in an earthquake to illustrate the extent to which we are trapped within ourselves. He suggests that a 'man of humanity in Europe, who had no sort of connection with that part of the world' might express platitudes on the disaster and voice philosophical reflections, but

> when all these humane sentiments had been once fairly expressed, he would pursue his business or pleasure, with the same ease and tranquillity, as if no such accident had happened ... If he was to lose his little finger to-morrow, he would not sleep to-night; but, provided he never saw them, he will snore with the most profound security over the ruin of a hundred millions of his brethren. (p. 136)

The impartial spectator explains why the 'active principles', which are 'generous' and noble', are capable of 'counteracting the strongest impulses of self-love'. Yet the 'benevolence which Nature has lighted up in the human heart' is a mere 'feeble spark'; a vast effort is required to project its rays far beyond the self (p. 137). Although he is reassured that God ultimately superintends the justice and order of the universe, Smith's conception of man's capacity to help others emerges as deeply pessimistic.

Lynn Festa has explored how imaginative sympathy could give a voice and 'a human face' to the victims of British and French imperialism in the eighteenth century in her study *Sentimental Figures of*

Empire in Eighteenth-Century Britain and France (2006). She examines the tension between the 'sociable benefits and pleasures of sympathetic affect and the desire to uphold the singularity of the self'.[52] According to this model, the roving impulse of 'vagrant affect' is checked by the selective operations of sentimentalism that select precisely which colonial subjects are humanised and which remain outside the pale. Festa justly remarks that the much-vaunted community of empire that was sometimes presented as a sympathetic ideal (by Burke and others) in fact referred only to European colonisers and excluded the indigenous inhabitants, who were merely objectified as victims, and she acknowledges the threat posed by 'unfettered sympathy' to a European sense of self-hood. But whereas Festa argues that physical distance was theoretically speaking an 'arbitrary barrier' to the operations of sympathy, this study explores in more depth the problems of imaginative blockage identified by Hume and Smith.[53] India in reality proved to be beyond the scope of the average metropolitan British mind although a remarkable feature of many British texts about India is their willingness to address this problem head-on and even to berate the imagination for its limitations.

The second and considerably more complex barrier to sympathy was what today is often termed 'cultural otherness'. The fruits of Orientalist scholarship introduced Indian art and literature to Britain often for the first time, sometimes (but by no means always) in the form of literal translations and often festooned with taxing nomenclature. The problem of otherness profoundly affected texts on India produced throughout this period precisely because sympathy was considered to be essential to the efficacy of a literary work. Both Augustan and Romantic literary critics agreed that literature's force derived from the reader sharing in the emotions and sentiments conveyed by the text, which raised obvious problems for exotica and representations of unfamiliar places such as India. Mary Wollstonecraft recognised as much in her review of Jones's *Sacontalá*, published anonymously in the *Analytical Review* in 1790, where she acknowledged that, on a superficial level, 'with respect to manners, we are all, more or less, under the dominion of prejudice, and so local are our senses, and even our judgement, that for a short time every thing [*sic*] strange appears absurd'.[54] For an Indian text to be transplanted successfully to Britain it must contain 'universally' recognisable features in order to appeal to the generality of mankind:

> Universal poetic similes ought to strike the senses, their aptness should be obvious at first glance, and they are, perhaps, often

rendered dear by reminding us of the first ebullitions of sensibility, and of the customs that have been long familiar to our memory. By numberless hidden, yet powerful springs, are we filled with admiration, or moved to sympathy; but we are seldom lost in either till wonder ceases.[55]

Wollstonecraft went on to conclude that *Sacontalá* was successful in surmounting these hurdles and concluded her review with the confident assertion that the play's 'poetic delineation of Indian manners, and the artless touches of nature' was capable of producing familiar sentiments that would 'come home to the human bosom in every climate'.[56] British writers on India faced a considerable aesthetic dilemma: should they strive for authenticity and trust to the curiosity of an enlightened readership, or accept that prevailing literary tastes were unwilling to digest unadulterated Indian subject matter and adapt their work accordingly? Leask has coined the term 'costume poetry' to describe writings that draped Oriental decoration over an essentially European literary aesthetic, creating a poetic form that was 'both culturally legible and translatable'.[57] Many texts on India betray an awareness of sympathy's limited power and came to be dominated by authorial strategies for surmounting aesthetic and moral otherness.

The most optimistic advocate for imaginative sympathy by far was Burke, who evolved a more efficacious sympathetic model in his *Philosophical Enquiry into the Origin of our Ideas of the Sublime and the Beautiful* (1757). The faith in the reach of the imagination he enshrined there was put to use in the later political campaigns he waged over India in the 1780s and 1790s. Burke's refusal to concede the barriers of geographical distance or cultural difference in the case of India marks out his position from that of Hume or Smith. This was partly due to two factors which he felt made India unique. First, Britain had personal connections there through the officials of the East India Company, who as fellow countrymen naturally animated the passions of their kinsmen and women. The British public's failure to take note of the alleged crimes of these individuals was, Burke felt, a sympathetic anomaly, for a sense of national moral responsibility should apply to them. Only the geographical remoteness of the East India Company's servants protected them from scrutiny. In his speech on Fox's East India Bill of 1 December 1783, he denounced 'the desperate boldness of a few obscure young men' who believed they could plunder the wealth of India unobserved.[58] Secondly, it behoved Britons to regard the native inhabitants of British India as fellow subjects since, under the various constitutional settlements imposed on India from 1765 onwards, Britain held a duty of care towards the Indian people. Burke maintained that it was both idle and morally wrong to submit to arbitrary barriers to the imagination, although he was willing to concede that representation of India required an exceptional affective intensity, 'for it is an arduous thing to plead against abuses of power which originates from your own country, and affects those whom we are used to consider as strangers'.[59]

Scope of the Book

The book is organised along broadly chronological lines and moves from the more overt sentimentalism of the late eighteenth century into the Romantic era, although it must be emphasised that representations of India from this period were in a process of continuous development. Sympathy was initially applied to the Indian victims of British colonialism but, after 1800, began to morph into an antipathy towards what were increasingly denounced as 'heathen' Indian practices. The period of literary history explored in this book coincides with the evangelical revival of the early nineteenth century as Clapham Sect evangelical Christians and dissenters gradually gained sway over the mainstream of religious culture in Britain.[60] This was of great importance to representations of India for Clapham Sect members were in the forefront of the political campaign to allow missionaries access to Britain's territories, which the East India Company had previously forbidden on security grounds. The battle to insert the so-called 'pious clause' into the Company's charter, which came up for renewal in 1813, saw an upsurge of depictions of Hinduism as monstrous and inhumane that drew upon precisely the same imaginative reflexes as earlier attacks on colonial violence.[61]

The opening chapter evaluates Burke's campaign to impeach Warren Hastings for 'high crimes and misdemeanours', which began in 1787 and ended with the former Governor-General's acquittal in 1795.[62] It discusses Burke's efforts to widen the scope of the British public's interest in colonial affairs beyond the domestic sphere, which manifested itself in popular opposition to nabobs and their effect on the British economy, the subject of several satirical plays. Burke initially sought to balance these home-grown concerns with what he saw as the East India Company's nefarious practices, but later sharpened his rhetoric into what others interpreted as a personal crusade. Drawing on his own confident assertion of classical rhetoric's power to arouse sympathy, prefigured in his *Philosophical Enquiry*, he brought unprecedented affective energy to representations of India in a bid to produce emotional clarity over Britain's duty to act. Yet the campaign against Hastings attracted widespread ridicule from commentators who saw Burke as at best over-zealous and at worst as a pathologically unbalanced demagogue. Scores of popular prints and reams of satirical literature attested to his failure accurately to gauge the strength of public opinion over India. Ultimately, Burke fell foul of Smith's maxim that 'the furious behaviour of an angry man is more likely to exasperate us against himself than against his enemies', or Hume's observation that a statesman speaking of 'distant ages and remote nations' wins less regard than the patriot serving his own country, for the former 'affects us with a less lively sympathy' on account of the 'obscure' nature of his cause.[63] Burke can thus be seen to have attempted to generate emotional connections between Britain and India through a straightforward application of sympathy. His failure highlighted the pitfalls that others faced in representing India and writing Orientalist literature and pointed to the aesthetic strategies that they adopted to avoid them.

Chapter 2 switches the scene to Calcutta and the work of Sir William Jones and the Asiatic Society he established there in 1784. Jones's scholarship explored links between Asia and Europe that he claimed originated from the biblical creation, which he used as the bedrock for his conviction that Indian culture contained sympathetic possibilities for European audiences. This formed part of a wider project – linguistic, anthropological and literary – to recognise Europe and Asia as offshoots of a single originary civilisation and so facilitate the means of imaginative sympathy between two disparate peoples. Crucially Jones was able to attain a close perspective on India after his arrival there in 1783. His 'Hindu Hymns', purportedly translations of Vedic texts but remodelled along the lines of the Pindaric ode, were feted by critics for disclosing, in the words of Alexander Chalmers, 'new sources of the sublime and the pathetic by familiarizing the scenery and manners of the eastern regions'.[64] Within the framework of imaginative sympathy, Orientalism was one way of forming bonds between what Jones, in his ninth discourse to the Asiatic Society, described as 'families of nations'.[65] He came to see in the Hindu doctrine of dualism and re-absorption the prospect of total sympathy or the imaginative escape from the self into the divine.

Chapter 3 remains in Calcutta, but explores how sympathy was redefined within the colonial contact zone, a change that paralleled the increasing tendency to denigrate the culture of sensibility in Britain. Threatened on one side by the debilitating heat of the Indian climate and by metropolitan pressure to cultivate civil society in India on the other, the raucous years that H.E. Busteed chronicled in *Echoes from Old Calcutta* (1882) were an embarrassment to Hastings and his London paymasters alike.[66] British colonists increasingly defined themselves in terms of their ability to resist India's climate and culture. In Britain, authors increasingly associated sensibility with spurious displays of emotion and French Jacobinism.[67] Driven by these bipolar forces, writers working in Calcutta or in touch with relatives there sought to absolve British colonists from the charge of relinquishing national identity in alien surroundings. Marie Louise Pratt's notion of the colonial 'contact zone' is useful in conceptualising the territorial space in which two cultures interact with reciprocal effects on the identities of both. Here, changes to the dynamics of sympathy were two-fold, for colonial authors sought to elicit esteem from their compatriots in Britain by proving themselves recognisable members of civil society, which in turn necessitated their own distinction from the Indian population by whom they were surrounded, a revolution in bodily practices that E.M. Collingham has described in terms of a transformation 'from nabob to sahib'.[68] These imperatives made colonial India a platform for proto-feminist women authors such as the diarist Eliza Fay and the novelist Phebe Gibbes – whose responses to *sati*, a recurring secondary theme in this study – demonstrate India's importance as a battleground for gender issues as well as a site for the consolidation of British and Indian national identities.

Meanwhile evangelical authors and missionaries were reconfiguring imaginative sympathy as gothic affect in the cause of Christian proselytising. Chapter 4 examines texts written by authors associated with the evangelical revival as attempts to dissever sympathetic links with modern India and Hinduism in particular. If the Orientalist movement employed a cosmopolitan, neoclassical aesthetic to affiliate the inhabitants of the ancient world, dissenters and evangelicals of various denominational hues turned to gothic *chiaroscuro* to depict 'monstrous' Hindu ceremonies and rituals unillumined by gospel truth. Spectacles such as *sati*, female infanticide and the ceremony of Juggernaut at Puri, Orissa (memorably recorded by Claudius Buchanan, Vice Provost of Fort William College in Calcutta) percolated into British gothic writing, which in turn influenced many subsequent eyewitness accounts. Somewhat ironically, indignant outbursts against Hinduism by members of the evangelical Clapham Sect lobby group led by Wilberforce and Lord Teignmouth used the same affective techniques as Burke when he railed against officially sanctioned oppression. Evangelicals discriminated between Hinduism's 'victims' – the sub-Brahminical castes purportedly in thrall to a vicious priesthood – and the combined forces of the religious authorities themselves, local potentates who stood to benefit from their power, and the East India Company, which subsidised Hindu religious festivals including the notorious procession of Juggernaut.[69] This opened up a three-way split in British imaginative conceptions of India that John Barrell has schematised as 'this, that and the other', or that Gayatri Chakravorty Spivak has defined as the subject, the 'self-consolidating other' and the 'absolute other', into which last category religiously motivated authors endeavoured to push Hinduism at the turn of the nineteenth century.[70] The Indian people on the other hand were supposedly clamouring for religious enlightenment. Henry Martyn, an evangelical East India Company chaplain who travelled to India in 1805, complained in his journal 'how many hundreds of millions of souls lying in heathen darkness there are, how many millions of heathen souls professing Christ'.[71] As Homi K. Bhabha has argued, even those Indians willing publicly to recant Hinduism lingered as hybrid figures in the evangelical imagination, seen as inveterately sly and mendacious and at the outermost margins of sympathy.[72]

The need for sympathy was nowhere more apparent than in the field of Romantic literary aesthetics. Chapter 5 explores the distinction made by literary critics in the Romantic period (authors of belles-lettres, poets, rhetoricians) between 'Oriental' texts in their raw, untranslated or transliterated state and what can properly be called 'Orientalist' literature: the adaptation of Eastern literary forms for the Western book market that played to the emotional dynamics of European audiences. The respective exemplars of these traditions were the Hindu epics the *Ramayana* and the *Mahabharata*, excoriated by James Mill in his *History of British India* (1817), and Thomas Moore's Indian poem *Lalla Rookh*, the publishing sensation of the same year. Southey's *Curse of Kehama* (1810) was invariably taken as a flawed attempt to render the Hindu idiom into English; as an awkward combination of classical Vedic cosmology and pro-missionary evangelicalism, the poem's conflicted sympathetic demands baffled the critics. Moore's infinitely more successful *Lalla Rookh* followed Byron's 'Eastern Tales' series published between 1813–16 (*The Giaour, The Bride of Abydos, The Corsair* and *The Siege of Corinth*) in artfully intermingling Western moral sentiment and Eastern particularities, revitalising interest in exoticism at a time when the missionary question threatened to eclipse India's potential as a site of fantasy. Moore's melodramas of doomed love and holy war updated the *Arabian Nights* tradition without forsaking the goodwill and aesthetic requirements of his readers.

The book comes full circle to find that sympathetic engagement with India became possible only through the medium of heavily 'Westernised' forms of representation, either through the 'costume poetry' of Jones, later reworked by Moore, or through the depiction of Indian suffering in uniquely affecting terms within European schemes of aesthetics, the discursive practice initiated by Burke. Evangelical writers appropriated this latter form of representation but adapted it so that sympathy might only be felt for the Indian victims of Brahminical (not British) cruelty, demonising the customs and institutions of India in the process. All of this left the possibility of representing the 'real' India in Britain in doubt, for in both cases the country and the people were surrendered to the widespread acknowledgement that culturally and geographically remote entities such as the subcontinent were beyond the range of European imagination. For all the influx of Orientalist knowledge occurring over this period, British representations of India continued to create familiar objects onto which the imagination could attach, creating an illusion of affinity which in reality bore little relation to Burke's ideal of sympathetic 'imperial justice'. Sympathy, in this sense, functions as what Pratt has termed an 'anti-conquest', a fallacy commonly found in sentimental writing of a 'utopian, innocent vision of European global authority'.[73] Yet even as Burke first advanced such a vision, the prospect of non-identification latent in eighteenth-century discussions of sympathy meant that his hopes for benign intervention were compromised by the contemporary unwillingness to look beyond European boundaries of understanding. It should be noted in passing that the limitations of sympathetic engagement were by no means confined to the colonial era and remain evident today. Charities and campaigners for international human rights still seek to stimulate the sympathetic imagination with graphic images of human suffering, only to find their cause displaced from the headlines the following day by domestic concerns. In crude prototype, Burke broached these issues and found the imagination wanting.

1
Edmund Burke and the Trial of Warren Hastings

The impeachment and trial of Warren Hastings, which began in 1787 and concluded with the acquittal of the former Governor-General in 1795, brought unprecedented attention to Indian affairs in Britain.[1] It also illustrated – in terms that, for Burke, were nothing less than tragic – the aesthetic difficulties inherent in constructing a sentimental depiction of India. For most of his hearers and for the British public at large, the remote and unfamiliar subcontinent simply eluded the scope of the sympathetic imagination, or was too easily displaced by objects closer to home. Nor did the trial's prodigious length favour Burke's cause. Hastings was charged before the House of Lords for 'high crimes and misdemeanours' on 18 February 1788. By the time of the verdict a full eight years later, 180 changes to the peerage (in their capacity as jurors) had taken place, and the Lord Chancellor (as judge), Lord Thurlow, who opposed Hastings, was replaced by Lord Loughborough, who supported him. Outside the courtroom, the French Revolution had shaken the political and social foundations of Europe and provided Burke with an alternative animus for his political philosophy. War with nearby revolutionary France easily effaced concerns over the East India Company's conduct in the 1770s, however much the theatre of war now extended to the Indian Ocean. Even the outpouring of literature in the 1770s and 1780s, much of which can be categorised as sentimental, which denounced the wrongdoings of British nabobs, placed domestic concerns centre stage at the expense of the Indian context.

The first sympathetic appearance of India in the literary culture of the period, therefore, can be said to have misfired. Yet out of Burke's failure was born the pattern for future sentimental representations of India, although the reasons for his lack of success were paradoxical in nature. As this chapter will explore in relation to his *Philosophical Enquiry into our Ideas of the Sublime and the Beautiful* (1757), and examples from his subsequent parliamentary speeches, Burke firmly believed in the affective force of classical rhetoric. His principal inspiration was Cicero, but Burke's application of formalised rhetoric to contemporary foreign policy problems (America, India and France) struck many onlookers as absurd over-inflation. Moreover, it reawakened the popular mistrust of rhetoric in all its forms that had lingered in Britain (and elsewhere) since the seventeenth century. Conversely, Burke was also ridiculed for his exhaustive, and exhausting, recitations of dry facts and figures over the course of the trial that counteracted the affective simplicity required for sympathetic engagement.

A commonly expressed objection to the trial of Hastings at the time was that it was a mere piece of political theatre designed to manipulate public emotion. Interest in the trial's opening sessions in Westminster Hall was at fever pitch, attracting a vast audience including William Cowper, Joshua Reynolds, Fanny Burney and Edward Gibbon, who flocked to hear Burke and his fellow managers for the prosecution Charles James Fox and Richard Brinsley Sheridan, and witness a spectacle that drew upon the full panoply of the British state. Entry tickets commanded high prices and their distinctive design, featuring the crest of the Deputy Great Chamberlain Peter Burrell, spawned satirical imitations and even imitations of imitations.[2] Sheridan was manager of Drury Lane Theatre and possibly responsible for some of the more theatrical elements of the proceedings, which included a canopied 'stage', complete with royal box, erected in Westminster Hall for the occasion. Speakers for the prosecution regularly passed out from exhaustion or spoke with such vehemence that spectators, including at one point Sheridan's wife, fainted in shock. As such, it has drawn interpretation from literary criticism as an episode shot through with cultural significance; Frances De Bruyn arguing, for example, that Burke conducted the trial in the medium of 'gothic romance', building a prosecution case not upon 'bare historical facts' but a 'literary paradigm which orders, explains, and at times even transforms the historical reality'.[3] David Musselwhite similarly argues that Burke's use of 'imaginative, romantic, theatrical and literary' language proved inadmissible in a court of law, and Hastings eventually gained an advantage by adhering to more conventional modes of discourse.[4] In the second of her two linked chapters on Burke and India in *The Rhetoric of English India*, Suleri takes a cue from Sheridan's management of the Drury Lane theatre to reveal how parts of his celebrated speech on the Begums of Awadh found their way into his stage tragedy *Pizarro* (1799) on Spanish colonial oppression in

South America.[5] His speech is even recalled in Hardy's *The Return of the Native* as an unforgettable *tour de force* performance, where it is compared to the concerts of the legendary castrato Farinelli.[6] Yet the trial must be seen as more than partisan rodomontade. Burke's strategy at the trial was designed to focus public indignation about a widespread set of issues upon the figure of Hastings, whom he held personally responsible for the alleged crimes, which included taking illegal bribes; presiding over a judicial murder; and more generally subverting the ancient usages and customs of the inhabitants of British India. Over the course of seven years, during which he amassed information on India and the affairs of the East India Company, Burke became convinced of the personal culpability of the former Governor-General, whom he introduced to the court as 'one in whom all the frauds, all the peculations, all the violence, all the tyranny in India are embodied, disciplined and arrayed', adding that 'you strike at the whole corps if you strike at the head'.[7]

Spurred on by his associates Sir Philip Francis, likely author of the 'Junius' letters and Hastings' implacable foe on the Supreme Council of Bengal, and his shadowy 'kinsman' William, Burke drafted 22 articles of charge, which for purposes of clarity he grouped under four headings: 'Benares', 'Begums', 'Bribes' and 'Presents'. The Benares charge concerned the alleged intimidation and unlawful arrest of the Raja, Cheit Singh, resulting in a popular uprising against the British in the city in 1780. The Begums charge involved allegations that Hastings had expropriated dowries belonging to the mother and grandmother of the Nawab of Awadh, and that his soldiers had tortured their household eunuchs while trying to extract information. The Bribes and Presents charges referred to assorted allegations of corruption and peculation, and additional secondary charges accused Hastings of having illegally precipitated a war against the Rohilla Afghans in 1773, and ordering the judicial murder of an informer-turned-blackmailer, Raja Nandakumar, in 1775. Numerous publications hostile to Hastings and the East India Company had carried information relating to the allegations in the years preceding the trial, and to a critical eye much appeared rotten in the state of Bengal. Burke attempted to sway judicial and public opinion together through the sheer weight of evidence.

Despite the legalistic minutiae upon which many of the charges hinged, Burke's campaign against Hastings may also be considered as an attempt to redefine sympathetic relations between Britain and its Indian dominions at an imaginative and ethical level. Nicholas B. Dirks has recognised the trial's significance as a turning point in the culture of empire, arguing that Hastings' acquittal 'not only put paid to the scandals of empire; it also raised empire above the possibility of scandal'.[8] This chapter concentrates on Burke's (and to a lesser extent Sheridan's) use of scandal to generate sympathetic capital in support of their cause. If eighteenth-century accounts of imaginative sympathy revolved around aesthetic responses to incidents of suffering, then the wrongdoings of the East India Company offered paradigms of sentimental distress to which (Burke hoped) the British public imagination would respond. Burke ought to be credited with a humanitarian sensibility, although it is important to recognise his complete eschewal of radical politics for all his reformist zeal. Several critical reappraisals of Burke have emphasised his long-standing faith in the imagination's power as a corrective to human misery, most notably Conor Cruise O'Brien's which replaced Sir Lewis Namier's view of Burke as a reactionary with the theory that Burke's 'great melody' against the abuse of power stemmed from his subliminal awareness of the plight of colonial Ireland.[9] More recently, Luke Gibbons has argued that instances of systematic injusice and oppression roused Burke to speak on behalf of those who were disenfranchised from the intricate web of feeling that constituted late eighteenth-century civil society.[10] Burke's utterances on the inalienable rights of colonial subjects were more often made on behalf of rajas than of *ryots*; however, no analysis of his speeches before and during the trial of Hastings should overlook his faith in the humanitarian potential of the imagination.

Burke's own contribution to moral philosophy, his *Philosophical Enquiry into the Origin of our Ideas of the Sublime and the Beautiful* (1757), is strikingly more optimistic about the outward scope of the sympathetic imagination than the comparatively sceptical accounts of Hume or Smith. The treatise, published when Burke was only 28, entered an already crowded field of enquiry into ideas of taste, judgement, the sublime and the operations of the passions. Nonetheless, it seems to have provided a yardstick for Burke's belief in imaginative sympathy that remained with him throughout his career. His four great political campaigns – the cause of Ireland, the separation of America from Britain, British India and revolutionary France – were defined by prodigious exertions of imagination. The *Philosophical Enquiry* identifies notably fewer barriers to the workings of imagination than Hume or Smith, insisting instead that 'it is by [sympathy] that we enter into the concerns of others; that we are moved as they are moved, and are never suffered to be indifferent spectators of almost anything which men can and do suffer'.[11] This is more akin to the modern concept of empathy, to invoke Philip Mercer's definition of the term, for it involves actively insinuating oneself into the life of another person rather than detachedly speculating how we might feel in the same situation.[12] For Burke, sympathy was one of the social passions, which 'must be considered as a sort of substitution, by which we are put into the place of another man, and affected in many respects as he is affected'; unlike Smith's impartial spectator, who sympathises only with those victims able to lower the pitch of their suffering to the gaze of a dispassionate onlooker, Burke's spectator of 'circumstances of real distress' is roused to assist no matter what their personal disposition may formerly have been, an idea rooted in the *Enquiry*'s earlier proposition that certain types of pain are capable of giving pleasure.

Burke locates the individual spectator within a divinely ordained web of sympathy: 'as our Creator has designed we should be united by the bond of sympathy, he has strengthened that bond by a proportionable delight; and there most where our sympathy is most wanted, in the distresses of others'.[13] In other words, we willingly incline our footsteps towards a scene of suffering, inasmuch as we are prompted to do so by innate feelings of compassion. The idea of sympathy as a universal bond recurred in Burke's speeches at the trial of Hastings, where he adapted it to the unique demands of a widespread empire. The *Philosophical Enquiry* emphasises the superior affective potential of real suffering as opposed to imitations of suffering in art or literature. The celebrated example of this is Burke's scenario of the 'state criminal of high rank' shortly to be executed in a public square, adjoining a playhouse which is staging 'the most sublime and affecting tragedy we have'. 'In a moment', Burke predicts, 'the emptiness of the theatre would demonstrate the comparative weakness of the imitative arts, and proclaim the triumph of real sympathy', the result of our ability to discriminate between what he calls a 'simple pain in the reality' as opposed to 'delight in the representation' of that 'which ... our heartiest wishes would be to see redressed' (p. 44).

As a scenario from 'the reality', the growth of empire posed new challenges and opportunities for the British sympathetic imagination. Art nevertheless plays an important role in Burke's moral philosophy as a form of school for the passions whereby the study of art and literature can train the mind how it should respond to suffering in real life. Gibbons reads this idea into Burke's patronage of the painter James Barry, whose painting *Philoctetes on the Isle of Lemnos* (1770) initiated a revival of the Greek concept of virtue in suffering, countering the neo-Stoicism of Adam Smith and others who sought 'to purge the body and its discontents from the public sphere'. The spectacle of Odysseus's marooned former comrade-in-arms nursing his festering wound was a seminal moment in the eighteenth-century legitimisation of emotional display, Gibbons argues – a development of crucial importance to Burke's political discourse.[14] Certainly where Smith saw neo-Stoicism as the means of bridging the gap between the victim in indescribable pain and the merely curious onlooker, the *Philosophical Enquiry* places greater reliance on the ready communicability of the passions, insisting that 'we take an extraordinary part in the passions of others, and ... are easily affected and brought into sympathy by any tokens which are shewn of them'. Burke saw classical rhetoric as one such token for eliciting this sympathy, for 'there are no tokens which can express all the circumstances of most passions so fully as words' (p. 158). The challenge to link the tenets of the *Philosophical Enquiry* to Burke's subsequent political writings and speeches has since proved irresistible, for the latter are festooned with precisely the aesthetic and rhetorical devices explored in the earlier work.[15] His lifelong admiration for Cicero's rhetoric became more evident during his encounter with Hastings in whom he found his very own Verres, the disgraced Roman governor of Sicily and the target of Cicero's Verrine Orations.[16]

There is ample evidence to suggest that the *Philosophical Enquiry* exerted a lasting influence on Burke's thought, and in the 1780s and 1790s commentators and satirical printmakers continued to associate him with his youthful sally into the world of letters, not least to undermine his self-assumed role of elder statesman. Hostile engravings made, for example, in response to the Fox-North coalition of 1783 and the East India Bill crisis of the 1780s typically feature Burke clutching a copy of his *Philosophical Enquiry* labelled 'Sublime and Beautiful' by a variety of artistic contrivances.[17] His critics persistently alluded to the *Philosophical Enquiry* to attack what they saw as Burke's intemperate and apparently conflicting outward displays of emotion at the trial, leading to insinuations of insincerity, insanity (one such depiction will be discussed in Elizabeth Hamilton's *Translation of the Letters of a Hindoo Rajah* in Chapter 3) and even sexual imbalance.[18] The satirist 'Anthony Pasquin' (aka John Williams) dismissed Burke as 'a non-descript Philosopher ... a Quixitonian Theocritus, who fights, laughs, and weeps in the same moment'.[19] The modern critic Olivia Smith, on the other hand, has defended Burke's 'assumption that emotions are not transitory and irrational but constitute a valid component of thought' and credits him with the inauguration of a 'politics of feeling'.[20] Burke's unabashed appeal to the emotions in the Marie Antoinette passage in the

Reflections on the Revolution in France (1790), composed midway through the trial, or the late pyrotechnics of his *Letters on a Regicide Peace* (1795) and *Letter to a Noble Lord* (1796), suggest that his faith in rhetoric as an aid to sympathy remained strong until the end of his career.[21]

Burke's speeches on India indeed demonstrate his belief that the imagination could vault boundaries of geographical distance, culture and history. For all the mockery Burke endured in his own lifetime for his campaigning on behalf of remote causes, the Victorian commentator Thomas Babington Macaulay singled out precisely these visionary powers as praiseworthy in various pieces of review journalism. Macaulay's review of the Revd G.R. Gleig's *Memoir of the Life of Warren Hastings* (1841) offers valuable insights into Burke's ability to transport himself into 'the past and in the future, in the distant and the unreal', the author perhaps recognising in Burke a kindred 'castle-builder':

> India and its inhabitants were not to him, as to most Englishmen, mere names and abstractions, but a real country and a real people. ... All India was present to the eye of his mind, from the halls where suitors laid gold and perfumes at the feet of sovereigns to the wild moor where the gypsy camp was pitched, from the bazaar, humming like a beehive with the crowd of buyers and sellers, to the jungle where the lonely courier shakes his bunch of iron rings to scare away the hyænas. He had just as lively an idea of the insurrection at Benares as of Lord George Gordon's riots, and of the execution of Nuncomar as of the execution of Dr. Dodd. Oppression in Bengal was to him the same thing as oppression in the streets of London.[22]

Macaulay is notably willing to validate Burke's claim that the mind can summon up people and places that are far removed geographically, although he does suggest that the ability to perform this imaginative feat is singular and perhaps unique. In an important reassessment of Burke's Indian speeches, Sara Suleri has challenged the omniscient imagination to argue that Burke's attempt to translate India into an idiom recognisable to fellow eighteenth-century Europeans was doomed to collapse into the unrealisable category of the sublime, something she associates with widespread contemporary perceptions of India as a 'land of perpetual surplus'.[23] Gibbons takes a different view of the role of the sublime in relation to sympathy, tracing the *Enquiry*'s multiple images of pain and suffering to Burke's formative experiences in colonial Dublin. The Cork famine of 1740–41, the judicial murder of the priest Nicholas Sheehy, and the arrest of one of his own relatives in connection with the 1760s Munster Whiteboy insurgency all represented for Burke what Gibbons calls 'exemplary events', vertiginously affective incidents that deeply scarred the young Burke's psyche. The crucial point for Gibbons is that the sublime defied visual or verbal representation: 'as if, the more disturbing the event, the greater the resistance to graphic clarity'.[24] Burke was certainly willing to harness the shock of the sublime, but as a political campaigner his goal was to replace obscurity with the beauty of natural order restored.

Burke's speeches on India therefore employed a dialectic of sublime concealment and sympathetic engagement, which sought (to use Macaulay's words again) to generate 'vivid pictures' out of 'darkness, and dulness, and confusion'. The visualisation of suffering constitutes only a preliminary act of recovery in an attempt to expose colonial victims to sympathetic view. This tendency of the European imagination to grasp an object has been seen as tantamount to virtual colonial possession, but Uday Singh Mehta has applauded what he calls Burke's 'conversation across boundaries of strangeness', respect for local customs and reluctance to impose a 'grid of Enlightenment rationality' on the objects of his compassion.[25] At first glance, an extract from Burke's opening speech before the House of Lords (15 February 1788) would appear to contradict this line of thought entirely. Addressed directly to the Lords who were trying Hastings' case, the speech represents his most grandiose claim for the global reach of the sympathetic imagination:

> Your lordships always had a boundless power and unlimited jurisdiction. You now have a boundless object. It is not from this country or the other, that relief is applied for, but from whole tribes of suffering nations, various descriptions of men, differing in language, in manners, and in rights, men separated by every means from you. However, by the Providence of God, they are come here to supplicate at your Lordships' Bar; and I hope and trust that there will be no rule, formed upon municipal maxims, which will prevent the Imperial justice which you owe to the people that call to you from all parts of a great, disjointed empire.[26]

Burke is arguing here that with the acquisition of Indian territories, the polity of Great Britain has expanded, and the jurisdiction of the House of Lords, acting here in its capacity as a court of law, has expanded accordingly. The power of the Lords is 'boundless' within the confines of the British state, but the object newly brought before them is boundless not because Britain has limitless territorial ambitions (as might be construed from this) but because the population of Britain's Indian dominions is now unimaginably vast. Suleri's Indian sublime raises its head but Burke does not submit to it, seeing no cause for defeatism in the face of this vastness, rather the reverse. He evokes sympathy for India through the scale of the wrongdoing ('whole tribes of suffering nations') and the immediacy of individual victimhood ('they are come here to supplicate at your Lordships' bar'). Burke demanded an especial exertion of imagination to endow every Indian victim of Hastings' rule with a human face, as though each were standing face-to-face in Westminster Hall. In this passage, Burke seeks to reduce the seemingly innumerable claimants on British justice to the paradigm of a single spectator and a single victim: justice administered individually but repeated millions of times over.

In this respect at least, Burke refused to be bound by the category of the sublime as Suleri defines it. However, he also employed its more conventional associations with obscurity and terror as a means of generating moral outrage. His primary means of doing this was to reconstruct horrific colonial crime scenes, which, as will be seen later in the chapter, drew on the ideas of terror first elucidated in the *Philosophical Enquiry*. Such crimes involved the sympathetic paradigm of victim (as object or sufferer) and villain (as author of the misdeed), into which role the late eighteenth-century figure of the nabob notoriously slipped. Burke's imagery grew out of public disquiet about the conduct of East India Company servants (sometimes referred as East Indians), who increasingly formed the subject of literature and public discourse from the late 1760s onwards. Most commentators have accurately noted that anti-nabob polemic contained both a foreign and a domestic dimension; for example, nabobs could be cast as hated manifestations of new money, as James Raven has demonstrated.[27] Some contemporary authors, such as William Cowper, recognised that serious crimes committed in India went unpunished because they were committed far away, writing in Book 1 of *The Task* (1783–84) that 'Thieves at home must hang; but he, that puts / Into his overgorged and bloated purse / The wealth of Indian provinces, escapes'.[28] And while wealthy nabobs sometimes made benign *deus ex machina* appearances in fiction, for example to redeem impoverished friends and relatives, more commonly their narrative function was domestic villainy.[29]

This sense of nabobs as a threat to the British way of life complicated Burke's attempt to harness sympathy for people suffering in faraway India. The nabob literature of the period is notable for its lack of detailed reference to the colonial sphere despite the supposedly Oriental habits of the returned East Indian. Macaulay again supplies a deft portrait of the literary nabob, 'with an immense fortune, a tawny complexion, a bad liver, and a worse heart', as described in his 1840 review of John Malcolm's *The Life of Robert Clive*.[30] Sympathetic currents were further conflicted by the personal connections of nabobs in British society. One illustration of this point is the friendship of Cowper, a critic of empire, and the embattled Hastings, whom he knew as a schoolboy at Westminster. A short poem captures the scepticism he felt towards the lurid allegations levelled against an individual he recalled as eminently humane:

> Hastings! I knew thee young, and of a mind,
> While young, human, conversable, and kind,
> Nor can I well believe thee, gentle then,
> Now grown a villain, and the worst of men.
> But rather some suspect, who have oppress'd
> And worried thee, as not themselves the best.[31]

Another is the case of Pitt, who, despite his doubts about Burke's campaign against Hastings, voted in favour of impeachment. As his contemporaries were keenly aware, Pitt was the great-grandson of Thomas 'Diamond' Pitt (1653–1726), whose fortune was established in 1702 with the acquisition of a 410-carat diamond, sold in 1717 for a staggering £125,000. This did not deter his grandson, William Pitt the Elder, the Earl of Chatham, from denouncing 'the importers of foreign gold' and 'Asiatic luxury', who threatened to overrun the country 'by such a torrent of private corruption, as no private hereditary fortune could resist'.[32]

The archetypal nabob, Robert Clive, whose receipt of £27,000 per annum for his role in establishing the victorious Mir Jafar as Nawab of Awadh (the so-called black *jagir*) made him the subject of a parliamentary enquiry between 1772 and 1773, also formed the object of domestic rather than colonial anxiety.[33] Just as nabobs stood accused of destabilising the British economy by importing the fortunes that had amassed in India through illegal private (i.e. non-Company) trade, so they were perceived to corrupt British civil society through their debauched Oriental habits, similarly imported. Nabob habits such as smoking hookahs and arranging erotic *nautch* dances were primarily perceived as injurious to Britain, for all their suggestion of an exotic (but absent) colonial dimension.[34] This fed into a deeper end-of-century anxiety about Britain's empire, which many feared resembled Rome's in becoming progressively weakened through exposure to the corrupting East: a recurrent theme of Gibbon's *Decline and Fall of the Roman Empire* (1776–88). Cowper wrote of British India in *The Task* as 'a mutilated structure, soon to fall', a fate brought on by the moral malaise at its core.

The nabob threat served, if anything, to direct public sympathy away from India and towards the established landed gentry, whose pre-eminence was challenged by the influx of East Indian super-wealth, part of a wider reaction against middle-class aspiration and the apparent triumph of trade over title.[35] New and ostentatious houses rose up out of the countryside to accommodate returned nabobs, and nabob fortunes were busily employed purchasing seats in Parliament. Fears about nabob electoral malpractice reached their peak at the 1784 General Election, when 60 members of the so-called 'Bengal Squad' deserted Fox for Pitt over the former's East India Bill, resulting in the dismissal of the Fox-North Ministry.[36] Many 'Old Whig' commentators saw the emergence of the nabob as symptomatic of a national decline: 'What is England now?' Walpole wrote to Sir Horace Mann in 1773, 'a sink of Indian wealth, filled by nabobs and emptied by Maccaronis! A senate sold and despised! A country overrun by horse races! A gaming, robbing, wrangling, railing nation without principles, genius, character or allies'.[37] The body of the nabob himself functioned as an index of Britain's corruption, for example Sir Thomas Barlowe in Eliza Fenwick's epistolary novel, *Secresy; or, The Ruin on the Rock* (1795), whose past crimes are only partially erased by his addiction to alcohol and opium (the quintessential emblem of imported Eastern depravity).[38]

One of the most popular novels of the later eighteenth century, Henry Mackenzie's *The Man of Feeling* (1771), written in the aftermath of Clive's appearance before Parliament, features a rare imaginative excursion into the Indian colonial sphere. In the short section entitled 'A Fragment: The Man of Feeling talks of what he does not understand – an incident', the sentimental hero, Harley, converses with a friend about the morality of the British military victories in India and asks 'what title have the subjects of another kingdom to establish an empire in India?'[39] Harley contrasts the 'equitable' trade of the early colonial period with the recent 'fame of conquest', and describes the spoils of trade as being 'covered with the blood of the vanquished'. The feelings of the reader are only fleetingly directed towards sufferers in India before more domestic concerns intrude. Harley laments the tendency to reward military conquest financially, arguing that this is what explains the modern absence of noble principle among Britain's generals.

The title of the fragment alerts us to Harley's benign naivety, although while the reader is invited to share his condemnation (which approximated Mackenzie's own view) colonial scrutiny collapses into anxiety about modernity and the proximate.[40] Mackenzie's sentimental fiction typified the problems facing imaginative enquiries into the colonial margin, however heartfelt.

Samuel Foote's satirical play, *The Nabob*, staged at the Haymarket Theatre in 1772, demonstrates the interplay of sympathy, India and the domestic in greater complexity. Clive's biographer, Mark Bence Jones, has described the extraordinary circumstances surrounding the composition of the play: Clive was defending himself in the House of Commons on 30 March 1772 and argued that public hostility to nabobs was widely exaggerated. Mindful of Foote's reputation for producing highly topical satires, Clive remarked that there were no nabobs 'sufficiently flagitious for Mr Foote to exhibit on the theatre in the Haymarket'. Foote dined with James Boswell and George Gray when Clive's speech was discussed, and within days he began work on the play, in which he played the part of the villainous Sir Matthew Mite himself.[41] India features as a proving ground for Mite's criminality and the wellspring of the vices he and his fellow nabobs have introduced to Britain. The principal joke against Mite (and by extension Clive) is his humble origins: from a school friend we learn that he was a 'Blue-Coat' boy at Christ's Hospital (established for orphans and foundlings) and a petty criminal in his youth (as was Clive).[42] The plot revolves around Mite's dealings with the Oldham family, whose name connotes their established social pedigree, and commences with Mite's tumultuous arrival in the locality.

Sir John Oldham has fallen on hard times and has contracted a debt of £10,000 to Mite, who, in predictably ungentlemanly fashion, demands the hand of the Oldhams' daughter Sophy in marriage in lieu of payment, a transaction that Mite considers to be on a par with the purchase of 'an antique bust or picture' (p. 36). Mite's vindictive entrance into polite society is figured as social revenge, that of the underdog striking back at those who formerly sneered at him. Through Foote's reactionary eyes, this is seen in a strongly negative light, for example when Mite fumes 'I will see if I can't bend to my will this sturdy race of beggars!', an indication that nabob corruption threatens to destroy the impoverished old order (p. 50). Despite *The Nabob*'s smattering of Oriental jargon, Mite's Indian misdemeanours are of secondary importance compared to the socio-economic danger he poses in Britain: he is seen damaging the economy through ostentatious spending, destroying food stocks to inflate prices, purchasing a rotten borough and planning to establish a seraglio complete with imported eunuch guards. The dramatic emphasis on Mite's disdain for *noblesse oblige* in Britain far surpasses any attention Foote grants to India.[43]

In the play's opening scene, where Sir John and Lady Oldham are deliberating over how best to respond to Mite's blackmail, there is a textbook example of how a single incidence of suffering and personal knowledge of the victim take precedence in the sympathetic imagination over suffering on a mass scale in a faraway location. Lady Oldham, quite understandably an anxious mother, subordinates the condition of multitudes of Indians to the plight of her own daughter faced with an undesired marriage to Mite. When Sir John suggests that Mite's better nature might prevail, Lady Oldham retorts 'His feelings! Will he listen to a private complaint, who has been deaf to the cries of a people? or drop a tear for particular distress, who owes his rise to the ruin of thousands?'[44] For the purposes of the drama, the sympathies of the audience at this point are engaged clearly not for the suffering 'thousands' in India but the immediately visible Sophy Oldham. The device occurs a second time when Sir John's son, Thomas, reflects on the seemingly insoluble bind in which Mite has placed his father: 'No wonder that so much contrivance and cunning has been an overmatch for a plain English gentleman, or an innocent Indian' (p. 11). Foote recognises that sympathy for India can only be transmuted through an affecting domestic incident. The resolution of the play reinforces Foote's criticism of the new wealth of empire as Thomas Oldham, interestingly an East India merchant himself but one who 'does his duty at home', secures a loan staked on the family's reputation in an apposite triumph of title over trade (p. 71). In the concluding scene, Lady Oldham remarks with characteristic hauteur that 'the possessions arising from plunder very rarely are permanent', and Thomas chides nabobs for 'introducing a general spirit of dissipation, [which] have extinguished labour and industry, the slow, but sure force of national wealth' (p. 66). The play exhibits a Gibbonian pessimism about the poisoned fruits of empire but resolutely privileges the British victims of such corruption.

It was little surprise that Foote's subject matter remained close to home since his satires catered to metropolitan audiences. Burke, however, deplored this narrow-mindedness on the part of the British public, and his newly awakened horror at nabob depredations in India explains his volte-face on East India Company politics between 1773 (when he opposed the Regulating Act as an attack on chartered rights) and 1781 (when he joined the House of Commons Select Committee charged with considering how 'the greatest Security and Advantage to this Country and ... the happiness of the Native Inhabitants may be best promoted', as Burke described its remit in his correspondence).[45] Where he had formerly regarded the East India Company as a bastion of mercantile freedom against royal patronage and party politics, what he later referred to as 'this cursed Company' came to embody the ways in which institutional intrigue in Britain bore malefic consequences thousands of miles away.[46] At the level of representation, Burke's aspiration was to transcend the insularity of anti-nabob invective to engage sympathy for the Indian victims of colonialism directly. With his reputation as an exponent of rhetoric, he was seemingly well placed to redefine imaginative engagement with a problematically obscure object such as India. His writings and speeches on India sought to bring life to what he saw as the pathos and tragedy unfolding in a distant land under the colonial yoke.

Appeals to the passions to create connections over barriers of geography and culture mark all of Burke's thought on India from around 1781 onwards, notably his speeches in the House of Commons on Fox's East India Bill (1 December 1783) and on the Nabob of Arcot's Debts (28 February 1785). In the first of these, Burke argued that it was necessary to adopt language that deviated from conventional standards of debate, owing to the unique epistemological difficulty in comprehending India:

> It is an arduous thing to plead against abuses of a power which originates from your own country, and affects those whom we are used to consider as strangers.
> I shall certainly endeavour to modulate myself to this temper; though I am sensible that a cold style of describing actions which appear to me in a very affecting light is equally contrary to the justice due to the people, and to all genuine human feelings about them.[47]

Here was a nod to Adam Smith's neo-Stoicism in his use of the infinitive 'to modulate': as the advocate of the suffering party he would have to lower the pitch of his emotions to those of the audience. Burke signalled his departure from Smith, equally, by intimating that he may be unable to do this, not only because he personally feels so passionately about the cause, but because the crucial problems of distance and cultural unfamiliarity (the Indians are 'strangers') compel him to employ stronger forms of representation. Burke promises that he will be 'very sparing of epithets either to persons or things' – an acknowledgement of his reputation for verbosity – but objects that Tacitus and Machiavelli, 'by their cold way of relating enormous crimes, have in some sort appeared not to disapprove them'. India's sheer alterity in relation to late eighteenth-century Britain, furthermore, meant that 'the very names of the sufferers are so uncouth and strange to our ears, that it is very difficult for our sympathy to fix upon these objects'.[48]

Suleri suggests that Burke harboured a 'subterranean understanding of the failures of classification' and spoke with unconscious irony when he surveyed the grand sweep of Indian geography, history and manners.[49] Was Burke really so pessimistic about the power of the imagination and its role in the formation of a viable imperial polity? While no imperialist in the nineteenth-century sense of the word, Burke's vision for colonial India, as throughout Britain's empire in general, required organic ties of affection and allegiance between government and governed, and where those did not exist Burke saw the necessity of creating them. The dry enumeration of place-names between 'Tartary' and 'Cape Comorin', which Suleri seizes upon as evidence for her interpretation, is dry precisely because it serves as a foil for the description of India's diverse populace that follows. This Burke confesses is difficult to quantify, but all the more important because India's splendour lies not in its physical vastness but in the human achievements of its civilisation:

> This multitude of men does not consist of an abject and barbarous populace; much less of gangs of savages, like the Guaranies and Chiquitos, who wander on the waste borders of the river of Amazons, or the Plate; but a people for ages civilized and cultivated; cultivated by all the arts of polished life, whilst we were yet in the woods. There, have been (and still the skeletons remain) princes once of great dignity, authority, and opulence. There, are to be found the chiefs of tribes and nations. There is to be found an antient [sic] and venerable priesthood, the depository of their laws, learning, and history, the guides of people whilst living, and their consolation in death.[50]

Burke compares the size and prosperity of Indian cities with their European equivalents and alludes to recent financial crises in Britain by describing how, in the past, Mughal credit houses vied 'with the Bank of England' to support 'a tottering state'; a scenario familiar, in other words, from Britain at the time with a rapidly escalating national debt.[51] This is less an attempt to register the futility of colonialism (as Suleri sees it) than a call for respect for a nation thrown into dependency (as Burke saw it) on Britain by the sheer vicissitude of history.

Mark Salber Phillips has distinguished between what he calls Burke's 'distanciative' and 'approximate' rhetorical devices, calculated to manipulate the emotions of his auditors in contrasting ways.[52] Emphasising the experiential differences between subject and object could lessen the flow of sympathy between them, although conversely it could cultivate esteem and foster objective historical understanding, as Hume understood. Accentuating points of connection, on the other hand, increased the emotional intensity of an imaginative encounter and so facilitated sympathy. What Phillips calls Burke's 'blatant presencing effects', for example the vivid rendition of sexual violence in his opening speech to the House of Lords, were moments when the classic spectator-object relationship of presence was employed. Burke's reconstruction of the glories of Indian civilisation in all its glory must therefore be read as attempts to span multiple gulfs of temporality, spatial and geographical difference through varying configurations of sympathy. How far removed from this ideal was the disdain of young East India Company servants, Burke argued, 'birds of prey and passage' who 'roll in one after another; wave after wave … with appetites continually renewing for a food that is continually wasting', who have neither the social acumen nor the intellectual maturity required to discharge the responsibilities of office. Among these whelpish adventurers, who 'drink the intoxicating draught of authority before their heads are able to bear it', Burke perceived an indifference to Indian society that he saw as tantamount to barbarism:

> The natives scarcely know what it is to see the grey head of an Englishman. Young men (boys almost) govern there, without society, and without sympathy for the natives. They have no more social habits with the people, than if they still resided in England … Were we to be driven out of India this day, nothing would remain, to tell that it had been possessed, during the inglorious period of our dominion, by any thing [sic] better than the ouran-outang or the tiger.[53]

Here was a double breakdown of sympathy: in India itself, between the ruling official cadre and the people whom they are under chartered obligation to serve, and between the people of Britain and India more generally, between whom, Burke believes, there should be a degree of reciprocal affection, which only the imagination can supply. Clearly Britain's sense of its obligations in India had to be reawakened if such abuses were ever to be corrected. Burke's first rhetorical move was to render the scale and nature of those abuses in idioms that British politicians would readily understand. Only then was he able to generate meaningful imaginative interchanges between his audience and the colonial object newly restored to prominence.

The speech on Fox's India Bill reveals both Burke's awareness of the difficulty of undertaking such a mammoth imaginative task but also his refusal to concede the impossibility of doing so. He admits that ordinarily 'the cries of India are given to seas and winds, to be blown about, in every breaking up of the monsoon, over a remote and unhearing ocean' but presents his own intervention as an imperfect but resolute corrective to collective failure of imagination in Britain (vol. 3, p. 403). In what may be a deliberate allusion to the analysis of judgement in Hume's *Enquiry*, Burke in his later speech on the Nabob of Arcot's debts acknowledged that 'the scene of the Indian abuse is distant indeed', but scornfully dismissed the 'optical illusion which makes a briar at our nose of greater magnitude, than an oak at five hundred yards distance' (vol. 3, p. 488). As a precursor for sympathy he tries to secure understanding, giving the reasons for his expansive account of India's situation: 'I think I can trace all the calamities of this country to the single source of our not having had before our eyes a general, comprehensive, well-connected, well-proportioned view of the whole of our dominions, and a just sense of their true bearings and relations' (vol. 3 p. 488). He berates the House of Commons for the lack of attention they had shown hitherto to Indian affairs, which he argued was the prime reason for their present neglect, not the obscurity of foreign nomenclature. If British legislators were to redeem themselves, they had to match the breadth of their understanding to the magnitude of the empire, or else 'at length our concerns are shrunk to the dimensions of our minds' (vol. 3, p. 488).

In the speech on Fox's India Bill, Burke compared the political geography of India with the contemporary Holy Roman Empire, equating the Nawab of Awadh with the King of Prussia, the Raja of Tanjore with the Elector of Bavaria and so forth. He announced that he intended to awaken sympathy by removing barriers to understanding posed by exotic-sounding names and contrasted this with Hastings' deliberate obfuscation of the situation:

> It is an empire of this extent … that I have compared to Germany … not for an exact resemblance, but as a sort of middle term, by which India might be approximated to our understandings, and if possible to our feelings; in order to awaken something of sympathy for the unfortunate natives, of which I am afraid we are not perfectly susceptible,

whilst we look at this very remote object through a false and cloudy medium. (vol. 3, p. 390)

As well as offering a succinct diagnosis of his own rhetorical methods, this passage is important in revealing the association in Burke's mind between graphic clarity and imaginative sympathy; in order to summon the requisite passions, the object of concern must be presented as it were before the eyes of an observer with the full force of immediacy. To an extent this was always the aim of classical oratory, but Burke was responding to the unique challenges posed by what (for his generation) was the unprecedented global stage upon which Britain suddenly found its political transactions enacted. His calls for ever greater exertions of imagination, seen by contemporary commentators as eccentric expressions of hyper-sensibility (and dubbed ironic by Suleri) were in some sense an attempt to come to terms with the challenges of Britain's imperial modernity. As O'Brien has argued, Burke's impassioned mellifluence, cruelly mocked in his own time, is one reason why he endures as a political theorist today and is increasingly recognised as a prescient critic of colonial practices. While Burke was clearly no bleeding heart liberal, his ideas of compassionate interventionism constitute his most significant contribution to humanitarian thought.[54]

His earlier speeches can legitimately be construed as outworks of certain of his aesthetic ideas in a political context. By 1788, the necessity of employing the rhetorical device of magnification in order to make Hastings' crimes comprehensible was clear to him. Accordingly, with his co-manager Sheridan's assistance, Burke drew on a wide range of effects to create a spectacle that he hoped would, given sufficient force of presentation, effectively reproduce the scene of suffering before the assembled peerage. Two contemporary cartoons published in 1788, shortly after the trial began, responded to Burke and Hastings' rhetorics of magnification and diminution. In the first (Figure 1.1), James Sayers accused Burke of exaggerating the charges by magnifying a 'Benares flea', a 'Begum wart' and 'Begums' tears' into an elephant, a mountain, and an ocean of tears respectively in his engraving *Galante Show: Redeunt Spectacula Mane* (6 May 1788); audience members leaving the booth are seen commenting 'finely magnified' and 'poor ladies they have cried their eyes out'.[55] Gillray responded only days later by showing Hastings reducing an elephant, a mountain and a massacre by British soldiers into mice and molehills with a camera obscura (Figure 1.2). This time the spectators are saying that the objects are 'charmingly diminish'd'.[56] Clearly neither party was to be trusted to give a faithful version of events

Figure 1.1 James Sayers, *Galante Show 'Redeunt Spectacula Mane'* (1788)
Courtesy of the Lewis Walpole Library, Yale University.

and the juxtaposed images highlight the inverted rhetorical strategies of the pro-Hastings lobby and Burke's fellow reformists.

As the readiness with which objects could be manipulated and inverted makes clear, the rhetorical potentialities of imaginative sympathy were highly unstable. Through the use of theatricality, Burke and Sheridan sought to direct sympathy onto the plight of India and opprobrium onto Hastings. The latter's human presence in the courtroom, however, significantly altered the flow of sentiment among the spectators. Suleri observes that Hastings appeared as the only human figure

Figure 1.2 James Gillray, *Camera-Obscura* (1788)
Courtesy of the British Museum.

in the otherwise completely abstract plan of the courtroom included in the *History of the Trial of Warren Hastings, Esq.* (1796), a popular narrative version of the official transcript.[57] In her diary, Fanny Burney recorded Burke's ceremonial entry into Westminster Hall on the opening day of the trial. Responding to his grim, inquisitorial presence, she conveys the play of emotions between herself, the prisoner, and what emerges as his seemingly pitiless accuser in a way wholly unintended by the managers for the prosecution:

> I shuddered, and drew involuntarily back, when, as the doors were flung open, I saw Mr. Burke, as Head of the Committee, make his

solemn entry. He held a scroll in his hand, and walked alone, his brow knit with corroding care and deep labouring thought – a brow how different to that which had proved so alluring when first I met him! ... How did I grieve to behold him now the cruel Prosecutor (such to me he appeared) of an injured and innocent man![58]

The fatal weakness of Burke and Sheridan's strategy, as revealed in Burney's account, was that the feelings of the audience gravitated not towards the suffering people of India but towards Hastings, in his sixties at the opening of the trial and well known in metropolitan society as a benevolent and cultivated gentleman. David Marshall foregrounds what he calls 'the figure of theatre' in eighteenth-century constructions of sympathy, and Burney is certainly disposed to construe Hastings' situation as dramatic spectacle.[59] In another passage from her diary, she offers an Aristotelian account of his plight, albeit one tinctured with the warm blush of sensibility:

What an awful moment this for such a man! – a man fallen from such height of power to a situation so humiliating – from the almost unlimited command of so large a part of the Eastern world to be cast at the feet of his enemies, of the great tribunal of his country, and of the nation at large, assembled thus in a body to try and judge him! Could even his prosecutors at that moment look on – and shudder at least, if they did not blush?[60]

As the final section of the chapter will show, a sizeable body of satirical literature produced over the course of the trial portrayed Hastings as a man unjustly made the victim of political opportunism, or as another Gillray cartoon depicted him, 'The Saviour of India assaulted by Banditti'.

P.J. Marshall, in his introduction to Burke's *Writings and Speeches* on India, wisely remarks that the trial's great length detracts from a clear sense of logical progression in Burke's arguments; nevertheless, it is possible to trace some overarching themes in his three great set-piece speeches.[61] Burke insisted on the universal validity of certain principles of justice, particularly the incompatibility of arbitrary power with the rule of law. Hastings had earlier used the notion of arbitrary power to defend himself during his trial before the House of Commons in 1786, arguing that in adopting this method of government he had simply been following centuries of Eastern tradition of rule by benign despotism. Burke seized on this to protest against Hastings' 'geographical morality', or abandonment of European moral norms outside Europe, an embryo form of moral relativism which he repudiated utterly. This line of defence was a concealing shroud, and 'Mr Hastings shall not screen himself under it'.[62] Burke insisted that moral laws were uniform throughout the world as, moreover, was criminal culpability:

> The laws of morality are the same every where, [and] there is no action which would pass for an action of extortion, of peculation, of bribery and of oppression in England, that is not an act of extortion, of peculation, of bribery and of oppression in Europe, Asia, Africa, and all the world over. (vol. 6, p. 346)

Neither the King of England nor the Mughal Emperor, Burke protested, was entitled to wield arbitrary power, still less a colonial governor answerable to Parliament. 'Law and arbitrary power are at eternal enmity', he insisted, 'I would as willingly try [Hastings] upon the law of the Koran, or the Institutes of Tamerlane, as upon the Common Law or the Statute Law of this Kingdom' (vol. 6, p. 365), reinforcing his point with a lengthy extract from the *Institutes Political and Military written originally ... by the Great Timur* (1783), which he had read during his involvement with the parliamentary select committee five years earlier.[63] But Burke's moral universalism was not the totalising system it seemed, for he spoke only of fundamentals and took care to preserve space for variety in local usages and customs, a hallmark of his political philosophy as a whole. By arguing for a common ground of human morality, however, he was able to extend the domain of imaginative sympathy worldwide. Hastings on the other hand, according to Burke, fooled the British public into thinking that the ways of the East were inscrutable to Europeans, and that India was both inaccessible and unreadable. The 'geographical morality' defence denied imaginative sympathy its role of moral overseer of empire.

The earlier discussion of Burke's speech on Fox's East India Bill examined some of the techniques used to generate cross-cultural similitude and remove stumbling blocks thrown in the way of imagination. The persistent problem of obscurity in the contents of the charges – one of which hinged on the legal definition of the Indian landowning class – was addressed both through a rhetoric of magnification and by subsuming regional technicalities in more generalised, emotive versions of the crime. The Begums charge, for example, was announced as having 'fraudulently alienated the fortunes of widows'; Hastings was accused of having 'without right, title or purchase, taken the lands of orphans and given them to wicked persons under him'; and through his agent Devi Singh, of having 'wasted the country' of three provinces, 'destroyed the landed interest, cruelly harassed the peasants, burnt their houses, seized their crops, tortured and degraded their persons, and destroyed the honour of the whole female race of that Country'; Hastings personally stood accused of 'avarice, rapacity, pride, cruelty, ferocity, malignity of temper, haughtiness, insolence' and a general abandonment of morality unprecedented in a British public servant. 'Do we want a cause, my Lords?' Burke railed at the Lords, 'You have the cause of oppressed Princes, of undone women of the first rank, of desolated Provinces and of wasted Kingdoms'.

The charges were mapped into a cross between fairy tale and medieval romance, but this was a strategy for reducing alien and complex legalistic jargon with a view to attaining moral clarity. Burke, in a sudden swell of optimism, paused to reflect on the transports of sympathy these transformations may have helped to inspire:

> I believe, my Lords, that the sun in his beneficent progress round the world does not behold a more glorious sight than that of men, separated from a remote people by the material bounds and barriers of nature, united by the bond of a social and moral community, all the Commons of England resenting as their own, the indignities and cruelties that are offered to all the people of India.[64]

Burke acknowledged the problem of spatial distance even as he marvelled at the possibilities imaginative exertion can bring to the ministration of colonial justice. In his long closing Speech in Reply (delivered between 28 May and 16 June 1794) he confronted the question of remoteness in connection with the Begums charge, posing the rhetorical question of whether the House of Lords, 'at nine thousand miles distance', was fit to be trying 'the titles of women buried in the depths of Asia, buried in the depth of the Seraglio, concealed from human eye?' Hastings, he contended, had sought to 'bury' his crimes in Oriental obscurity so opaque he never dreamed the British Parliament would dare try to penetrate it. Burke restated his determination not to founder in the sublime, arguing that nothing relating to Britain's duty of care should escape the eye of parliamentary scrutiny: 'If we did not bring this case before you as the heaviest aggravation we should betray our trust as representatives of the Commons of Great Britain, which I hope we never shall'.[65] Burke's lonely quest during the Hastings trial can be summarised as a struggle of sympathy against the sublime. His efforts to bring affective simplicity out of infinite complication were threatened on all sides by the limits of imagination, beyond which lay sublime obscurity. This led to critics labelling him as Quixotic for pursuing politics into the phantasmic realms of the mind. It can – and should – also be seen as a refusal to mystify the exercise of unchecked authority.

The trial speeches, whose length restricts their widespread availability as critical texts, reveal the extent and ambition of Burke's claims for the moral imagination and sympathy. In his opening speech (16 February 1788), Burke set out a vision of what the *Enquiry* described as 'the great chain of society'.[66] In an under-recognised set piece of his mature political philosophy he described the subjection of humanity under God, laying particular stress on the social and moral obligations imposed by our participation in a universal sympathetic nexus:

> We are all born in subjection, all born equally, high and low, governors and governed, in subjection to one great, immutable, pre-existent law, prior to all our contrivances, paramount to our very being itself, by which we are knit and connected in the eternal frame of the universe, out of which we cannot stir.[67]

In the context of the impeachment and trial of Hastings, the implications of Burke's words are unmistakable: sympathy operates globally and a person is compelled to intervene wherever suffering is detected.[68] Burke coined the important concept of 'sympathetic revenge' to describe the mechanism whereby imperial justice is meted out; referring to Bacon's idea of revenge as 'a kind of wild justice' (from his essay written in 1625), he sketched how this might work in his closing speech of 28 May 1784:

> That wild stock of revenge, regulated but not extinguished, transferred from the suffering party to the communion and sympathy of mankind. This is the revenge we feel and which we would be sorry that all the false, idle, girlish, novel-like morality in the world should extinguish in the breasts of us who have a great public trust to maintain.[69]

The notion of an original 'wild stock', which 'submits to culture' and 'yields all the charming fruits of justice' tallies with the credo memorably expressed in his *Appeal from the New to the Old Whigs* that 'art is man's nature', and Burke is explicit about the need to cultivate sympathy, which, for all its dependency on affect, is in the first instance a civilised art. Thus natural emotions experienced at the scene of suffering must be channelled in ways consistent with the wider demands of civil society, as in Sheridan's speech on the Begums charge (6 June 1788), where he hailed the social utility of moral promptitude as a means of targeting the miscreant figure of Hastings:

> You see that strong Cherub Truth, empowered by that will which gives strength to an infant's arm. ... It calls now to your Lordships. It is the weak but clear tone of that Cherub Innocence, whose voice is more persuasive than eloquence, more convincing than argument; where look is supplication; whose tone is conviction. It calls upon you for vengeance upon the oppressor, and points its heaven-directed hand to the detested author of its wrongs.[70]

Doubtless the scene was enlivened by Sheridan raising a trembling finger towards the prisoner.

This much might be categorised as a humanitarian ideal of sympathy which Burke, and by proxy Sheridan, believed operated universally to correct moral abuse. Burke may have rejected the impenetrability of the sublime as a barrier to sympathy, but it should be noted that elsewhere (and more opportunistically) he used the emotive qualities of obscurity coupled with gothic tropes as weapons against Hastings. Here, Burke drew on ideas of the sublime familiar from his *Enquiry*, comparing Hastings to such terrifying creatures as monsters, tigers, vultures, and even a vampire; he had 'a heart blackened to the very blackest, a heart dyed deep in blackness, a heart corrupted, vitiated and gangrened to the very core'.[71] Such was the vitriol of Burke's attack on Hastings that the editor of the *History of the Trial* included a 'Curious Collection of Mr Burke's Abuse of Mr Hastings' as an appendix, whilst the satirist John Williams ('Anthony Pasquin') in his *Authentic Memoirs of Warren Hastings*, wrote, 'Had this furious, implacable, but *pitiable* man, existed in the remoter ages, and foamed and bellowed forth his malediction, similar to his present mode, his irrational ferocity would have drawn an exorcism from the church'.[72] Even his closest allies feared that Burke had gone too far in his use of gothic horror. One passage from his opening speech (18 February 1788), which swiftly became notorious, recounted atrocities allegedly committed in the northern Bengalese district of Rangpur by Devi Singh's minions (an episode not strictly related to the main charges at all); describing the seizure of land and property from tenants unable to pay exorbitant rents, Burke reconstructed a scene of sexual violence so graphic that Sheridan's wife fainted in the public gallery of the House of Lords, in a veritable climax of sentimental indignation. The passage reveals an artful interplay of sympathy for women and children and antipathy for their torturers, who subvert the intimacy scenes of infancy into a site of sexualised brutality:

> They [the victims] were dragged out naked and exposed to the public view, and scourged before all the people. ... In order that nature might be violated in all the circumstances where the sympathies of nature are awakened, where the remembrances of our infancy and all our tender remembrances are combined, they put the nipples of the women into the sharp edges of split bamboos and tore them from their bodies. Grown from ferocity into ferocity, from cruelty to cruelty, they applied burning torches and cruel slow fires (My Lords, I am ashamed to go further); those infernal fiends, in defiance of every thing divine and human, planted death in the source of life, and where that modesty which more distinguishes man even than his rational nature from the base creation, turns from the view and dared not meet the expression, dared those infernal fiends execute their cruel and nefarious tortures where the modesty of nature and the sanctity of justice dare not follow them or even describe their practices.[73]

Burke trespassed at the bounds of modesty himself in relating the torturer's practices, invoking the sublime to sidestep representations that would be truly outrageous even while they gleaned extra force from the semi-concealment of his account.

Ever since Burke wrote that 'pain is much stronger in its operation than pleasure', and Adam Smith asked readers to imagine that 'our brother is upon the rack', bodily violence, torture and death remained potent emblems of sympathetic identification in eighteenth-century moral philosophy and, by extension, the vocabulary of political investigation.[74] Work by Elaine Scarry and the late Susan Sontag has sought to account for the phenomenon of witnessing the spectacle of a victim in pain, an experience, Scarry and Sontag both agree, immeasurably intensified by the onset of modernity and the age of photographic and now digital reproduction.[75] Sontag remarks that Burke's aesthetical formulation of suffering significantly came 'at the beginning of modernity', and perhaps we may count Burke as the forerunner of the modern war photographer when he brought home the scenes of violence associated with colonial misrule overseas.[76] Then, as now, distractions close to home trump distant suffering. A sample of the satirical literature and prints produced as direct responses to the trial reveals not only the partisanship surrounding the trial of Hastings but also the widespread failure of British commentators to transcend domestic politics as Burke exhorted. Pro-Hastings titles tended to focus on the absurdity and futility of Burke's project, but even satires directed against Hastings repeated the domestic accusations familiar from earlier nabob literature. An example of this was Elizabeth Ryves' anonymous three-canto mock epic, *The Hastiniad* (1785), an extended verse commentary on the entire Hastings saga, purporting to be composed in honour of Marian Hastings' triumphant return to Britain (she left Calcutta just over a year before her husband). Building up his reputation as an arch nabob, Hastings had courted criticism by presenting the King and Queen with a large ivory bed, and Ryves accordingly describes how the ocean 'groans beneath the weight / Of gold and iv'ry's precious freight', as Marian Hastings' entourage approaches the British coast.[77] Ryves concentrates on the Oriental splendour of the Hastings' establishment, insinuating that the treasures therein had been obtained through unmentionable crimes. Joseph Richardson and Richard Tickell's spurious epic, the *Rolliad* (1795), mostly consisting of Scriblerian prose commentary on fragments of a non-existent poem, likewise alluded to the Oriental pomp of the 'BENGAL SQUAD', criticising their influence over the King and the Pitt Ministry:

> There too, in place advanc'd, as in command,
> 'Above the beardless rulers of the land,
> 'On a bare bench, alas! exalted sit,
> 'The pillars of Prerogative and PITT;
> 'Delights of Asia, ornaments of men,
> 'Thy Sovereign's Sovereigns, happy Hindostan.'[78]

Ralph Broome's poetic trial commentary, *Letters from Simpkin the Second to his Dear Brother in Wales* (1788), like Gillray, depicted Burke as 'Quixote-like', and poked fun at his susceptibility to rumours circulated by Philip Francis, reversing Burke's own generalisation of the charges against Hastings to satirise their lack of substantive content: 'He [Francis] told him long Stories "of Damsels distress'd," / "Of extirpated Nations, of RAJAHS oppress'd"; / "Of HASTINGS'S having compell'd the NABOB, / His *Kindred*, his *Mother*, *Grandmother* to rob----".'[79]

Most revealing of all, perhaps, is James Sayers' engraving *The Last Scene of the Managers Farce* (Figure 1.3), published at the end of the trial in 1795, which shows how public interest in the trial ebbed away over

Figure 1.3 James Sayers, *Last Scene of the Managers Farce* (1795)
Courtesy of the Lewis Walpole Library, Yale University.

its long duration. Burke, in a high rage as always, is seen conjuring black smoke from a cauldron containing the articles of charge, while his co-managers Fox, Francis and Sir James Erskine try to restrain him. Burke is sinking into a pit of hellfire through a trapdoor next to the cauldron, marked 'Exit in Fumo'. Meanwhile, a bust of Hastings bearing the legend '*Virtus repulsae nescia sordidae incontaminatibus fulget honoribus*' (Virtue, repelling sordid wickedness, shines with uncontaminated honour') stands irradiated amidst the smoke, testifying to the sympathy he attracted despite the disgrace heaped upon him. Sayers conveys the tedium with which the trial was by then associated, showing a rat clutching the familiar ticket labelled 'Permit the Bearer to Pass & Repass 1787 renewed 1795', and a snail wending slowly across the Managers' Box.[80] If Burke had called for an especial effort of imagination on the part of the British public in the 1780s, interest in India's plight, at least as presented by him, had all but vanished by the mid-1790s.

Burke's position throughout the trial was that no British governor of a far-flung province should escape justice simply on account of the obscurity of colonial outposts, a scenario that would later become a familiar part of the narrative of empire (Conrad's Kurtz was the most notorious offender). While Burke was a critic of British colonial practices as they were then constituted, he had no wish to relinquish any part of Britain's territorial possessions, and in a way he and Hastings were merely arguing about the best method for making British India secure. Refusing to confine himself to the parochial concerns of the nabob controversy, Burke applied ideas of imaginative sympathy germinated in his *Philosophical Enquiry* to widen the horizons of the British national consciousness. Metha describes Burke's writings and speeches on India overall as 'an extended tutorial system to his compatriots to help them perceive certain relations both between things within India and between things in India and in Britain so that the moral sentiments appropriate to such relations would be awakened in them'.[81] The problem was the extreme variety in the strength of imaginative sympathy between events in one country and the other. To configure aspects of the relationship between Britain and India in a way that Burke felt the new circumstances of empire demanded was not necessarily to succeed in rousing the moral sentiments. As we have seen, there were numerous barriers and complexities at hand to thwart the free flow of sympathy for India.

Ironically, it was Hastings whom imperial historians commonly viewed as 'sympathetic' in his dealings with India; through his adoption of indigenous forms of government, knowledge of local languages and extensive patronage of Oriental scholarship he has acquired a reputation as a progressive and culturally tactful Governor-General. Hastings' biographer Sir Charles Lawson, for example, remarked that 'the longer Europeans live in, work for, and sympathise with India, the more they should realise the magnitude and difficulty of grafting Western upon Eastern modes of thought', an apologia for Hastings' divergence from British governmental norms.[82] Similarly, Percival Spear in his study *The Nabobs* (1932) described Hastings' 'Anglicist' successor Cornwallis as having had 'no previous knowledge of the country, and a lack of that imaginative sympathy which would have made up for his ignorance'; again the inference is that imaginative connections are made most easily at a local level.[83] If Burke's campaign to impeach Hastings foundered through the over-ambitious claims he made for the reach of imagination, the technique he engendered of representing distant suffering before a mass audience perhaps lacked only the technological means to disseminate real images of violence rather than verbal accounts of them. The next chapter will explore sympathetic connections made in India itself by the Orientalist scholar Sir William Jones, testing the assumption that proximity to the colonial contact zone effected a level of imaginative engagement that, tragically, evaded Burke.

2
'No Less Pious than Sublime': The Sympathetic Vision of Sir William Jones

Only a year before the collapse of Burke's impeachment campaign, on 22 May 1794, Sir John Shore (later Lord Teignmouth) rose before the Asiatic Society in Calcutta to lament the death of its founding president, Sir William Jones. As an Orientalist scholar and judge who believed that India should be governed according to its own traditions, Jones seemed to embody the tolerant attitude to Indian culture that Hastings claimed to represent. Like Burke, Jones has been acknowledged as making an important contribution to the discourse surrounding contemporary India, and trying to assimilate India and the East more generally into the European imaginative landscape. Less frequently noted but equally pertinent is the shared interest of the two men in sympathy as a lynchpin of imaginative engagement with India. The term occurs at key moments in Jones's writings, and underlies a great deal of his published work produced both before and during his decade serving as a puisne judge in the Calcutta Supreme Court. Jones evolved a more sophisticated model of sympathetic engagement with India based on the capacity of Eastern poetry and religion to convey the passions and so complicated the spectator-object relationship between Britain and India predicated by Burke. This was reinforced by Jones's physical proximity to his objects of enquiry. In a letter to his former pupil Earl Spencer in 1787, Jones revealed his awareness of this advantage, writing that 'in Europe you see India through a glass darkly: here, we are in a strong light; and a thousand little *nuances* are perceptible to us, which are not visible through your best telescopes'.[1] Unlike Burke who was obliged to vault the span of geographical distance through imagination, Jones was able to consider the intrinsically sympathetic qualities of Indian culture at first hand.

Physical closeness was, of course, deemed to be powerfully conducive to sympathy and Jones seems to have sought to achieve intimacy with India in two interrelated ways: firstly, through acquired knowledge, in the belief that knowing about an object was tantamount to imaginative possession, an instinct seen later in the letter to Spencer when Jones comments that '*things* are my great object; since it is my ambition to know *India* better than any other European ever knew it' (vol. 2, p. 751). And secondly, in terms of physical immediacy, through his ready access to native speakers, original texts and local detail that he felt was essential to a genuine understanding of the place. Indeed, during the long waiting period before his appointment to the India bench, Jones complained to Gibbon that were he unable to reside in India, he would abandon his Oriental studies altogether: 'I shall ... entirely drop all thoughts of *Asia*, and, "deep as ever plummet sounded ... drown my *Persian* books"' (vol. 2, p. 481).[2] He was more sensible still of the importance of location after his arrival, writing to John Eardley-Wilmot in 1789 of his 'vast and interesting study, *a complete knowledge of India*, which I can only attain in the country itself' (vol. 2, p. 848).

Jones can be understood as a thinker for whom proximity was of paramount importance, whether as a matter of scholarly accuracy or a means of firing the poetic imagination. His poetry, literary criticism and translation of the play *Sacontalá* (1789), originally by Kalidasa, are all marked with a desire for authenticity that flows from this ideal of knowledge as something that is at once comprehensive and intimate. Jones wanted his translations and adaptations of Eastern verse to bring the reader into a sympathetic relationship with the culture of the places where the originals were produced, which involved reproducing it in authentic form but adapting it so that it was still capable of operating on European passions, the test of what Jones argued were 'the finest parts of poetry, musick and painting' in his essay 'On the Arts, Commonly Called Imitative' (1772).[3] Eastern expressions of the primary passions were, for Jones, the beau ideal of poetry and the diametric opposite of the neoclassical doctrine of mimesis.

Jones's motives for acquiring knowledge of India and the East have been called into profound question ever since Said described his work as a sustained project 'to gather in, to rope off, to domesticate the Orient and thereby turn it into the province of European learning'; for Said, Jones's eagerness to grasp hold of his subject finds its counterpart in the compulsive acquisitiveness of colonial power. Worse still, the taxonomies he created actually helped to subjugate the East into something that could be readily categorised and dominated:

> To rule and to learn, then to compare Orient with Occident: these were Jones's goals, which, with an irresistible impulse always to codify, to subdue the infinite variety of the Orient to 'a complete digest' of laws, figures, customs, and works, he is believed to have achieved.[4]

Jones certainly insisted that India and the East were legible to the European gaze, but for reasons as much to do with his wish to preserve an idea of universally communicable passions as the imposition of colonial hegemony. Said's conclusions have, of course, been the subject of much debate and might be said to have divided commentators ever since.[5] In some respects, it is possible to portray Jones as exactly the kind of colonial codifier that Said made him out to be, not least through his zeal to translate Hindu law into English culminating in the publication of his *Institutes of Hindu Law; or, the Ordinances of Menu* (1794).[6] In common with most of his contemporaries, he also believed that the forms of representative government appropriate for Britain were not applicable in India. In a reference to his radical pamphlet, *The Principles of Government, in a Dialogue between a Scholar and a Peasant* (1782), he wrote to Lord Ashburton in 1783 that 'India must and will be governed by an absolute power', and to Edward Hay in 1784 that 'such a system is wholly inapplicable to this country, where millions of men are so wedded to inveterate prejudices and habits, that if liberty could be forced upon them by Britain, it would make them as miserable as the cruellest despotism'.[7]

Jones's reputation has fluctuated from one pole of postcolonial thought to the other, before settling in the more nuanced territory of contemporary literary scholarship, with its attention to the social and historical contexts of British colonial culture. In the decades before Said's *Orientalism*, Jones's sympathetic stance towards India was often taken as a paradigm of humanist scholarship. As late as 1945, Jawaharlal Nehru wrote in *The Discovery of India* that 'to Jones and many other European scholars, India owes a deep debt of gratitude for the rediscovery of her past literature', a remark that reveals Western Orientalism's complex and sometimes controversial relationship with the Bengal Renaissance.[8] A.J. Arberry, writing in 1946, described how 'in India, with a new world of knowledge and experience to explore, his mind, which recognised no frontiers of race and colour ... was free to pasture at will over the rich broad plains of wisdom human and divine'.[9] And Raymond Schwab and David Kopf credited Jones and his generation of Orientalists with the creation of a golden age of 'cosmopolitanism, classicism and rationalism' and an 'idea of tolerance' that allowed them 'to transcend alienation from another culture'.[10] Jones's biographer Garland Cannon, responding to Said's intervention, insisted on the 'spirit of kinship and unity' that breathes through Jones's writings, which 'helped to stimulate a new Renaissance in the Western mind'.[11] Yet Kate Teltscher has rightly cautioned against any 'hagiography' of Jones, arguing that posthumous images of him as 'some kind of scholar-saint' disguised the reality of his participation in the colonial establishment.[12] Perhaps the most sophisticated analysis of Jones's career has come from Rosane Rocher, who proceeds from the premise that 'for Jones, individual scholarship and professional duties were porous categories'.[13] Evaluating Jones's achievements in terms of a binary opposition between East and West is ultimately a fruitless exercise, and indeed his own search for an approach to India that was both aesthetically pleasing and actively useful can even be said to have anticipated the hermeneutic challenge Said posed in his 1984 paper, 'Orientalism Reconsidered', where he called for a new form of knowledge 'that is non-dominative and non-coercive' yet alert to the terms of its own production within a society 'deeply inscribed with politics'.[14] As critics of Said were quick to point out, the notion of finding any culturally neutral ground from which to mount an enquiry into a given culture is perhaps entirely chimerical.[15]

An excessive amount of postcolonial positioning also distracts from the true significance of Jones's efforts to gain unsullied access to Indian culture and language, namely his wish to clear away the confusing welter of geographical contingencies that might impede the flow of sympathy between reader and subject. Marshall has remarked on the tendency of Jones's writings to 'show a concern for feeling and emotion alien to other writers on Hinduism' and this trait significantly points towards the centrality of the passions to Jones's systematic method of engaging with India.[16] Jones pursued the study of Eastern languages as a means of tapping the wellspring of Orient poetic genius as it expressed itself in pure outpourings of emotion, authentic offerings that might then revivify the stale classicism of European literature, an idea Jones explored in his essay 'On the Poetry of the Eastern Nations' (1772). Jones's theory of poetry has long been placed in the lineage of 'expressive' poetics analysed by M.H. Abrams in *The Mirror and the Lamp* (1953) but has a complex relation with his scholarly writings that remains deserving of more critical attention.[17] Jerome McGann is right to regard these as 'a vast set of contextual commentaries for his poetry and the originals upon which he drew', but McGann's characterisation of Jones's scholarship as exhibiting 'a certain kind of rationalist neo-Platonism – distinctively English [sic], distinctively Enlightened', while accurate, serves to elide the emphasis on the passions and the emotions that pervade Jones's imaginative writing.[18] While it must therefore be borne in mind that the many permutations of sympathy available by the late eighteenth century sprang from European moral philosophy's study of the rational mind, 'enlightened' rationalism for Jones functioned as a necessary precursor to sympathy by clearing away mental obstructions to affinity between European readers and the East.

Jones's *Poems, Consisting Chiefly of Translations from the Asiatick Languages* (1772) saw Jones presenting specimens of Eastern literature as worthy of aesthetic consideration by the European reader. In the preface to his *Grammar of the Persian Language* (1771), to which Jones had appended his earlier 'Traité sur la poesië orientale', there is a perceptible embarrassment about the work's obvious complicity in advancing the colonial project, as Jones refers witheringly to 'servants of the company' receiving 'letters they could not read, and were ambitious of gaining titles of which they could not comprehend the meaning'; only the prospect of material spoils, it seemed, would induce Europeans to study Eastern languages: 'interest was the magick wand which brought them all within one circle; interest was the charm, which gave the languages of the East a real and solid importance'.[19] Despite the overtly literary nature of much of its contents, Jones compiled the *Grammar* in hopes of receiving patronage from the East India Company, but there is a palpable sense at this early point in his career that he wished linguistic scholarship and colonial administration were not so densely intertwined.[20] The 1772 *Poems* sought to make a mark upon the apparently more disinterested realm of poetry, and accordingly Jones proffered different reasons for publishing the work than those given in the *Grammar*. In the preface, the reader encounters Jones's characteristic diffidence about the status of literature in relation to the utility of official and judicial writing but tellingly he recommends a study of the languages for their own sake in order to recommend 'to the learned world a species of literature, which abounds with so many new expressions, new images, and new inventions'.[21] Yet the seeming emphasis on novelty is misleading, for the 1772 *Poems* as a whole aspire towards an encounter with an originary moment in poetry, which for Jones was located specifically in the remote Oriental past and predicated on authentic expressions of the passions transmitted to the reader through sympathy, the operative principle of artistic genius.

Readers and critics of the 1772 *Poems* have struggled with the stubborn problem of the work's diffuse range of contents, which comprise 'Solima', 'The Palace of Fortune: An Indian Tale', 'The Seven Fountains: An Eastern Allegory', 'A Persian Song of Hafiz' (published earlier as part of the *Grammar*), 'A Turkish Ode on the Spring' and two translations of Petrarch, 'An Ode of Petrarch' and 'Laura: An Elegy', in addition to the two subjoined essays, 'On the Poetry of the Eastern Nations' and 'On the Arts, commonly called Imitative'.[22] Jones added to the confusion by undercutting the merits of Oriental poems with his notorious remark in the preface that he does not intend to place them 'in competition with the beautiful productions of the *Greeks* and *Romans*; for ... we always return to the writings of the ancients, as to the standard of true taste', but the logic of the volume as a whole actually counteracts this superficial Eurocentrism.[23] Later in his career, Jones was at pains to stress the parity, and in many respects the superiority, of Hindu epic poetry.[24] Yet the 1772 *Poems* proceed in four stages to construct a reasoned theory of poetic sympathy and a demonstration of Eastern poetry as a faithful embodiment of that theory. Jones's first overall argument, as set out in the essay 'On the Poetry of the Eastern Nations' (encountered, it is reasonable to assume, after the reader has finished the poems themselves) is that 'the poets of *Asia* have as much genius as ourselves' and 'more leisure to improve it', with 'some peculiar advantages over us' that mean 'their productions must be excellent in their kind'.[25] One preoccupation of the essay is to defend Eastern poetry against Voltaire's accusation that religious tyranny had stunted the progress of the arts across the Islamic world and the tendency of European commentators more generally to dismiss the form as irredeemably florid, mounting an initial defence of the Oriental landscape as a worthy source of artistic inspiration. He describes the Arabian landscape as 'a perfect garden, exceedingly fruitful, and watered by a thousand rivulets' and a likely site of the biblical Garden of Eden (one of several that Jones would suggest throughout his career; p. 321). This together with the profusion of gloomy and terrible objects in the desert wastes provided ample sources for beautiful and sublime poetic imagery. Moreover the Arab life al fresco spent 'in the plains and woods' meant that figures drawn from the natural world could be employed with greater propriety than by European 'inhabitants of cities' (p. 322). Jones next suggests the possibility (without unequivocally endorsing it) that the hot climate has caused 'the *Asiatics*' to 'excel the inhabitants of our colder regions in the liveliness of their fancy, and the richness of their imagination' (p. 326). This significantly shifts the debate away from external objects and the poetic imagery derived from them towards the interiority of poetic genius, allowing Jones to discount mere contingencies of 'climate, manners, and history' (p. 329). As a consequence he is able to assert that the Persian poet Ferdusi and Homer both 'drew their images from nature herself, without catching them only by reflection, and painting, in the manner of modern poets, the *likeness of a likeness*' (p. 334).

From this point, Jones is able to bear in on the originary moment of poetic creation free from the accretions of modern Occidental artifice. Zak Sitter has called attention to the shades of meaning the concept of imitation bore for Jones and earlier purveyors of Oriental literature, maintaining that Jones was critical of the counterfeiting of emotion rather than the delineation of external objects, without which, indeed, no representational art could exist.[26] The first essay traces the descent of Eastern poetry from its pure origins, a migratory process of borrowing and imitation whereby the productions of the Persians were carried into India by 'the descendants of *Tamerlane*' and continues to his own day amongst 'the *Indian* poets who compose their verses in imitation of them' (p. 335). This tradition, although weakened over the passage of time, based on a faithful delineation of nature and an uncultivated articulation of the passions, was to be the means of revivifying a European poetic lexicon long since grown moribund. Not having yet been to the East himself, the Eastern promise Jones offers is bibliographical rather than experiential:

> I cannot but think that our *European* poetry has subsisted too long on the perpetual repetition of the same images, and incessant allusions to the same fables: and it has been my endeavour for several years to inculcate this truth, *That, if the principal writings of the Asiaticks, which are reposited in our publick libraries, were printed with the usual advantage of notes and illustrations, and if the languages of the Eastern nations were studied in our places of education, where every other branch of useful knowledge is taught to perfection, a new and ample field would be opened for speculation; we should have a more extensive history into the history of the human mind, we should be furnished with a new set of images and similitudes, and a number of excellent compositions, would be brought to light, which future scholars might explain, and future poets imitate.* (p. 336)

But Jones's wish for '*a more extensive insight into the history of the human mind*' recalls us to his conviction that true poetry was defined by the expression of the passions rather than the reiteration of images and similitudes, a phrase that connects the first essay cogently with the assertion in the second that the 'greatest effect' of poetry, music and painting 'must be sought for in the deepest recesses of the human mind' (p. 338). The essay 'On the Arts, commonly called Imitative', whilst geographically non-specific also carries forward the earlier suggestion that the absence of figurative art and '*dramatick poetry*' in the Islamic world was proof that the artistic first principle is 'entirely distinct from *imitation*' (p. 338). Instead Jones posits his celebrated definition of poetry as 'originally no more than a strong and animated expression of the human passions', which anticipated Wordsworth's better-known formulation of poetry as 'the strong expression of powerful feelings' by over 20 years (p. 339).[27] Abrams placed the second essay in a lineage of eighteenth-century theories of expressive poetry that included John Dennis, Bishop Robert Lowth and the ideas of primitivism expounded by Scottish conjectural historians such as Henry Home, Lord Kames, and saw in it a confluence of ideas 'drawn from Longinus, the "old doctrine" of poetic inspiration, more recent theories of the emotional and imaginative origin of poetry, and a major emphasis on the lyric form and in the supposedly primitive and spontaneous poetry of the Oriental nations'.[28] The primitive power of Eastern antiquity, like the utterances of the rural north-west of England, possessed an exemplary ability to transmit emotion from one person to another. Ancient music was according to Jones 'a delight to the soul, arising from sympathy and founded on the natural passions always lively, always interesting, always transporting'. Jones claimed that in demonstrating the nature of the 'true poetry', he has shown what it 'really *was* among the *Hebrews*, the *Greeks* and *Romans*, the *Arabs* and *Persians*'.[29]

Sympathy arises from the sincerity of emotional expression, an insight which led Jones to privilege the primitive, the heartfelt and the extempore over the insincere artifice of modernity exemplified by the mannered absurdities of the fugue in music and the acrostic in poetry, indications of the 'false taste' of contemporary Europe (p. 344). Like the Arab tribes, poets ought to be close to nature for they are most likely to succeed 'by assuming nature's power' and through sympathy cause 'the same effect' on the imagination as nature's 'charms produce to the senses' (p. 346). Modern urbanised poets shut off from the natural world could only arouse weaker sentiments 'analogous to those, which arise in us, when the respective objects in nature are presented to our senses' (p. 346). Reading the two essays in sequence reveals Jones's circular logic that Eastern poetry must be 'excellent' because it articulates the passions and is consequently conducive to sympathy, and that 'the finest parts of poetry, musick, and painting ... are expressive of the *passions*, and operate on our minds by *sympathy*'. Jones juxtaposed this artistic ideal with 'the inferior parts' of art which 'are descriptive of natural *objects*, and affect us chiefly by *substitution*' (p. 346). He appealed to a universal standard of taste whereby we judge an artwork not according to how faithfully it reproduces the appearance of external objects (for this would naturally vary from place to place) but by the artwork's power to inspire emotion in us, an effect that must transcend locality 'since the *passions*, and consequently, *sympathy*, are generally the same in all men, till they are weakened by age, infirmity, or other causes' (p. 346). This transcendental standard of taste was clearly grounded on a physiological understanding of the passions that derived from earlier eighteenth-century moral philosophy.[30] Hence it is instructive to read the contents of the 1772 *Poems* in reverse order, for only at the close of the second essay does Jones insist that there is not 'the least *imitation* in the preceding collection of poems' (p. 344). Sitter reads the diffuseness of the collection as a strategy to dramatise the 'successful assimilation' of Oriental difference 'within the field of English letters'. But additionally by adopting a transcendental view of the poems' regional origins by showing them to be matter of mere contingencies Jones is able to contend that he is presenting the sympathetic quality of the works unadorned. His principal remaining problem was linguistic, for despite his desire to turn the sympathetic rays of the poems directly onto the reader, he was still compelled to translate the works into English, albeit by (in Sitter's words) 'guaranteeing the fidelity of these mirrors' as well as 'guarding the purity of the lamp's flame'.[31] Jones decided to cut his losses by proving only 'the authenticity of those *Eastern* originals, from which I profess to have translated them', doing so by providing detailed textual references and the locations of manuscripts, and turned the situation to his advantage by exploiting the added sympathetic potential of familiar English literary forms of expression.

Like Burke in his Indian speeches, Jones set about calibrating Oriental details for appreciation by the European imagination. Thus in the translation of 'Solima', he explains that he 'selected those passages, which seemed most likely to run in our measure', metre of course being an essential component of poetry's mnemonic function.[32] In 'The Palace of Fortune', Jones claims to have 'given a different moral to the whole piece' and with 'The Seven Fountains' to have 'taken a still greater liberty with the moral allegory'. 'An Ode of Petrarch' was added 'that the reader might compare the manner of the *Asiatick* poets with that of the *Italians*, many of whom have written in the true spirit of the

Easterns', and the Petrarchan 'Laura: an elegy' was 'inserted with the same view'.[33] His intention is to retain the spirit if not the letter of his originals, for it is here and not in geographical incidentals that poetry's sympathetic power resides.

It was therefore not inconsistent for Jones to present his poems as authentic whilst in fact adapting them to accentuate their European literary and moral resonances, retaining only a covering of what he called Eastern 'dress' or 'costume'.[34] Of far greater importance was the need to translate the emotive essence beneath into a recognisable idiom in order to produce an approximation of the original reader's passions in contemporary European reading audiences. This logically determined a high degree of borrowing, allusion and intertextual references to the European literary canon in the so-called translations, justified on the basis that the makeup of the human passions, and so the sympathetic response to a text, was universally the same, as set out in the essay 'On the Arts, commonly called Imitative'. John Guillory's notion of a 'compositional matrix' explored in *Cultural Capital* (1993) offers a valuable approach to Jones's strategic adoption of a vernacular poetic diction that is almost continuously intertextual 'as though it were the anonymous distillation of literary sententiae'.[35] The sensation of encountering individual works in the 1772 *Poems* (as with Gray's 'Elegy Written in a Country Churchyard' discussed by Guillory) is of wandering through a library of familiar half-remembered texts with an uncanny feeling that one has read them before; an effect no doubt heightened by the many subsequent Romantic borrowings from Jones's works. The circumstances in which Jones composed 'The Palace of Fortune: An Indian Tale' indeed may have heightened his referential frame of mind, for he related to Althrop how he had 'dined and supped' with Samuel Johnson, Oliver Goldsmith, the lawyer Robert Chambers and Thomas Percy before sitting up to write his poem until the small hours.[36] In consequence 'The Palace of Fortune' may be fairly regarded as the product of an intertextual conversation, reflecting the diverse tastes and fields of interest of those present at Johnson's club that evening.

The original material for the poem was derived from Alexander Dow's *Tales Translated from the Persian of Inatulla of Delhi* (1768), specifically part of 'the story of Roshana', which tells of an ambitious young maid's journey to a magical palace, her encounter with various allegorical representations of worldly temptation and her final rejection of them in favour of filial piety.[37] Dow himself explains how he adapted his translation 'in order to bend it to the Persian idiom' but has nevertheless 'retrenched many of the redundancies of [the] author, so in purely textual terms Jones's version can be regarded as third-hand.[38] However, by implanting a multitude of canonical references, Jones hoped to replicate the sympathetic force of the original version. The protagonist's name is Maia, which, as Michael J. Franklin observes, reflects both the Sanskrit *maya* (illusion) and the English 'May'.[39] The second signification summons up a multitude of imaginative associations, not least the true season for poetry and the anti-heroine of Chaucer's Merchant's Tale who forewarns the astute reader of young female innocence tainted. The opening of the poem pursues the theme of a fall from grace as 'some fiend' whispers to the Tibetan maid that she is fair, which awakens her vanity and a desire for admiration. A Hindu goddess duly descends in 'a golden car ... by two fair yokes of starry peacocks drawn' (pp. 37–8).[40] The poem by and large follows the Persian original: Maia is borne to a magical palace where she beholds the pleasures of the senses in a series of mirrors, before finding herself alone in a depopulated landscape, from where she ultimately begs to be transported back to her parents' home. Several distinctive features are also retained, such as the crystal palace on pillars of ice and goddess's opal throne suspended in mid air.[41] Yet the minute description of the goddess's attendants ('Webs half so bright the silkworm never spun', 'Transparent robes, that bore the rainbow's hue / And finer than the nets of pearly dew / That morning spreads o'er every opening flower') are reminiscent of Mercutio's 'Queen Mab' speech in *Romeo and Juliet*, Act 2, Scene 4 (p. 38). The entire poem is similarly shot through with canonical, classical and even scriptural echoes in order to replicate the charms and, crucially, the expressiveness of the original tale. The 'lovely stripling' who represents sexual pleasure, when he petitions the goddess to 'Grant me to feed on beauty's rifled charms, / And clasp a willing damsel in my arms', invokes the archetypal expression of Oriental sexuality, the *Song of Songs*: 'her bosom fairer than a hill of snow / And gently bounding like a playful roe' (p. 42). At length, 'grown senseless with delight', Maia sees an emerald ring and slips it onto her finger, whereupon 'the palace vanish'd from her sight, / And the gay fabrick melted into night' (p. 47), putting the reader in mind of Prospero's speech on mutability from *The Tempest*, Act 4, Scene 1 ('the cloud-capp'd towers, the gorgeous palaces ... shall dissolve'). When Maia returns to her parents' abode, the 'rosy-finger'd dawn' that illumines the scene is unmistakably Homeric (p. 50).

Canonical recognition could facilitate the flow of sympathy up to a point but in 'The Seven Fountains', based on the tale of the three calendars from the *Arabian Nights*, Jones presents a significantly Christianised version of the original in order to engage the moral sense of his reading audience.[42] Jones uses footnotes to explain the (none too complicated) workings of the allegory as the poem progresses. The plot tells of a prince, accompanied by 'ten comely striplings' (representing 'the follies of youth') who journeys to 'a glittering isle' (representing 'the world') (p. 15). The prince's boat and companions mysteriously vanish from sight, to be replaced with a 'band of damsels' (representing 'the follies and vanities of the world'). These lead him to a lavishly bejewelled palace inside which are seven golden doors, concealing the fountains of sight, hearing, smell, taste, touch and 'the sensual pleasures united', which serve the ironic purpose of raising European expectations of an Oriental tale as a repository of hedonistic excess.[43] But here Jones deviates from the original moral lesson. In the *Arabian Nights* version, the prince opens the seventh and final gate and enters an Islamic paradise garden in which stands a black horse. The horse's tail strikes out his right eye as a punishment for curiosity, leaving him to rejoin his ten companions, all of whom have been blinded identically. Perhaps feeling that readers may find this excessively harsh, Jones applies positive and quite possibly protective censorship to offer his hero an opportunity for redemption when he encounters an 'aged sire' (representing religion), who confronts him with the state of his immortal soul. The elder then rows the prince for three days over a dark sea to 'a lovelier island', where the repentant hero is rewarded with eternal life, and 'o'er walks of jasper takes his flight, / And bounds and blazes in eternal light', so importing an eschatological trajectory firmly rooted in the Christian tradition (p. 30). Such adaptations certainly test Jones's claim for authenticity, but according to the logic of the 1772 *Poems* as a whole, the act of providing a moral that would stir the reader to the sympathy fulfilled the true purpose of the original.

Not all his contemporaries were convinced of the authenticity of Jones's offerings, Walpole writing in 1772 'I think Mr. Jones's [book] is a blunder of *oriental* for *ornamental*, for it is very flowery, and not at all Eastern'.[44] Others, like Elizabeth Montagu, who wrote of the 'gayety and splendor [sic] in the poems which is naturally derived from the happy soil & climate of the Poets & they breath Asiatick luxury, or else Mr. Jones is himself a man of most splendid imagination', were enchanted, whilst Alexander Chalmers, writing in 1810, came closer to an understanding of Jones's aims with his praise for the poems having 'opened new sources of the sublime and the pathetic' and for 'familiarizing the scenery and manners of the eastern regions'.[45] Jones seemed to be regretfully aware of his status as an untravelled Orientalist and, as his reputation as a scholar and as a lawyer grew, he increasingly expressed a wish to experience India at first hand. Throughout the early 1780s, he confessed his anxiety over his appointment to the India bench after the death of Stephen Lemaistre in 1778, which depended on patronage from Lord Shelburne and without which he would have insufficient funds to marry his future wife and the editor of his posthumous works Anna Maria Shipley. There can be no doubt that India intensified as an object of intellectual desire above and beyond Jones's personal material concerns in the 1780s. Jenny Sharpe has forcefully argued that India's reality as a colonised space offered British Orientalists not only direct access to the relics of antiquity but also the chance to impose 'a moral order represented by ... Orientalist inquiry' with British India at its centre.[46] India furthermore offered Jones the next best thing to the primal moment of human civilisation as an object for research with all the invigorating possibilities for European culture that entailed.

Before and after his arrival in India, Jones's scholarship systematically attempted to solve problems for a sympathetic appreciation of India in the contested realm of late eighteenth-century mythography. Whereas Burke embarked on an equivalent project with a view to inspiring pity for a suffering nation, Jones's objective was for the cultural productions of India, excelling in expressions of the passions, to be appreciated by European audiences. As for Burke, this involved positioning India in ways that would optimise the interchange of imaginative sympathy between European audiences and Eastern creativity. One obvious problem was the destabilising effect that the 'discovery' of Hinduism in the earlier eighteenth century had on established Judaeo-Christian epistemology. French radical *philosophes* including Pierre Bayle, Diderot, Charles François Dupuis, Volney and Voltaire had seized on the fact that Hinduism apparently pre-dated the accepted Creation date of 4004 BC by thousands of years in order to use it in Marshall's words 'as a stick to beat Christianity'.[47] British mythographers who tended to the more orthodox view scrambled to rebuff the assertions of their French counterparts, which resulted in a spate of treatises attempting to reconcile Christianity with the newly explored religions of the East.[48] Jones likewise upheld the traditional chronology as part of a sustained demonstration that the peoples of East and West shared a single epistemological domain, which was vital if sympathetic relations were to exist between them. He was, however, critical of his friend Jacob Bryant's proposal in his *New System; or, An Analysis of Ancient Mythology* (1774) that the ancient inhabitants of the Earth all formed part of the lineage of Noah. Bryant euhemeristically argued that Greek and Roman mythology consisted of retellings of the deeds of the Ammonites, descendants of Noah's son Ham, or Ammon. Jones was unimpressed by his friend's methodology, writing in 1777 to Viscount Althorp that 'I reckon his Ancient Mythology among my books of entertainment', adding that 'I cannot help thinking his system very uncertain. I see no reason to hunt for explanations of old fables, many of which had no foundation at all except in the poet's imagination'.[49]

Instead Jones famously approached the question of human affinity through the study of language. If he was not exactly the 'father of modern linguistics', as Cannon has dubbed him, he promulgated the theory that parallels in grammatical structure and vocabulary between Greek, Latin, Persian and several Celtic dialects indicated a common ancestry between them to an unprecedentedly large audience.[50] In 1779 Jones wrote to his friend the Polish prince and Orientalist Adam Czartoryski, 'How so many European words crept into the Persian language, I know not with any certainty'.[51] Another acquaintance of Jones, Nathaniel Brassey Halhed, had caused a sensation the previous year with his *Grammar of the Bengal Language* (1778), whose preface reported a remarkable discovery made in India:

> I have been astonished to find the similitude of Sanskrit words with those of the Persian and Arabic, and even of Latin and Greek: and these not in technical or metaphorical terms, which the mutation of refined arts and improved manners might have occasionally introduced; but in the main ground-work of language, in monosyllables, in the names of numbers, and the appellations of such things as would be first discriminated on the immediate dawn of civilization.[52]

Spurred on by this and similar findings, Jones began to contemplate the existence of an ancient and now lost primal language, whose origins he speculated might lie in the remote region of central Asia known to the Romans as Scythia. 'Many learned investigators of antiquity', he wrote to Czartoryski, 'are fully persuaded, that a very old and almost primæval language was in use among these northern nations, from which not only the Celtic dialects, but even the Greek and Latin, are derived'.[53] Jones's understanding of human history and his quest for a pure form of poetry were both undergirded by the hypothetical existence of a primeval language, which potentially stood as a sympathetic lingua franca for the diverse inhabitants of the world. He was acutely aware that the material evidence for such a meta-language was only available in the East itself.

Jones's presence in India changed the nature and tone of his writings as he immediately exploited the potential of his new situation. Immediately after his arrival in Calcutta in September 1783, we find Jones sending out for local information to supplement his researches that, prior to this point in his career, were perforce theoretical rather than applied. To Richard Johnson he wrote for 'some poetical names of *places* in India, where *Camdeo* may be supposed to resort, like the *Cyprus* and *Paphos* of the Greek and Roman deities'.[54] In January 1784, he dispatched a proof of his 'Hymn to *Cāmdew*' to Wilkins and speculated to John Hyde that a 'book in strange characters' produced by native witnesses at a trial, 'which they called *Zuboor*', might be the Psalms of David written 'in old Hebrew or Samaritan'.[55] The same month, he instituted the Asiatic Society 'for the purpose of enquiring into the History, civil and natural, the Antiquities, Arts, Sciences, and Literature of *Asia*', whose founder members included Hyde, Wilkins, William Chambers, Francis Gladwin, Jonathan Duncan and Charles Hamilton.[56] The first volume of their published transactions, *Asiatick Researches*, appeared in Calcutta in 1788, widely regarded as a seminal moment in the intellectual engagement of Europe with Asia.[57] The Society's work also saw a shift towards empiricism in the way of thinking and writing about India, enabled by its members' physical proximity to the objects of enquiry and, it is not unreasonable to assume, their professional training as administrators, lawyers, soldiers and engineers.[58] The early contributors to *Asiatick Researches* present their articles as plain 'observations', 'accounts', 'descriptions' and 'translations', bound together by Jones's annual discourses, which aspired towards a more totalising form of Orientalist knowledge.[59]

Jones, as President, sought to fuse the particles of localised discovery gathered in by the Society's members into a coherent whole. Aware as he was of barriers towards the sympathetic appreciation of India, in his discourses and essays he tried to clear away what was problematic, obscure or objectionable about India and replace it with what was appealing to the rational mind as well as the emotions, the union of which, he believed, might lead to a complete or sympathetic understanding. Thus he describes the intention of the essay 'On the Gods of Greece, Italy, and India' (written in 1784 but published in a revised form in 1788) as to 'infer a general union or affinity between the most distinguished inhabitants of the primitive world.[60] In order to do this, as several critics have commented, he effectively rendered Hinduism as a Western classical religion complete with a Graeco-Romanesque pantheon.[61]Among the parallels suggested in this essay were the facts

Figure 2.1 Arthur William Devis, *Sir William Jones* (1793)
Courtesy of the British Library.

that Hindu and Roman poems invariably begin with an invocation of a deity (to either Ganesa or Jupiter); both cultures believed in a single divinity (Menu and Saturn) who personified rainfall and fertility and who was also worshipped as a lawgiver; and (related in the Puranic account of the life of Menu) there is an account of a great deluge to cleanse the world of sin, which includes the construction of an ark.

Jones equates Lakshmi with Ceres as goddesses of abundance, whilst Indra and Jupiter command the visible universe, wielding thunderbolts to symbolise their power. His objective was not just to suggest similarities but to fix the 'affinity' between the ancient inhabitants of the world well within the established Creation date 'at the time when they deviated, as they did too early deviate, from the rational adoration of the only true GOD'.[62]

Jones was aware of the high stakes posed by Hinduism's claim to primacy and threw down the gauntlet to the radicals with the challenge that 'either the first eleven chapters of *Genesis*, all allowances being made for a figurative Eastern style, are true, or the whole fabrick of our national religion is false' (vol. 3, p. 325). The anniversary discourse 'On the Hindus' (1786), and the essays 'On the Antiquity of the Hindu Zodiac' (published 1788) and 'On the Chronology of the Hindus' (written in 1788 and published in the second volume of *Asiatick Researches* in 1790) worked towards an accommodation of Hindu world history within the parameters of Judaeo-Christian belief, the prerequisite for Jones's bid to divest Hinduism of its apparent strangeness and contradiction of Christianity. The essay 'On the Hindus' considers the life of Krishna, 'the Indian APOLLO', which Jones places approximately 3000 years before his time of writing. Jones calculates the age of Rama, to be coeval with the dispersal of the peoples at Babel, to have fallen around 4000 'years ago' and supposes the 'dark interval of about a *thousand* years' between this and Krishna's birth to have been 'employed in the settlement of nations, the foundation of states and empires and the cultivation of civil society' (vol. 3, pp. 37–9). Thus there remained a comfortable 2000 years for the events related in the Pentateuch in a successful reconciliation of Hindu and Christian chronology. 'I am sensible, how much these remarks will offend the warm advocates for Indian *antiquity*', Jones concluded with a swipe at his French opponents, 'but we must not sacrifice truth to a base fear of giving offence: that the *Vēdas* were actually written before the flood, I shall never believe; nor can we infer from the preceding story, that the learned *Hindus* believe it' (vol. 3, pp. 343–4). By this means even India's most pronounced alterity could be passed off as French intransigence.

Jones's reconstruction of Hindu chronology did not claim to be definitive, but, as Marshall points out 'he had done enough to set the minds of most Christians at rest'.[63] In place of the disturbing claims French radicals made for Hinduism chronologically, Jones predicated philosophical, moral and imaginative points of connection between the Indian and the European and Christian traditions, with the object of showing that the essence of Indian culture was worthy of intellectual attention and, of equal importance, capable of engaging the European mind imaginatively and emotionally. Inden has interpreted this aspect of the Orientalist project as providing 'an orderly facade for Indian practices' but in addition it is important to acknowledge the importance of Jones's rearrangement of Indian strangeness into a legible object for the European gaze as a logical prerequisite for sympathetic understanding.[64] In his essay 'On the Gods of Greece, Italy and Rome', Jones asserted that Vedic philosophy bears a strong resemblance to 'the *Sicilian, Italick*, and old *Academick* Schools', referring to the belief that Pythagoras was tutored by Brahmins whilst in India (vol. 3, p. 384).[65] The essay 'On the Mystical Poetry of the Persians and the Hindus' maintained that Hinduism, far from containing an alien system of morality, bore vestiges of divine revelation that manifested themselves in an 'emblematical theology' (vol. 4, p. 234). The third anniversary discourse, 'On the Hindus', contained Jones's most memorable assertion of affiliation in his observation that 'the *Sanscrit* language, whatever its antiquity, is of a wonderful structure; more perfect than the *Greek*, more copious than the *Latin*, and more exquisitely refined than either' (vol. 3, pp. 34–5). This helped to demonstrate his hypothesis that 'the inhabitants of *Asia*, and consequently, as it might be proved, of the whole earth, sprang from three branches of one stem', the bedrock of his connective outlook on world history (vol. 3, p. 191). What Sharada Sugirtharajah has dubbed Jones's attempts at 'making Hinduism safe' involved the removal of obvious moral objections and historical and religious complications posed by Hinduism's reported antiquity and was lent crucial credence by his presence in India and consequent access to Brahmin lore.[66]

His mock-heroic poem, *The Enchanted Fruit; or, the Hindu Wife* (published in Gladwin's *Asiatic Miscellany* in Calcutta in 1785 and subsequently in London in 1787) reflects Jones's rapid acquisition of local knowledge and, very probably as a consequence, exhibits a strongly antiquarian bent to an almost Scriblerian degree.[67] The poem's subtitle, 'An Antediluvian Tale, Written in the Province of Bahar', anchors the poem within the confines of the Pentateuch and its Indian setting recalls readers to the vestiges of divine truth Jones believed were discernible in Hindu legend. The plot is derived from the Mahabharata and tells of the five Pandava brothers and their polyandrous wife Draupadi. It is set in the '*Dwāpar Yug*', or Brass Age of the Hindus, as described in the essay 'On the Chronology of the Hindus', when vice and virtue existed in the world in equal portions. Jones employs multiple strategies to clear obscure and morally problematic elements from the original away, in the opening lines enfolding what might be regarded as Oriental exaggeration in a string of negations that return the reader comfortably to familiar ground: the '*Setye Yug*', or Golden Age of the Hindus, is 'delightful! Not for cups of *gold*, / Or wives *a thousand centuries* old; / Or men, degenerate now and small, / Then *one and twenty cubits* tall' – the stuff of Asiatic hyperbole – but rather 'because /*Nature* then reign'd, and *Nature's Laws*'.[68] The European imagination is guided away from the monstrous size of the characters towards their blissful existence in an obviously Edenic landscape. The mock-heroic mode also helps to detract from the scandal of Draupadi's polyandry by comparing her to a specimen of Linnaeus, the 'learned northern *Brahmen*', who identified that the flower '*Polyandrian Monogynian*' is impregnated by the pollen of many others (p. 83). The oddities of the original are doubly framed by European faith and science, an Orientalist act in Said's terms, certainly, but a familiarising tactic intended to placate the reader's moral scruples no less.

As the group walk through a temple garden replete with authentically Indian flora (all duly enumerated) the biblical allusions intensify before they chance upon a tree that 'above all others tower'd', bearing 'aloft a solitary fruit' 60 cubits high (p. 85). Whilst this obviously forebodes a loss of innocence, in a deft inversion of gender it is a man who brings about the Fall when Erjun shoots down the fruit with his arrow. Krishna descends amid flashes of scarlet lightning and, terrified, the six agree to confess their greatest crimes and faults, causing the fruit to rise by ten cubits at a time back towards the bough. In a litany of familiar sins, the Pandavas admit to revenge, rage, intemperance, avarice and pride, whilst Draupadi herself admits to vanity and, finally, allowing a Brahmin to kiss her cheek, which in a symmetrical reversal of Genesis restores the state of primeval bliss. Jones places another frame around his poem in a didactic challenge addressed directly to the European woman reader:

> Could you, ye Fair, like this black wife,
> Restore us to primeval life,
> And bid that apple, pluck'd for *Eve*
> By him, who might all wives deceive,
> Hang from its parent bough once more
> Divine and perfect, as before [?] (p. 95)

Most remarkable of all is the appearance of Britannia, 'Guardian of our realm', who responds to Jones's challenge in an extended coda by asking 'are the fair, whose heav'nly smiles / Rain glory through my cherish'd isles, / Are they less virtuous or less true / Than *Indian* dames of sooty hue?' Britannia slays the demon of scandal, 'bane of mortals', in its cave and enjoins British womenfolk to 'reign at will, victorious Fair, / In *British*, or in *Indian*, air!' But far from signifying colonial domination, Jones's poem has in fact withdrawn entirely to the polite society of European Calcutta, revealed when he bids British women to reign over the hearts of 'rhyming bards and smiling beaux' (p. 97). It is they, not the characters of Hindu mythology, who need protection from scandal by the time the poem's deliberate draft towards colonial domesticity is completed. Hinduism in this transitional poem has indeed been made safe to the point of being tidied away completely.

Although it received favourable reviews when it was published in Britain, critical hindsight renders *The Enchanted Fruit* a transitional work that represented only a preliminary removal of obstructions to a sympathetic appreciation of Indian mythology.[69] Jones proffers a more creative and complex sympathetic vision when he considers the origin and scope of Indian expressive arts, which for him were exemplified in the sublime mysticism of Hindu poetry and music. Jones's nine hymns to Hindu deities published between 1784 and 1799 daringly attempted to address these ineffable qualities and, more than any other of his works, put into practice the theory of poetic sympathy proffered in the 1772 essays. Rather than articulating his verse in the persona of a Hindu worshipper, as he might have done, Jones writes about the act of poetic creation as a European Orientalist for all his celebration of the affective force of religious ecstasy. In so doing he seeks to impart something of the powerful emotions he describes and, at significant intervals when he steps forward in his own right, summons up himself. The poems are in one sense hymns about hymns, whose ironic self-reflexivity fortuitously lays bare the sympathetic workings of poetry.

Jones's most overt attempt to posit a sympathetic relationship between Britain and the inhabitants of India comes in the 'Hymn to Lacshmí' (composed in 1788), which celebrates the Hindu goddess of fertility, described as 'the CERES of *India*'.[70] Towards the end of poem occur topical references to the Bengal famine, mythologised as the consequences of mankind's 'vices', which 'excite' the frown of the goddess, and Britain's role in ameliorating the suffering. Torrential rain followed by plagues of 'warping insects' blight the crops, whilst 'drought unceasing leaves the hills 'gasping' and the woods 'mute', 'Till Famine gaunt her screaming pack lets slip'. A powerful description of a dying mother and child who 'drops expiring, or but lives to feel / The vultures bick'ring for their horrid meal' culminates in a direct appeal to the goddess to 'preserve thy vot'ries: be their labours blest! / Oh! bid the patient *Hindu* rise and live' (p. 162). In what Franklin has called an uncharacteristic 'Serampore mood' on Jones's part, the Hindu deity fades away to be replaced with British reformism with the power to correct the 'erring mind' of the Hindu (p. 162n). The poem's chiasmic final line reminds readers of the sympathetic duty they owe to the Hindus, for 'though mists profane obscure their narrow ken, / They err, yet feel; though pagans, they are men' (p. 163). The hymn's prefatory argument similarly employs pathos to cement the relationship. Recalling that the Brahmin who related the story 'was frequently stopped by tears', Jones chides readers who may think that 'the wild fables of idolaters are not worth knowing' with the fact that the poem's theological foundations 'are devoutly believed by many millions, whose industry adds to the revenue of *Britain*'. He insists on the reality of a sympathetic relationship between European colonisers and the Hindus 'whose manners, which are interwoven with their religious opinions, nearly affect all *Europeans*, who reside among them' (p. 154).

The affective qualities of Hindu manners and religious opinions provide a unifying logic for the hymns, which emphasise the power of Indian mythology to move the passions and the purity of the theology that permeates them. Jones, since the 1772 essays, had argued that Oriental verse excelled in forceful expressions of the passions through song. His essay 'On the Musical Modes of the Hindus' (written in 1784 but published in an expanded version in 1792) consolidated this idea and, as Bennett Zon has shown, attempted to reconcile Jones's Popeian description of music as 'poetry, dressed to advantage' in the earlier essay by demonstrating that the two forms combined became, in Zon's words, 'the greater Romantic force of heightened emotional expression.[71] The essay considers the affective power of music to result from different vibrations in the air playing on the auditory nerves as if on a stringed instrument. The feelings thus aroused have the capacity to raise associated ideas, which, particularly when reinforced with the signification of words, stir the mind to contemplative thought. Jones was fascinated by the seven 'Rágas', or Indian musical modes, which he felt 'properly signifies a *passion* or *affection* of the mind, each mode being intended ... to move one or another of our simple or mixed affections'.[72] He records that in the time of Krishna the Hindus possessed 16,000 musical modes but contemporary musicians tended to employ around 36, 'and the rest very rarely applied to practice', although these could be augmented and varied according to the season of the year and the desired emotional effect. Mode and poetic metre could both be chosen 'according to the change of subject or sentiment in the same piece'.[73] It is thus possible to speak of '*poetical modulation*' and to regard the musician as emulating the poet when modular shifts are used to trace changes in sentiments and ideas. Far from regarding Indian music as a series of harshly dissonant and alien sounds, as the music critic Charles Burney had done, Jones argued that, like all true music, it was closely allied to natural passions that were fundamentally the same in all the peoples of the world.[74] In this respect, India and Europe were in harmony with each other both melodically and emotionally.

The preliminary argument to 'A Hymn to Sereswaty' (1785) describes the consort of Brahma and '*Goddess of Harmony*' who produces 'the seven notes, an artful combination of which constitutes *Musick* and variously affects the passions'. Her 'RÁGMÁLA, or *Necklace of Musical Modes*' represents 'the most beautiful union of Painting with poetical Mythology and the genuine theory of Musick' and provides successive stanzas for the poem.[75] The hymn opens with the goddess leading forth 'sev'n sprightly notes' which depict the power of music to play the full octave of human emotion. The naming of each passion aims to call the feeling itself into being through sympathy:

> Young Passions at the sound
> In shadowy forms arose,
> O'er hearts, yet uncreated, sure to reign;
> Joy, that o'erleaps all bound,
> Grief, that in silence grows,
> Hope, that with honey blends the cup of pain,
> Pale Fear, and stern Disdain,
> Grim Wrath's avenging band,
> Love, nurs'd in dimple smooth,
> That ev'ry pang can soothe;
> But, when soft Pity her meek trembling hand
> Stretch'd, like a new-born girl,
> Each sigh was music, and each tear a pearl. (p. 116)

The hymn unfolds as a versified account of Jones's belief that primitive Oriental song, which 'like the full Ganga, pours her stream divine, / Alarming states and thrones', retains echoes of 'primeval Truth', elevating human feeling to the plateau of the divine. Nared, the son of Sereswaty and Brahma, 'Creative spreads around / The mighty world of sound' by playing the 'fretted *Vene*', the instrument with which he is pictured in the engraving that accompanied the hymn (p. 117).

Thus Sereswaty, 'Queen of the flowing speech' and 'joy of mortal' hearts teaches 'mystic wisdom' through song, the union of poetry and melody, which alone can inspire pure emotion (p. 122).

The affective power of love, supposedly the strongest of human emotions, is explored in Jones's 'Hymn to Camdeo' (which had appeared in 1784 as part of *A Discourse of the Institution of a Society*), whom the argument describes as 'evidently the same with the *Grecian* EROS and the *Roman* CUPIDO' (p. 99). Like those ineffable beings, Camdeo is addressed as a 'potent' god and a 'pow'r unknown', whose workings operate directly on the human frame, conveyed through the repetitive emphasis of 'I feel, I feel thy genial flame divine' (p. 100). For all the disorientating ravishment of such emotion, Camdeo is celebrated as 'God of each lovely sight, each lovely sound, / Soul-kindling, world-inflaming, starry-crown'd, Eternal *Càma*', uniting the erotic suggestiveness of loveliness together with enlargement of the soul (p. 101). The god's power is portrayed in terms of love's physical impact, for he fires from his bow, whose string is twisted with bees ('how sweet! But ah, how keen their sting!'), arrows tipped with 'five flow'rets ... Which thro' five senses pierce enraptured hearts' (p. 102). But if the Indian god – whose weaponry is familiar but contains culturally specific detail – inflicts emotional excesses on his votaries, Jones steps back from such abandonment, having earlier praised love's 'consort mild, *Affection* ever true' (p. 101). The closing couplet offsets European affection with Oriental passion as the poet bids the god 'Thy mildest influence to thy bard impart, / To warm, but not consume, his heart', inviting the European reader to endorse his greater capacity for self-restraint (p. 103).

Such moments of critical distancing from the excessive affect of Oriental poetry are offset by Jones's intense and apparently sincere interest in the doctrine of absorption. In his view poetry's highest purpose, exemplified in Oriental compositions, was not simply the arousal and articulation of passion but the elevation of the poet and (through sympathy) the reader towards the divine, the primary source of poetic inspiration. Jones pursued this decidedly Romantic concept in his essay 'On the Mystical Poetry of the Persians and Hindus' (published in *Asiatick Researches* in 1792) in which he calls for the reader's forbearance towards what he admits 'seems on a transient view to contain only the sentiments of a wild and voluptuous libertinism'. Were this true, the poetic creations of the Hindus (and Jones's translations of them) would be deemed unfit for European eyes and, more importantly, moral sensibilities. By way of defence, he exonerates this problematic feature of Indian verse as 'natural, though a warm imagination may carry it to a culpable excess' before reverting to the primitivist argument that 'an ardently grateful piety is congenial to the undepraved nature of man' and so confronting Europeans with the debasement of their own spiritual condition. John Drew has provided an exceptionally detailed commentary on Jones's Neoplatonism, which is perhaps at its most evident in this essay.[76] However, Jones's reclamation of impassioned love serves the additional purpose of coherently linking Oriental expressiveness to the prospect of moral improvement – even perfection. As part of a consideration of love, where he also cites Isaac Barrow at length, Jones appeals to Necker's comment that 'love, by disengaging us from ourselves, by transporting us beyond the limits of our own being, is the first step in our progress to a joyful immortality', positing the sympathetic experience of love as a form of divine agency on which point enlightened Europeans and '*Védántis* and *Súfis*' would concur. Thus Jones is able to justify his opening claim that the superficial eroticism of Persian and Hindu religious poetry in fact 'consists almost wholly of a mystical religious allegory'. Love for another person, by taking us outside our own selves, is but a small step on our journey towards the divine.

Jones's allegorical interpretation of Hindu theology and understanding of its sympathetic potential is seen towards the end of his 'Hymn to Súrya' (composed in 1786), which is addressed to the Indian sun god, or 'PHŒBUS of the *European* heathens'. The prefatory argument portrays the god as a derivation of the 'enthusiastick admiration of the Sun' at a time when 'the primitive religion of mankind was lost amid the distractions of establishing regal government, or neglected amid the allurements of vice' and the closing segment of the poem is at pains to stress Hinduism's descent from primeval belief (p. 144). The pretext for such reflective comment comes when, having enduring a fit of sunstroke, Jones self-referentially hymns the god 'with no borrow'd art', attesting to the sincerity of his entreaty as well as the primacy of expressiveness over imitation as a poetic medium. He prays for herbs 'cull'd by sage *Aswin* and divine *Cumàr*' to assuage the pain before on bended knee pleading his scholarly accomplishments to the god as one who 'draws orient knowledge from its fountains pure, / Through caves obstructed long, and paths too long obscure' (pp. 151–2). Jones metaphorically purges Hindu knowledge of its obscurantism in order for the vestiges of divine truth it bears to seep through:

> Yes; though the *Sanscrit* song
> Be strown with fancy's wreathes,
> And emblems rich, beyond low thoughts refin'd,

> Yet heav'nly truth it breathes
> With attestation strong,
> That, loftier than thy sphere, th' Eternal Mind,
> Unmov'd, unrival'd, undefil'd,
> Reigns with providence benign (p. 152)

Jones therefore offers a bold defence of Indian poetry's moral worth but with the important caveat that only the European scholar possessed enough objective judgement to recover its innate and eminently worthy meaning. According to this Orientalist logic, it falls to Jones to strip the latter-day accretions of Hindu tradition from the original.

Accepting the view that the expression of emotion and the capacity to be moved by the utterances of others could enlarge the soul in this way, the 'Hymn to Náráyena' (published in the *Asiatic Miscellany* in 1785), often hailed as Jones's most brilliant imaginative creation, seeks to portray the Hindu doctrine of emanation and reabsorption as an act of total sympathy through the sublime immersion of the self in the divine nature. The poem contains what in the light of Jones's earlier disparagement of mimesis constitutes an ingenious demonstration of why the imitation of external objects is not only futile but actively delusory. The essay 'On the Mystical Poetry of the Persians and Hindus' contrasts the love of god, which alone 'is *real* and genuine love' for that of all other objects, which 'is *absurd* and illusory'.[77] The world of things is but a veil hung between god and his creation, which it falls to mortals to draw aside:

> Nothing has a pure absolute existence but *mind* or *spirit*; that *material substances*, as the ignorant call them, are no more than gay *pictures* presented continually to our *minds* by the sempiternal Artist; that we must beware of attachment to such *phantoms*, and attach ourselves exclusively to God, who truly exists in us, as we exist solely in him; that we retain even in this forlorn state of separation from our beloved, the *idea* of *heavenly beauty*, and the *remembrance* of our *primeval vows*; that sweet musick, gentle breezes, fragrant flowers, perpetually renew the primary *idea*, refresh our fading memory, and melt us with tender affections, and by abstracting our souls from *vanity*, that is, from GOD, approximate to his essence, in our final union with which will consist our supreme beatitude.[78]

The Neoplatonic view that material substances (the only subject matter employed by the imitative artist) are an illusion that must be dispelled recurs in the prefatory argument to the hymn, which constitutes a concise disquisition on Vedic metaphysics, as Jones continues that 'many of the wisest among the Ancients', Hindu philosophers among them, believed 'that the whole Creation was rather an *energy* than a *work*, by which the Infinite Being, who is present at all times in all places, exhibits to the minds of his creatures a set of perceptions, like a wonderful piece of musick, always varied, yet always uniform'. This illusion of the material world is called 'MÁYÁ, or deception'. The same doctrine was propounded by the Platonic philosophers of 'the *Ionick* and *Italian* schools', but in case there was any room for doubt, Jones maintains that the theory is 'as different from any principle of Atheism, as the brightest sunshine from the blackest midnight'.[79]

The hymn's irregular pulsing metre conveys a sense of spiritual quest as Brahma, 'wrapt in eternal solitary shade' wills into being a companion deity, 'Primeval MAYA', who presents to her lord a casket 'with rich *Ideas* fill'd, / From which this gorgeous Universe he fram'd' (pp. 108–9). This refers us back to the argument's distinction between 'the Divine Essence and Archetypal *Ideas*', described in 'the sixth book of PLATO'S *Republick*', indicating that, for the Hindus, the world of ideas originates from a single and pre-existent godhead (p. 106). It is vital to note that in the poem Brahma plays the role of agent only, not instigator. Having moulded the physical forms of the universe, the god is next encountered, like Milton's Satan, in a moment of existential crisis:

> Rapt in solemn thought
> He stood, and round his eyes fire-darting threw;
> But, whilst his viewless origin he sought,
> One plain he saw of living waters blue,
> Their spring nor saw nor knew.
> Then, in his parent stalk again retir'd,
> With restless pain for ages he inquir'd
> What were his pow'rs, by whom, and why conferr'd

In the midst of these doubts, he hears 'Th'unknown and all-knowing Word' of 'NARAYEN', which commands him: 'no more in vain research persist: / My veil thou canst not move – Go; bid all worlds exist' (p. 110). The poem moves on to a complex (and initially perplexing) account of the Hindu doctrine of emanation, which should be distinguished from the more mainstream British Romantic conception of pantheism seen in Wordsworth's 'Lines written a few miles above Tintern Abbey' (1798) or Shelley's 'Hymn to Intellectual Beauty' (1817), both of which depict the divine spirit co-mingled with the objects of nature.[80] Jones employs a different cosmology, one in which the 'spirit of spirits' allows mortal beings to take pleasure in the natural world, illusory though it is:

> Omniscient Spirit, whose all-ruling pow'r
> Bids from each sense bright emanations beam;
> Glows in the rainbow, sparkles in the stream,
> Smiles in the bud, and glistens in the flow'r
> That crowns each verbal bow'r (p. 111)

The Romantic pursuit of nature thus disturbingly morphs into the lure of a siren as it becomes clear that contemplation is not enough for the soul seeking enlightenment. The poet in the climax of the poem purges his senses and achieves nirvana or absorption into the Supreme Being:

> Hence! vanish from my sight:
> Delusive Pictures! Unsubstantial shows!
> My soul absorb'd One only Being knows,
> Of all perceptions One abundant source,
> Whence ev'ry object ev'ry moment flows:
> Suns hence derive their force,
> Hence planets learn their course;
> But suns and fading worlds I view no more;
> GOD only I perceive; GOD only I adore (p. 112)

The illusoriness of the created world dissolves completely into a state of pure feeling. Jones is thus able to dispense with the view that much Hindu poetry revels in carnal lust in favour of an allegorised vision of the soul's yearning for reunion with the divine. The highest artistic expressions have the power to kindle a corresponding spiritual desire in the reader, which for Jones and other advocates of expressive poetry represented the noblest function of sympathy.

Jones's translation of Kalidasa's play, entitled *Sacontalá; or, the Fatal Ring* (1789) can be read as a dramatisation of human separation from the divine, the long yearning (according to the doctrine of metempsychosis played out over the course of successive lives) for reunion and the final reconciliation of 'our supreme beatitude'. Despite Jones's modest commendation of the play in the preface as nothing more than 'a most pleasing and authentick picture of old Hindû manners', it was enthusiastically received in the Romantic period as a sublime allegory of the human relationship with the divine (p. 216).[81] Goethe famously apostrophised in 1791 'Nenn' ich, *Sakuntalā*, Dich, und so ist Alles gesagt!' ('When I name you, *Sakontalā*, everything is said!').[82] The preface explains how Jones learned of the existence of Sanskrit plays from a Brahmin and acquired a copy of the finest example, which 'assisted by' his Indian teacher, he translated into Latin and afterwards 'word for word into English' and arranged into seven acts (p. 216). He related the substance of the plot (which ultimately derives from the *Mahabharata*) in a long letter to Spencer written between 3 September and 22 October 1787.[83] Act I tells of the love of King Dushmanta for Sacontalá, the forest nymph and foster daughter of the sage Canna, whom he meets whilst hunting antelope. He falls in love with Sacontalá, courts her and the pair are married. Shortly afterwards, Dushmanta is called away to his capital Hastinápura, leaving word that Sacontalá should join him there and claim her place as queen. As a keepsake, he gives her an emerald ring engraved with his own name. Read allegorically, the pure love of Dushmanta and Sacontalá stands for original bliss and their mutual attraction for one another is expressed as the compelling sympathetic union between god and creation. When he is momentarily summoned away by his officers, he complains that 'my body moves onward; but my restless heart runs back to her; like a light flag borne on a staff against the wind, and fluttering in an opposite direction' (p. 232). The natural order demands that the human and the divine, figured by Kalidasa and enforced by Jones as ardent lovers, exist sympathetically together.

The breach comes when Sacontalá, distracted by Dushmanta's absence, neglects to pay her obeisance to an itinerant hermit, 'the cholerick Durvásas' (p. 253). Enraged at his treatment, the holy man pronounces the imprecation that Dushmanta will forget about his wife, 'as a man who is restored to sobriety forgets the words which he has uttered in a state of intoxication' (p. 253). After Sacontalá's maidservant pleads to the hermit for clemency, he softens the curse to ensure that that the king's memory will return when he looks upon his ring. Sacontalá, who is pregnant, is adorned for her nuptials and leaves her tearful foster father for the journey back to Dushmanta. In a dramatic change of scene, the action shifts to the capital where the king, embodying the soul sundered from heaven, has forgotten his bride and instead dotes on his other wives. However, a song performed behind the scenes awakens a faint memory of his former love, although he is unable to recall its object. Jones here proffers the suggestive idea that the associations of ideas raised by the sympathetic power of song are necessarily weaker intimations of a higher truth, as Dushmanta struggles to identify the genuine reason for his sadness:

> Ah! What makes me so melancholy on hearing a mere song on absence, when I am not in fact separated from any real object of my affection? – Perhaps the sadness of men, otherwise happy, on seeing beautiful forms and listening to sweet melody, arises from some faint remembrance of past joys and the traces of connections in a former state of existence. (p. 265)

This notion seems fully in accord with Jones's belief that true art elicits emotion in others rather than mimetically replicating external forms. The song plays on Dushmanta's affections but imperfectly since he is not only parted from Sacontalá but also in ignorance of the fact.

The idea occurs twice more in the play when the association of the mimetic function of art with illusion (*maya*) and expressiveness with intimation of the divine appears with greater didactic explicitness. The pregnant Sacontalá and her party arrive at the court, where she presents the ring to Dushmanta but, mortified, discovers that it has gone, one of her attendants speculating that it must have slipped from her finger whilst she was performing her ritual ablutions. Dushmanta, under the hermit's curse, forswears all knowledge of his marriage to Sacontalá in an allegorical enactment of the soul's repudiation of god. The forsaken Sacontalá returns to her ashram, whilst the king remains 'entangled in a labyrinth of confused apprehensions' (p. 265). The moment of revelation comes when a fisherman, who has found the ring inside the belly of a fish, brings it to the palace and so breaks the hermit's spell. Having arriving at a painful consciousness of his actions, Dushmanta commissions a painting of Sacontalá but finds the likeness to be 'infinitely below the original', comparing himself to 'a traveller who negligently passes by a clear and full rivulet, and soon ardently thirsts for a false appearance of water on a sandy desert'. Artistic representation is shown to be not merely inadequate as a means of accessing the divine but dangerously illusory, whilst on the other hand the king is able to find a modicum of consolation through the exercise of his 'warm fancy' (p. 279).

The plot is resolved in the final act when Dushmanta, as a reward for slaying a race of gigantic genii at Indra's command, is deposited by Mátali, Indra's charioteer, on the beautiful mountainside where Sacontalá now resides with her son, Dushmanta's heir (the future Emperor Bharata). The mourning weeds in which she is originally glimpsed signify the sorrowful vigil she has kept for her absent husband 'with a mind perfectly pure', suggesting the enduring love of god for errant mortals (p. 293). When Dushmanta is finally reunited with his wife and son, he declares that he has 'reached the summit of my earthly happiness', whereupon it falls to the god Casyapa to provide a closing recapitulation of events: 'when the gloom was dispelled, his conjugal affection revived; as a mirror whose surface has been sullied, reflects no image; but exhibits perfect resemblances when its polish has been restored' (pp. 295–6). The epiphanic reunion with god is ambiguously figured here as an image in an untarnished mirror, but within the scheme of the allegory the revival of 'conjugal affection' signifies the sympathetic inclination of the soul towards god. Jones's translation of *Sacontalá* offers nothing less than a vindication of the principle that the highest function of art and poetry operates through imaginative sympathy and not by imitation, but he elevates emotional affect to the status of transcendental revelation. Once Jones had settled in India, he did come to regard Hindu mythology, once it was purged of its latter-day accretions, as no less capable of arousing sublime passions as the primeval texts of the Old Testament. *Sacontalá* allegorises the sympathetic relationship between mankind and the divine including the pangs of separation and yearning for restoration, the original wellspring (in Jones's view) of Oriental love poetry.

For all his advocacy of the sublime possibilities of Hindu culture, no appraisal of Jones can ignore the coercive undertones latent in eighteenth-century conceptions of imaginative sympathy, highlighted in his case by his position in the cockpit of colonial government. The consanguinity identified by Jones's extensive researches into the early inhabitants of the world did not necessarily imply equality, especially where those links were established only in the farthest reaches of antiquity. Jones's reconfigurations of Eastern religions too have drawn the ire of postcolonial critics, especially his manipulation of Hinduism to conform to Judaeo-Christian systems of ideas.[84] What is required for an understanding of Jones's conflicting and deeply involved position in India is what Rocher has called 'fine-grained analyses of the interwoven and constantly reconfigured tapestry of scholarship' in place of the 'single dimension of colonial predators and victims' that stemmed from the approach inaugurated by Said.[85] Something of the ambiguity of Jones's thought may be seen in his second Anniversary Discourse to the Asiatic Society (delivered in 1785), which accepts the view of 'Europe as a *sovereign Princess*, and *Asia* as her *handmaid*' and comments that 'reason and taste are the prerogatives of *European* minds, while the

Asiaticks have soared to loftier heights in the sphere of imagination'.[86] The preceding discussion has sought to illuminate the value that Jones in fact placed on imagination, elsewhere regarded as a subordinate faculty of the mind. Yet equally suggestive is Jones's view, expressed in the introduction to the first volume of *Asiatick Researches*, that 'there is an active spirit in European minds, which no climate or situation in life can wholly repress'.[87] The following chapter will explores how the idea of an innate difference in the makeup of sensibility, which elsewhere in his work Jones seems at pains to deny, compromised the notion of global kinship predicated on the sympathetic exchange of the mutually transferrable passions.

3
Sympathy in a Hot Climate: British and Indian Subjects at the Turn of the Century

Jones's fellow European writers in Bengal at the end of the eighteenth century were engaged in nothing less than the construction of a new notion of sensibility, one adapted for the rigours and cultural complexities of colonial conditions. This new culture stemmed in large part from the outcome of an earlier intellectual debate about the effects of a debilitating climate, but bore ramifications for the exercise of imaginative sympathy in the colonial contact zone that E.M. Forster intuited in his introduction to Eliza Fay's *Original Letters from India (1779–1815)* (1925 edition). Forster felt that the 'deportment' of Britons in India in the late eighteenth century was characterised by a tangible hardening of attitudes towards the country and its inhabitants. He noted that 'the English are no longer traders, soldiers, adventurers, who may take up what attitude suits them towards the aborigines; they are acquiring racial consciousness and the sense of Imperial responsibility'.[1] Forster holds Fay's letters to be both representative and unrepresentative of this behavioural development. Consciously alluding to Jane Austen's novel of a similar title, Forster continues that Fay is 'in her sense, as in her sentiment, the child of her century ... her floods of tears and fainting fits are always postponed until a convenient moment: they never intrude while she is looking after her luggage or outwitting her foes' (p. 14). In other words, she is prone to extravagant displays of emotion insofar as she is a product of the age of sensibility, but her colonial environment and the rigours of travel somehow steeled her personality. Indeed, as will be seen, Fay's self-reliance and independence of spirit have made her a figure of admiration amongst many feminist critics.[2]

A tough-minded independent woman she undeniably was, but environmental factors too exerted an influence on Fay and other writers based in India at this time. Notions that the Asiatic climate was debilitating and corrosive to a healthy European sensibility had long been current in Britain, chiefly derived from Montesquieu's influential treatise *L'Esprit des Lois* (1748; translated as 'The Spirit of the Laws' by Thomas Nugent in 1750), which initiated the theory often referred to as climatic determinism. As the preceding discussion of Jones demonstrated, there was a latent tendency in Orientalist thought to contrast European diligence with Eastern dissipation, but the tenets of climatic determinism raised more fundamental questions for Europeans living in the so-called torrid zone. Generations further on, Montesquieu's thinking implied, colonial communities would inevitably succumb to their environment, and contemporary cartoons of nabobs with jaundiced complexions, not to mention the all too real death rolls of Company servants felled by disease, pointed to precisely this effect taking hold on Europeans exposed to their surroundings. This possibility was countered by a conscious insistence on the part of colonial authors that a normative sensibility could be preserved intact, and so European identity might continue unalloyed in the torrid zone. Furthermore, a more hermetically sealed version of sensibility evolved as a response to concerns about climate and the possibility of inculturation by Indian surroundings (the danger of 'going native'), based less on somatic affect and more on an innate moral sense and identity. This paralleled the transition from sensibility to moral sentiment that is a widely observed feature of late eighteenth-century counter-revolutionary literary culture in Britain. However, the colonial modification of sensibility contained several distinctively Indian elements, notably a preoccupation with climate as a litmus test of European subjectivity. As a consequence, it became easier for Britons to feel sympathy for one another on the basis of national character, whilst Indians were increasingly shut out from the colonial economy of sentiment.

The culture of sensibility, as it was defined in the early to mid eighteenth century, encouraged individuals to think of their bodies as porous and intimately affected by external stimuli and situations. Anna Jessie van Sant has called this 'organic sensitivity', or the body's responsiveness to external sensations.[3] India's heat and humidity were considered particularly ill-suited to women, with the result that European colonial communities tended to suffer from a significant gender imbalance. Efforts to correct this included the notorious 'fishing fleet', a seaborne influx of women eager to secure East India Company officials as husbands, and a more general attempt to replicate European patterns of domestic life in India. Yet the 'problem of sensibility' that Markman Ellis identified as taking place around the turn of the nineteenth century also spelled changes for the culture of sensibility in Britain. Gillray's depiction of Sensibility in his 1798 print *The New Morality* as a ragged *sans-culotte*, weeping over a dead bird and a copy of Rousseau while Louis XVI's head lies disregarded at her feet, illustrated forcefully the association of sentimental excesses with French Jacobinism.[4] Men and women were expected to rely on inner moral sense rather than an external display of virtue, which helped to seal the body against malefic outside influences. The gradual replacement of a heightened form of sensibility with inner fortitude can be seen as a specifically colonial solution to the perils of climatic determinism. A resolution to defy the depredations of a hot climate became associated with British individuals overseas, and arguably lives on in a certain type of obstinate holidaymaker.

E.M. Collingham has provided a colonial corollary to this process in her persuasive account of the transition of British bodily practices in India from what she calls 'nabob to sahib'.[5] Self-belief, coupled with a need to overmatch native displays of power, resulted in the progressive isolation of colonial officials from the population. Partly this involved an element of political theatre as the British authorities assumed ever more prestigious mantles of Indian rule. But it also resulted from a rejection of Montesquieu's findings on the determining power of the climate. Anxiety about the climate marked the fledgling literary culture of Calcutta, as did concern about the ensuing fluidity of the passions and whether sympathy for colonised culture posed a threat to the European self, as the nabob controversy in Britain seemed to suggest. Elizabeth Hamilton's novel *Translation of the Letters of a Hindoo Rajah* (1796), a reading of which forms the conclusion to this chapter, mounts a defence of the colonial community in India based on the author's reverence for her brother, the Orientalist Charles Hamilton. Colonial publications (which are taken to include books written both in and about colonial India) reveal the changing nature of British sentimental encounters with India, as sympathy, conceived in terms of a cosmopolitan engagement with the world, gives way to the idea that the colonial self should be inured to its environment. Responsive sensibility was replaced with an innate moral sense, which perhaps inevitably aligned British identity closely with the doctrines of Christianity.

The contemporary debate about the influence of climate on the body polarised around the exchange between Montesquieu's *The Spirit of the Laws* and Hume's essay 'Of National Characters' (1748), written in response. Hume provided an alternative and ultimately countervailing view of how identity might be constituted in Asiatic surroundings. Montesquieu investigated, together with a host of other factors, the influence of hot and cold climates on the human frame, raising troubling possibilities for European colonists in tropical climates whose bodies, and by extension characters, were not impervious to their locale: 'the children of Europeans born in the Indies', wrote Montesquieu, 'lose the courage of the European climate'.[6] British colonial authors responded to this disturbing supposition either by demonstrating the continued sensitivity of their own sensibilities to show, *pace* Montesquieu, that national character could survive transplantation to the Indies; or alternatively by seeking to shift the grounds of sensibility from an emphasis on somatic impressionability to the idea of an internalised morality. Both responses suggested fundamental differences between Europeans and Indians that profoundly altered the dynamics of the colonial sympathetic encounter. Indeed Jones's comment that 'there is an active spirit in *European* minds, which no climate or situation can wholly repress' stood at the crux of these two lines of thought.

Montesquieu's examination of climate formed part of his broader enquiry into which code of laws was suitable for any given country, the overall goal of *The Spirit of the Laws*. The implications for sympathy are visible when he discusses the relationship between bodily conditions (including climate) and the mind. Montesquieu argues that, just as climate affected the geography of the different regions of the world, so the characters of the inhabitants were also shaped in symbiotic relation to the environment. Book 14, 'On the Laws in Relation to the Nature of the Climate', begins 'If it is true that the character of the spirit and the passions of the heart are extremely different in the various climates, *laws* should be relative to the differences in these passions and to the differences in these characters' (p. 231). Following the physiological accounts of human nature contained in the work of Locke and Hartley, Montesquieu proceeds to explain how different air temperatures affect both the body and mind. Cold air, he writes, has the effect of contracting the body's surface fibres, strengthening the metabolism and quickening the flow of blood. Hot air, by contrast, relaxes and lengthens these fibres, causing weakness of heart and an ungovernable receptivity to pleasure and pain. For this reason, 'the people in hot countries are timid like old men', while 'those in cold countries are courageous like young men'. These ideas undergirded Montesquieu's ideas of national character, typified by the 'Muscovite' who 'has to be flayed before he feels anything', or the inhabitant of warmer climes whose 'soul is sovereignly moved by all that is related to the union of the sexes' (pp. 232–3). Montesquieu proceeded to describe the climate's effect on morals, remarking how generosity of spirit (the origin of sympathy) appears to deteriorate as the traveller progresses from north to south:

> As you move towards the countries of the south, you will believe that you have moved away from morality itself ... The heat of the climate can be so excessive that the body there will be absolutely without strength. So, prostration will pass even to the spirit; no curiosity, no noble enterprise, no generous sentiment; inclinations all will be passive there. (p. 234)

Here was the quintessence of Oriental despotism, whose rubric *The Spirit of the Laws* placed on a quasi-scientific footing. By theorising the popular contemporary belief that Europe was a more propitious environment than Asia, Montesquieu contributed to the myth that non-Europeans were sensual, effeminate and fit only for enslavement beneath a tyrannical government.

But climate theory raised worrying possibilities for European nations too, and Britain and France in particular, then in the process of expanding their East Indian empires. Although, in his *Voyages* (1676), Tavernier opined that 'a hundred European soldiers would have little difficulty routing a thousand Indian soldiers', Bernier had warned in his earlier *Histoire de la dernière révolution des États du Grand Mogol* (1670–71) that 'in the third generation' the warlike Persians who settled in India took on 'the indolence and cowardice of the Indians'.[7] The long-term threats to any European colonial settlement were obvious: in Montesquieu's system, the body became acclimatised to its new living environment within two or three generations, a process colloquially referred to in Britain as 'going native'. Riding to the rescue of the European colonial enterprise came Hume's essay 'Of National Characters' (1748), which refuted what its author believed were Montesquieu's mechanistic simplifications. Hume instead described discrete national economies of manners, formed through the circulation of sympathy. His essay begins with the uncompromising statement that 'if we run over the globe, or revolve the annals of history, we shall discover everywhere signs of sympathy or contagion of manners, *none of the influence of air or climate*' (emphasis added).[8] National character, he argued in direct opposition to Montesquieu, derived from both 'physical' and 'moral' causes, and the latter were far more powerful in their operations than the former. Nobody, for example, would attribute the difference in manners between Wapping and St James's to the variations in the air or climate between those two places. Maintaining the sceptical line that philosophers should attend only to historical precedents rather than speculation, Hume asserted that, throughout history, the rise of letters and networks of sociability were pre-eminent determinants of national character, for 'the human mind is of a very imitative nature; nor is it possible for any set of men to converse often together, without acquiring a similitude of manners, and communicating to each other their vices as well as virtues' (p. 115). Here sympathy begins to be confined to 'a set of men', the kinship of the coffeehouse. If climate theory had any basis in fact, Hume continued, turning his guns directly on Montesquieu, it may be said to account only for the vulgar differences in human behaviour such as the propensity of northern peoples to strong liquor and of southern peoples to sexual promiscuity. Such vices may be overcome, he insisted, by the cultivation of polite society (p. 123).

Hume's conclusions had direct ramifications for the colonial environment: 'the same set of manners will follow a nation, and adhere to them over the whole globe, as well as the same laws and language. The SPANISH, ENGLISH, FRENCH, and DUTCH colonies, are all distinguishable between the tropics' (pp. 117–18). Provided that colonisers cultivate sympathy for each other, European identity could be preserved in the face of corrupting influences such as climate or the snares of Oriental decadence. Collingham argues that bodily practices among eighteenth-century British colonists were the product of a 'dialogue between Indian and British ideas of the appropriate ruling body', and that 'forms of luxury and nobility which would have been seen as illicit in Europe at this time were legitimised as appropriate within the context of an Indian style of government in a tropical climate'.[9] Collingham rightly continues that the adoption among Britons of Indian forms became progressively less acceptable after 1800. Early colonial print culture expounded an uneasy sense of Britishness that was at variance with Jones's sympathetic encounter with India.

As Hume described, print culture was a powerful emblem of European civic society in itself, for the circulation of print was deemed to facilitate communal sympathy. Texts printed in late eighteenth-century Calcutta reveal a desire to foster a *sensus communis* amidst the isolation of the colonial margin, which could be achieved primarily by imitating metropolitan forms. A somewhat vainglorious editorial column of 1791 in the Calcutta newspaper *The World* made the claim that:

> The civilized world affords no similar instance in the rise and culture of the arts, and to such perfection as Calcutta this day affords ... 'In splendour London now eclipses Rome' ... and in similar respects,

Calcutta rivals the head of empire. But in no respect can she appear more eminently so, as in her publications.[10]

If print culture was taken as a barometer of political and social change, as Paul Keen has argued, then Calcutta exhibited all the signs of a community vigorously responding to both external and internal developments.[11] These efforts manifested themselves in numerous artistic and social spheres. Under Hastings's governorship, the self-proclaimed 'city of palaces' had undertaken an extensive programme of improvements, whose results were clearly seen in the topographical views of the city painted by Thomas and William Daniell during their visit there in 1786 (exhibited between 1786 and 1788 as *Views of Calcutta*).[12] Neoclassical accents in the city's architecture were intended to invoke the civilising spirit of imperial Rome (Figure 3.1), and in his *Travels in India* (1793), the painter William Hodges praised the 'liberal spirit and excellent taste' of his patron, attributing to Hastings the commission of the first building in the city 'which deserves the name of architecture'.[13] Before 1780, Calcutta had much squalor about it: old Fort William, once the centrepiece of the British administration, had been badly damaged during the capture of the city by Siraj-ud Daula in 1756, and St Anne's Church, completely destroyed during the fighting, was slow to be replaced, leading Fay to complain as late as 1781 'how indifferently we are provided with respect to a place of worship; divine service being performed, in a room (not a very large one) at the Old Fort; which is a great disgrace to the settlement'.[14] By the 1780s, New Fort William had been built and a public subscription fund had been raised to build St John's Church, construction of which began in 1787.

William Hickey's *Memoirs*, which described his sojourns in India first between 1770 and 1779 then between 1783 and 1790, referred to the undeveloped manners that contributed to the poor reputation of colonial settlers in Bengal. The community there was coarse, disputatious and provincial, weaknesses the more cultivated Hickey deplored.[15] The Victorian historian and editor of the *Calcutta Review*, Sir John Kaye, commented on this period in an 1844 editorial entitled 'The English in India: Our Social Morality', blaming the malaise on the absence of the social checks and balances that would arise from a more extensive and variegated community. By acknowledging sympathy's importance among a group, Kaye hints at the Oriental corruption of the colonial social margin:

> There are saving influences in a multitude. The variety of character, of motive, and of habit, which it presents, can scarcely fail to exercise

Figure 3.1 Thomas Daniell, *View of Calcutta* (1786–8)
Courtesy of the British Library.

a restraining power over the individual. When a man knows that he is in the society of kindred spirits; that not only will nobody frown upon his vices, but that every member of the limited society, into which he is thrown, is addicted to the same vices, it would be strange indeed, if he did not give way to all the impulses of his corrupt nature. But when he knows that he is surrounded by others, whose opinions, tastes, and habits are widely different – who will turn away with disgust from open profligacy, and religiously keep aloof from the profligate – he restrains those natural impulses, and subjects himself to a course of moral training, which he soon acknowledges to possess its worldly advantages, even in a vicious state of society.[16]

The arrested social development of British colonists is often attributed to the shortage of women. The historian Suresh Chandra Ghosh calculates that in 1810 there were 250 European women in Bengal compared to 4000 men, an imbalance that at the time was acknowledged as a grave social deficiency.[17] Print culture had the unique capacity to supply this lacking sense of community, even within a relatively confined social milieu such as Calcutta at the turn of the century. As will be seen, the inhabitants set considerable store by the need to establish and maintain a form of literary culture along metropolitan lines. Without this there could be no civil society, and without the resulting sympathy between them, British colonists might succumb to their iniquitous surroundings.

The history of Calcutta's early print culture testifies to this struggle between social and what were perceived as anti-social forces in the colonial community; the latter including, among others, the many Portuguese residents of the so-called Black Town. Authors were preoccupied with the state of manners in the settlement and its formative history bore out Kaye's opinion that there was great need of improvement. For whilst Hastings and his governing circle approvingly countenanced learned publications such as the *Asiatick Researches*, the city's newspapers, not deemed so conducive to polite society, struggled to throw off official censorship. The Dutchman William Bolts first appealed for the establishment of a printing press in a notice pinned to the door of the city's public post office in 1768, but it was not until 1780 that James Hicky (no relation to William) produced the first edition of his *Bengal Gazette; or, Calcutta General Advertiser* on 29 January 1780, advertised as 'a weekly political and commercial paper open to all parties, but influenced by none'.[18] Bernard Merrick and Peter Reed's rival *India Gazette; or, Calcutta Public Advertiser* followed on 18 November of the same year, printed with types originally intended to produce Bibles, procured from the Swedish missionary John Zechariah Kiernander. Merrick and Reed secured government support for their paper (including exemption from postage fees), while the more scurrilous *Bengal Gazette* paid the price for the incessant stream of invective against the Governor-General. The *Bengal Gazette*'s regular 'Poets' Corner' was, as H.E. Busteed noted, predominantly a vehicle to expose Calcutta's prominent citizens 'to public odium and contempt veiled under the most obvious nicknames', and Kaye earlier lamented that 'society must have been very bad to have tolerated such a paper'.[19] Hicky was arrested and prosecuted for publishing libels and his printing equipment was eventually seized by judicial order in March 1782. In India, Hastings wielded powers that would have been denied him in Britain, and faced with a threat to public order he acted to silence his tormentor.

Thereafter, the rise of colonial letters continued apace with new titles appearing in succeeding years. Among the new titles Nair records was the semi-official *Calcutta Gazette; or, Oriental Advertiser* (edited by Francis Gladwin) of 1784, the *Bengal Journal* and the *Oriental Magazine; or, Calcutta Amusement* of 1785, the *Calcutta Chronicle and General Advertiser* of 1786, the *Calcutta Advertiser* of 1787 and the *Asiatic Mirror and Commercial Advertiser* of 1788, all issued on a weekly and occasionally on a monthly basis.[20] The government, which initially shared its counterpart in London's 'fear of printing', as Graham Shaw puts it, eventually relaxed controls as print culture in Calcutta was regarded as increasingly respectable, seen in such polite titles as the *Oriental Asylum for Fugitive Pieces* (1788), which provided a forum for amateur poetry.[21] If the prodigious rise of print filled Calcutta with pride, there was a certain irony in the fact that the colonists' imitation of metropolitan forms lent many publications an outmoded provincial air. At the very moment that British authors were tending to 'break with or seek places beyond centralised and traditional cultural authorities', as McGann describes British literature on the cusp of Romanticism, colonial writers signally failed to capitalise on their marginal status; rather, they imitated earlier conventions of sensibility as strenuously as possible.[22] The pseudonymous Emily Brittle's *The India Guide; or, Journal of a Voyage to the East Indies, in the year MDCCLXXX, in Poetical Epistle to her Mother* (1785), for example, parodied Christopher Anstey's *New Bath Guide; or, Memoirs of the B-----r---d* [Blunderhead] *Family, in a series of poetical epistles* of 1766.[23] The printer George Gordon was expressly summoned from Britain to produce the book to London standards, a task he performed at Messinck's press.[24] Presented as a series of letters home to the narrator's mother, *The India Guide* depicts the foibles of late eighteenth-century Calcutta life, a throwback world of rakes, knaves and bewigged beauties reproduced in the light satirical tone of Anstey's original. 'Brittle' considers the situation 'of young ladies embarking for India' in the breathless spirit of sentimental conduct literature:

> Every feeling heart would wish to soften the inconveniences to which they are exposed, and every liberal mind to lull, by respectful attentions, the ennûi of a six months confinement; – but how often is the contrary the case? How often is their sensibility wounded by the vulgar freedoms of an unpolished society! how often is innocence doomed to blush in vindication of insulted virtue![25]

Emily's fears reflected concern about the lack of feminine influence on colonial life, but the lexicon of sensibility ('feeling heart', 'soften' and 'blush') is redolent of a style that was less and less fashionable in Britain.

Such conspicuous treatment of the somatic trials faced by women made India a perfect testing-ground for the transformations of sensibility, a point that modern critics repeatedly connect with emergent feminism. Balachandra Rajan has argued that the traditional gendering of Asia as feminine and Europe as masculine made India the 'theatre for a narrative of [female] self-affirmation', going on to contend that 'the novel about India was originated by women'.[26] Female authors certainly dominated writing about British India at this time but, as will be seen, female characters did not so much draw strength from an atmosphere perceived to be liberating as react against an environment perceived to be dangerous. The hot climate, the licentiousness of the local culture and the ribald conduct of fellow-colonists all threatened to overwhelm the delicate faculty of sensibility.

In the non-fictional sphere, Fay's *Original Letters from India* engage directly with the challenges that a colonial environment, not least the rigours of the outward journey, posed to traditional notions of sensibility. The *Letters* were originally published posthumously in Calcutta for the purpose of settling Fay's estate. She had divorced her husband for 'criminal conversation' in 1781, and after an unsuccessful career as a merchant trading between the subcontinent, Britain and the United States, Fay died insolvent in India in 1816. In 1779, Anthony Fay had sought employment as a barrister in the Bengal Supreme Court. Accompanying her husband, Fay traversed the Ottoman Empire as an infidel, braved the perils of the Egyptian desert and was incarcerated by

Hyder Ali's forces at Calicut before finally arriving in Calcutta in 1783, after a journey totalling 12 months – an itinerary that would have made mincemeat of Marianne Dashwood. Eliza's epistolary narrative exhibits a consistent determination on the author's part to surmount the supposed delicacy of a female constitution. Fay displays her mettle early on in the *Original Letters* when she records that a pet pigeon blew from the ship during a gale in the eastern Mediterranean. As if in defiance of Hogarth's figure of sensibility weeping over a bird, Eliza admits she was a 'good deal vexed' by the accident but, 'notwithstanding my fondness for the bird, ... I could not even wish that, a ship running eight knots an hour, should be hove too, and a boat sent out after a Pigeon'.[27] The reality of life on shipboard required a stiffening of the sinews that all but ruled out effusive shows of personal distress. Between Cairo and Suez, the nature and intensity of her trials worsened dramatically. The Fays and their party found themselves infidels in the Ottoman Empire, in constant danger of attack from Arab marauders. Here, too, Fay experienced the desert heat for the first time, and she gives a vivid account of how her spirits flagged as the wilderness encompassed the party. Her account demonstrates how the absence of human civilisation was perceived to depress the passions:

> When we had proceeded some distance on the Desert; when all traces of human habitation had vanished – ; when every sign of cultivation disappeared; and even vegetation was confined to a few low straggling shrubs, that seemed to stand between life and death as hardly belonging to either – ; when the immeasurable plain lay around me, a burning sun darted his fierce rays from above, and no asylum was visible in front, my very heart sunk within me. (p. 97)

Fay here feels cut off from the social sustenance that the European self requires, while physical conditions sap her bodily energy. Further into the desert, the party encounters an Englishman who has been robbed by bandits and appears to be succumbing physically to the melancholy contemplation of his misfortune. Fay is convinced that the torrid climate has exacerbated his decline: 'The extreme heat of the weather so overwhelmed him, that he resigned all hope of life ... I fear his heart is breaking, as well as his constitution' (p. 99). Montesquieu cautioned that since the bodily frame enshrined the mental faculties, both suffered equally when exposed to intemperate conditions. Fay's narrative of her desert crossing combines ideas of human nature drawn from both Montesquieu and Hume, but she takes pride in her own ability to resist the much-vaunted rigours of the Indian climate. When the ship drew near the Malabar coast, she boasts that 'the climate seems likely to agree very well with me, I do not mind the heat, nor does it affect either my spirits, or my appetite' (pp. 108–9).

On landing in Calicut, the Fays were faced with a challenge of a very different order, for their arrival coincided with the hostilities leading up to the Second Mysore War of 1780–84. On the orders of Hyder Ali, a detachment of troops led by an English mercenary, 'the redoubtable Captain Ayres', seized the ship and imprisoned its captain, passengers and crew in a disused fort (p. 115).[28] Fay casts her incarceration in 'a horrid dark place scarcely twenty feet square, swarming with rats' as a trial of sociability (p. 135). The Fays spent a miserable Christmas in these conditions, relieved only by the discovery of a more spacious storeroom beneath a trapdoor, and the remembrance of her family. Fay draws consolation from the imagined company of distant relatives, which compensates in part for the absence of a 'congenial mind to which I could declare my feelings, sure of meeting with a sympathizing affection, as I so delightfully experienced in the company of my beloved sister'. Imaginative sympathy here upholds the self through its power to replicate familial bonds (p. 111). The Fays were eventually released in February 1780, thanks to the good offices of a Jewish merchant in the town who negotiated on their behalf with 'that fell tiger Hyder Ali' (p. 167).[29] These successive examples of imaginative sustenance can be seen as a deliberate attempt by Fay to present herself as resistant to the influence of the climate and distressing occurrences. They also demonstrate the colonial subject's need to block out external circumstances – in this case the Oriental world – to preserve individual identity.

Isobel Grundy observes of Fay that she writes as a 'detached observer, now satirical and now sympathetic', a world away from the heroines of sentimental fiction whom she occasionally purports to imitate.[30] Fay in fact exercises various shades of sympathy in her consideration of *sati*, which on the one hand she describes as 'that horrid custom of widows burning themselves with the dead bodies of their husbands' suggesting an affinity with the female victims (p. 202). Some male British witnesses of the rite, including William Hodges, who, whilst profoundly affected by what he saw, depicted a Hindu widow walking proudly to the funeral pile, had a tendency to regard *sati* as the pinnacle of female devotion to their husbands.[31] Fay rejects this interpretation entirely and instead criticises the desire of men throughout the world to subjugate their wives, expanding her point into a critique of European women who might readily submit to such treatment themselves:

> This practice is entirely a political scheme intended to insure the care and good offices of wives to their husbands, who have not failed in most countries to invent a sufficient number of rules to render their wives subservient to their authority. I cannot help smiling when I hear gentlemen bring forward the conduct of the Hindoo women, as a test of superior character, since I am well aware that so much are we the slaves of habit *every where* that were it necessary for a woman's reputation to burn herself in England, many a one who has *accepted* a husband merely for the sake of an establishment, who has lived with him without affection; perhaps thwarted his views, dissipated his fortune and rendered his life uncomfortable to the close, would yet mount the funeral pile with all imaginable decency and die with heroic fortitude. (p. 203)

Fay's sympathy modulates from Indian to European women before twisting into a critique of women who unthinkingly sacrifice themselves to their husbands. She ends almost by adopting the husband's viewpoint on the excessive materiality of some English wives. Her observations promote female agency and compare, to a degree, with Mary Wollstonecraft's arguments in *A Vindication of the Rights of Woman* (1792). Given the colonial setting, Fay notably disregards cultural differences between Hindu and European women whose behaviour is the same '*every where.*'

Fay is similarly dismissive about the effects of the Indian climate once she lands in Madras, now recovered from the desert sun and in a position to comment more objectively on environmental determinism. She expresses scorn for the gluttonous behaviour of the British residents, who blame their various medical conditions on the heat. The Europeans in Madras, she finds, are 'languishing under various complaints which they call incidental to the climate, an assertion it would ill become a stranger like myself to controvert'; she is under no illusions about the real cause of such illnesses, adding a possible play on Montesquieu: 'I see very plainly that the same mode of living, would produce the same effects, even "in the hardy regions of the North"' (p. 162). Generational differences seem to account for the divergence of views on this point, with old India hands more likely to attribute their habits to the climate, for which they were castigated in Britain. Witness James Johnson's later medical treatises *The Oriental Voyager* (1807) and

The Influence of Tropical Climates on European Constitutions (1813), which duly acknowledged the oppressive heat and humidity of Asia but argued that 'moral and physical temperance' was the surest mode of avoiding ill health, and that 'most of the precepts that apply to the regulation of [the passions] in cold climates, will be equally applicable here'.[32]

Fay's *Original Letters from India* can be regarded as a first-hand demonstration of the 'new' sensibility in action and how it was tested by the unique demands of a colonial setting. The author celebrates her own physical hardiness, in contrast to earlier expectations of feminine propriety in which extreme sensitivity to events would have been considered a virtue. Phebe Gibbes's novel *Hartly House, Calcutta* (1789) found a different solution to the crisis of colonial sensibility, one that emphasised British isolationism from Eastern threats. It is no coincidence that the novel was probably written in Britain; Gibbes's letters to the Royal Literary Fund reveal that her son was stationed in Bengal and indeed died there.[33] It is therefore reasonable to assume that her novel was based on letters home that Gibbes received from him, especially since her depiction of late eighteenth-century Calcutta is thoroughly convincing, complete with the names of individuals known to have lived there at the time. A doggerel poem published in the *Calcutta Gazette* on 26 August 1784, for example, alludes to the hospitality of East India Company surgeon Bartholomew Hartly:

> Oh, but dear Jack, I'll tell you partly
> Of Breakfast given by Doctor H—y,
> For I could only go to one,
> And just dropped in as that was done,
> A concert too and then a dance,
> This H—y sure was bred in France.[34]

Despite its status as a work of fiction, *Hartly House, Calcutta* appears to have been intimately connected to the social reality of late eighteenth-century Calcutta, and reflects a mixture of concerns about life in India with the perceptions of an onlooker based in England. Gibbes, as metropolitan onlooker, casts an element of moral anxiety over the entire situation, in particular about the climate, disease and sexual mores. The novel has been interpreted as a study of female liberation, but more accurately is preoccupied with the wayward sympathies of its heroine, Sophia Goldbourne, whose name intimates the mercenary reasons behind her presence in India. For some commentators, Sophia's India functions as a liberating space where European constraints of gender and sexuality are cast off.[35] There is certainly an element of sexual transgression in the novel but it also forms part of a morality tale as Sophia learns to inoculate herself against the triple dangers of heat, disease and sexual licence before her eventual return to England.

Hartly House, Calcutta is not in fact straightforwardly celebratory of the colonial way of life. A cautionary note is sounded immediately in Sophia's opening letter to her friend Arabella in England. Her dismissal of her friend's warnings alerts us to Sophia's fanciful and vain nature, in addition to the physical and moral dangers of climatic and materialistic excess:

> The grave of thousands! – Doubtless, my good girl, in the successive years of visitation, the eastern world *is*, as you pronounce it, the grave of thousands; but is it not also a mine of exhaustless wealth! the centre of unimaginable magnificence! An ever blooming, an ever-brilliant scene?[36]

Sophia accompanies her widowed father to Calcutta who plans to find a suitable husband for her. By suitable, he naturally means a European Company servant, although Sophia declares that she has no desire to become a 'nabobess'. Worse still, her courtship with the British officer, Edmund Doyly (another authentic Calcutta name) is threatened by her infatuation with her young Brahmin tutor, for whom she experiences a mutual attraction at a relatively early stage in the novel. This character, in contrast to later colonial novels, appears within a polite social setting and is susceptible to the same degree of passion as Sophia. At the height of their chaste romance, he tells Sophia that she is 'the loveliest of women' before retiring from the room 'with more emotion than quite accorded with his corrected temper, as if he had felt he had said too much'.[37] The Brahmin sits within the sympathetic compass of the novel and Nussbaum has interpreted the colonial setting as a rare opportunity for women to exercise domestic power: India serves as 'a mirror for the display of the Englishwoman's sexual desire … Love's empire and the power it brings are most easily flaunted in romance, in the past, or in the empire abroad, since its exercise at home is severely restricted by convention and civility'.[38] Rajan likewise interprets Sophia's sexual interest in the Brahmin as a rejection of 'the masculine principle which the West embodies, in favour of a feminine alternative'.[39] Playful as it may be, Sophia's behaviour surely invites a more censorious response from the reader. Despite the earlier eighteenth-century vogue for interracial love stories with their daring piquancy, Sophia's narrative trajectory points clearly back towards Britain and away from India, in part to shield her, in Franklin's words, 'from the spectre of miscegenation'.[40]

There is a subtle antagonism at play in *Hartly House, Calcutta*, possibly due to the nature of the novel's composition. An appreciative view of Indian life and culture, together with an accurate account of the city of Calcutta, reached Gibbes from her son, but it is tempered by her desire to sell her book in the British marketplace, hence the silent and disapproving gaze emanating from Arabella in London, whom Sophia tellingly chastises for her 'European *sang froid*'. Gibbes surely intends readers to fear for her heroine when, on her first disembarkation at Calcutta, she declares that 'the European world faded before my eyes, and became *orientalised* at all points'.[41] From her very arrival, the East flows into Sophia's alarmingly receptive self. The novel, on the other hand, contains passages about the elevated doctrines of Hinduism, taught to Sophia from her Brahmin tutor (and in all likelihood transmitted home by Gibbes's son). These sometimes seem to echo Burke's tendency to contrast Hindu purity, exemplified in 'the corrected and confirmed principles of the Gentoos', with the practices of Europeans, 'who have waded through the blood of millions, to bring home gems of inconsiderable value'. This leads Sophia to confess that she is 'ashamed to know myself a European', and blushes 'to feel how superior' Hinduism is 'to all that Christianity can boast, of peace and good-will towards men' (p. 136).

Sophia's sympathies are divided between admiration for Hinduism's philosophical tenets and the gentility of her Brahmin admirer, and revulsion for Hindu ceremonial practices. The most ambiguous point in the novel comes when Sophia appears to convert to Hinduism: she writes to Arabella that, 'ashamed of the manners of modern Christianity ... I am become a convert to the Gentoo faith, and have my Bramin to instruct me *per diem*' (p. 199). She nonetheless detests the Hindu customs of rope-swinging, mortification of the flesh and the practice of abandoning dead or dying relatives to the alligators of the Ganges. Sophia's sentimental description of *sati* as an 'affectionate and voluntary sacrifice' marks the beginning of the end of Sophia's dalliance with sexual and social experimentation (p. 182). Grundy and Nussbaum both berate Sophia for failing to find as a woman common cause with the victims, comparing the act to the British female 'sacrifice' of marriage. Rather than exploring the 'radical potential' of such a move, Nussbaum argues, Gibbes curtails Sophia's romance with the Brahmin's death and obliges her to learn to 'respond to her own marriage with patience and submission'.[42] Grundy contrasts Sophia's passivity over *sati* with Fay's 'robust desire to reform Indian gender relations'.[43] Yet these critics do not explore the role of climate in bringing Sophia's Eastern experiment to a premature end. Gibbes is explicit about the danger posed to her heroine's mind and body from the insalubrious conditions in which she finds herself, and a possible alternative reading is that Sophia's return to England forestalls the final capitulation of her pliant sensibility.

From the moment of her arrival in India, Sophia is quick to register the dangers posed to her by daily exposure to 'vertical suns'. She is alert to the shortcomings of colonial society and bemoans 'the fatigue of veiling our distresses from vulgar optics, by gaudy trappings and the pomp of retinue' and yearns for 'the social intercourse of the sons and daughters of Liberty and intellectual cultivation'. Significantly, she insists that she will never 'become habituated to what I now languish under, and cease to sigh for one delightful strole [*sic*] in St James's Park, unincumbered by palanquins, kitessan-bearers, the clamour of har-carriers, etc., etc' and repeatedly cites James Thomson's 'Summer' (1727) from *The Seasons*, exhorting 'Tyrant Heat' to 'intermit thy wrath! / And on my throbbing temples potent thus / Beam not so fierce'.[44] She even jestingly speculates that Thomson himself must have spent time in India in order to describe her situation so accurately.[45] Sophia is compromised by her environment as well as liberated by it. Apparently forgetting her dismissal of Arabella's comments on the subject, she declares that the extensive burial grounds of the city 'bear a melancholy testimony to the truth of my observations on the short space of existence in this climate'.[46] When she falls ill and fears for her life, her concern for her national and religious identity segues into a longing for mild British weather:

> Be assured, however, that I shall depart, if my hour is now come, in the true faith of an European – the faith confirmed by all around me – that there is no climate more salubrious than Britain – no people more blessed – no days more pleasurable, or nights more tranquil, than her temperate air bestows. (p. 172)

This rejection of her Indian surroundings complicates any idea that the colonial environment offered an affirming life choice for contemporary British women.

Sophia's own theory of climatic determinism holds that Europeans, 'having received their birth in the happy zone' of a temperate climate and passed their youth 'under the same healthful meridian', are able to withstand 'the Eastern sun for ten or twelve years of their mid-life with tolerable satisfaction' (p. 85). This sense of a colonial 'time limit' perhaps explains why, towards the end of the novel, Sophia's Brahmin dies from fever, she marries Doyley, and finally the couple sets sail for England in an abrupt narrative closure. If this denouement suggests Gibbes's desire to shield British national character from malign influences, an incidence of rape towards the end of the book confirms the risk of moral deterioration among the European community in India. News reaches Sophia that a British officer has raped an India woman, as Grundy points out, a crime that Gibbes presents primarily in patriarchal terms as an affront to the girl's father.[47] Sophia remarks that 'I now rejoice, more than ever, that I am about to leave a country, where fiend-like acts are, I fear, much oftener perpetrated than detected'.[48] The episode represents the slaying of her Orientalist ideals as she stands on the brink of domestic life in England. Far from representing a defeat for Sophia, the voyage home offers salvation. Her youthful experimentation is seen to be redeemed through marriage and repartition, whilst she is purged of her sympathetic immersion in the East.

Elizabeth Hamilton's *Translation of the Letters of a Hindoo Rajah; written previous to, and during the period of his residence in England* (1796) deploys its satirical thrust in almost exactly the opposite direction. This produces a very different set of sympathetic affiliations from those shown in Gibbes's novel, which ultimately restores its heroine to the comforting environs of British civic society. Hamilton's tale, like Gibbes's, was written under the influence of a brother who served in India, in this case the prominent Orientalist Charles Hamilton, best known as the author of *An Historical Relation of the Origin, Progress, and Final Dissolution of the Government of the Rohilla Afghans in the Northern Provinces of Hindostan* (1787) and translator of the *Hedàya; or, Guide: A Commentary on the Mussulman Laws* (1791). Between 1788 and 1792, brother and sister lived together and through his conversation, Hamilton tells us in the novel's 'Preliminary Dissertation on Hindu History, Religion and Manners' ... 'the names of the most celebrated Orientalists became familiar to [my] ear'.[49] Charles Hamilton served as the British Resident of Awadh but died of tuberculosis while on leave in London in 1792, and is the 'much-lamented brother' of the novel's dedication. We may assume that Charles Hamilton provided many of the novel's observations from the life, but the exemplary status Hamilton grants her brother's fictionalised appearance in the story, one of a group of Orientalist scholars who receive acutely sympathetic characterisation, reveals that she is inclining the reader's sentiments towards British colonists and indeed has been described as a 'novel-writing apologist' for Hastings.⁵⁰ Hamilton's use of sympathy is selective: she locates pockets of virtue in India and Britain, but tellingly makes no reference to Oriental corruption at the hands of the climate, rather the reverse. Her object is to expose failings in British culture and society, using an Indian narrator – the eponymous raja – to undermine the notion of inherent European moral rectitude. Hamilton depicts sympathy between groupings of morally upstanding individuals, whose moral sense increasingly contrasts with the false sensibility of what her novel shows to be a debased metropolitan society.

Given her personal connection to Orientalist scholarship, it should come as no surprise that Hamilton enthusiastically endorses the model of 'sympathetic colonialism' promoted under Hastings. Indeed, as Susan B. Egenolf points out, Hamilton's desire to position herself as a professional author in a field typically dominated by male scholars led to an accentuation of her pro-Hastings stance.⁵¹ The preliminary dissertation fosters sympathy for Hindu India at the expense of its Mughal conquerors, a characteristic Orientalist strategy but an ironic one in the light of her brother's researches into Islamic law, and presents British colonisers as restorers of a lost but once great civilisation. In common with other writers on the subject, Hamilton comments on the 'ignorance, and apathetic indifference with regard to affairs of the East, which is frequently to be remarked in minds, that are in every other respect highly cultivated, and accurately informed'.⁵² After this customary gauntlet to the domestic imagination, Hamilton evokes sympathy for the 'Hindoos under the mild and auspicious government of their native Princes', who are contrasted with 'the intolerant zeal and brutal antipathy of their Mohammedan invaders' (vol. 1, p. xl). Only under British rule did the relationship between governors and governed modulate from that of master and slave to the more affectionate bond of fond parent and child: 'that unrelenting persecution, which was deemed a duty by the ignorant bigotry of their Mussulman rulers, has, by the milder spirit of Christianity, been converted into the tenderest indulgence' (vol. 1, p. xliii). Hamilton thus apprises the reader of sympathy between colonising Britons and colonised Indians, although as the above extracts indicate, Britain played the role of spiritual and cultural preceptor, reinscribing the sympathetic imbalance between the two countries.

The novel opens with an account of a textbook sympathetic encounter between a colonial official and an Indian nobleman, Zāārmilla, raja of Almora, whose lands we learn have been overrun by Rohilla Afghans. Writing to his friend and correspondent Māāndāāra, the raja describes how, in the confusion of the retreat following the Battle of Cutterah (1774), he stumbled upon a dying English officer, the saintly Captain Percy, whom most commentators agree is modelled on Charles Hamilton. Percy it transpires is an Orientalist, who, as Zāārmilla relates, 'spoke to me in the Persian language, of which, as well as the Arabic, and the different dialects of Hindostan, he was *perfect master*'. He had set out from Calcutta several months before 'with an intention of travelling through the northern parts of Hindostan, in order to trace the antiquities of the most ancient of nations', and became caught up in the fighting presumably against his will (vol. 1, p. 8). Percy dies of his wounds despite Zāārmilla's ministrations, but not before he implants in the raja such a warm sense of British virtue that the latter resolves to visit England. Inspired by Percy's copy of the New Testament, which he calls 'the Christian Shaster', Zāārmilla delivers a panegyric on English benevolence in his letter to the more sceptical Māāndāāra. This appears to take the form of a deeply ironic indictment of empire:

> Benevolent people of England! it is their desire, that all should be partakers of the same blessing of liberty, which they themselves enjoy. It was doubtless with this glorious view, that they send forth colonies to enlighten, and instruct, the vast regions of America. To disseminate the love of virtue and freedom, they cultivated the trans-Atlantic isles: and to rescue *our* nation from the hands of the oppressor, did this brave, and generous people visit the shores of Hindostan! (vol. 1, p. 14)

But Hamilton is ultimately at pains to reform imperial morals, and goes on to depict the cadre of sympathetic individuals in British India as the engineers of such change. Over the course of the novel, true sympathy comes to be firmly tied to evangelical Christianity, its impulses derived from a religiously motivated desire to succour the needy. This makes Hamilton's notion of colonial sympathy personal rather than systematic in nature and reflected a significant new religious coloration to colonial relations.

Hamilton's belief in sympathy as one of the human virtues stood in opposition to what she regarded as the abstraction of speculative theory.[53] Gary Kelly has identified Hamilton as an anti-Jacobin writer on account of her opposition to the various new philosophies emerging in Britain around that time, arguing that through the guerrilla tactics of the footnote she engaged with political subjects that were ordinarily considered off limits for women authors, an anti-Jacobin hallmark.[54] Recent commentators have given more nuanced readings of Hamilton's political opinions, which Harriet Guest has described as combining an apparently reactionary distaste for the follies and vanities of contemporary life with a progressive view of education, seeking to remodel the domestic sphere (for both men and women) 'as the site of the values which should govern public life', a theme pursued in her influential *Letters on Education* (1801; republished as *Letters on the Elementary Principles of Education*, also 1801).[55] Among the most potent weapons in Hamilton's imaginative armoury were sympathy and religion, united in *Translation of the Letters of a Hindoo Rajah* in the character of Percy and, towards the close of the novel, the raja himself. Hamilton's view was that Christianity in its soundest and least pretentious form confounded all attempts by profane philosophical systems to usurp it, a subject elaborated in her later satirical novel *Memoirs of Modern Philosophers* (1800). The wounded figure of Percy dispensing wisdom from the New Testament is in this respect set up as an exemplar, the very type of colonial hero upon whom Colley argues 'Britons were encouraged to concentrate their emotional and moral gaze' by an East India Company eager to divert attention away from the material rapacity of colonialism.[56]

The novel juxtaposes groups of virtuous Orientalists and their friends with a wider British society that has grown vicious and uncaring. The raja's steady disillusionment with Britain begins when Māāndāāra, doubtful of his friend's naive opinions, forwards him three letters written by the Brahmin Sheermaal, who has recently visited England and finds it to be a land of rampant profanity where the wellsprings of sympathy have dried up. Card games are played with such devotion the Brahmin assumes they are a form of worship ('pooja'), while the severity of the justice system, the institution of slavery and modern philosophy, whose purpose seems to be 'to extirpate from society' all regard for the doctrines of the Bible, combine into a Hogarthian tableau of moral, religious and social degeneracy. Worst of all, as the Brahmin sees it, is the hypocrisy of British public condemnations of *sati* while women on the streets of London are left to suffer the ravages of poverty, disease and prostitution: 'Callous, and unfeeling Englishmen! they endure to behold with their own eyes, sacrifices in one year exceeding in number, all that, in the course of revolving years, perished on the altars of Asia!'[57] This has the effect of reversing the sympathetic gaze, so that an Indian character of unimpeachable moral standing may critique spectacles of suffering in Britain, while decrying as 'callous' and 'unfeeling' people in England who are alert to distant social problems but pay no regard to those close at hand. Again, this is easily construed as a pro-Hastings manoeuvre, combined with the belief that, in contrast to the universal application of 'system', charity begins at home.

Kelly sees this tendency to agitate for social reform despite an ostensibly conservative narrative voice as characteristic of the British anti-Jacobin novel, yet it was also a feature of the 'Oriental spy' genre of satirical literature.[58] This tradition began in the late seventeenth century with Giovanni Paolo Marana's *Letters Written by a Turkish Spy* (1692–1723) and continued with Montesquieu's *Lettres Persanes* (1721), Lord Lyttelton's *Letters Written by a Persian in England* (1735), Horace Walpole's *Letter from Xo Ho, a Chinese Philosopher in London* (1757), Oliver Goldsmith's *Citizen of the World* (1762) and later Southey's *Letters from England: by Don Manuel Alavarez Espriella* (1807). One salient feature of this mode of writing was that East and West were criticised jointly; thus Hamilton satirises Zāārmilla's regressive ideas on female education whilst faddish European notions of atheism and philosophical necessity are similarly lampooned. This levelling effect partly erased Eurocentric moral distinctions between Europeans and Asians, and in Hamilton's novel the naive Indians are actually elevated above the cynical inhabitants of England. This creates a complex sympathetic dynamic, whereby readers are more attracted to the Brahmin and the raja's point of view and simultaneously obliged to question their geographically inflected ideas about sensibility. Anne K. Mellor has argued for Hamilton as an early practitioner of standpoint theory, who consciously occupied a subaltern narrative position in order to demonstrate 'that oriental despotism begins at home, in Britain'.[59]

Sheermaal's narrative is only the first of two 'Hindu spy' episodes, for Zāārmilla, not persuaded by the Brahmin's letters, sets out to find the truth for himself. (The novel's dual setting probably resulted from the novel originally having been conceived as two separate works.) The raja's journey downriver by boat, accompanied by Percy's friend Captain Grey, gives him the opportunity to study the British in a colonial environment at first hand. As they travel deeper into British territory, Zāārmilla's impressions are increasingly favourable: up country, the Mughal states were marked by 'universal silence' and 'ruined villages'; in Bengal, by contrast, the 'flourishing state of the country' attests to the good stewardship of Hastings.[60] Zāārmilla's sighting of a peacock provokes a lively footnote from Hamilton, refuting the claims of William Belsham in his *Memoirs of the Reign of George III to the session of Parliament ending A.D. 1793* (1795) that, under Clive's administration, the peacocks of Bengal had become extinct.[61] Thus both author and character work in tandem to promote positive impressions of Bengal under British rule at a time when the state of the country was hotly contested.[62] These colonial scenes consolidate ideas of British virtue in opposition to the dissipation of the Mughal Empire, which Hamilton implies became so due to moral lassitude not the debilitating climate (which would otherwise affect Britons too).

Colonial virtue, through Orientalist eyes, comes to be regarded as a sympathetic affinity for ancient Hindu civilisation. Nearing Calcutta, Zāārmilla's point of embarkation for England, he meets with another group of British officers stationed at Chunar. They too are Orientalists, who devote their leisure time to the study of Sanskrit and Persian, a restorative enterprise which, Hamilton suggests, serves to propitiate the violence of conquest, Mughal and British:

> The time of vacation from immediate service wasted by the Musselman Commanders in voluptuous indolence, is spent by these more enlightened men, in studies which add to the stock of knowledge, and do honour to the genius of their country. It is by these strangers that the annals of Hindostan, which her barbarian conquerors have sought to obliterate in the blood of her children, shall be restored![63]

When Zāārmilla is finally introduced to Hastings, he compares him both to the Mughal emperor Akbar, who was regarded as an exemplar of Islamic enlightenment by many European commentators, despite the anti-Muslim drift displayed elsewhere in Hamilton's novel, and his court historian, Abu'l Fazl, although 'superior to both, in schemes of sound and extensive policy; as well as in that pure, blessed spirit of humanity, which has distinguished every act of his administration'.[64] This is Orientalist propaganda on a grand scale, culminating in a eulogium that is all the more persuasive for being articulated by an Indian nobleman:

> The pious Hindoo, no longer forced to submit to laws, that are repugnant to the spirit of his faith; no longer judged by the unhallowed ordinances of strangers, beholds with extactic gratitude, the holy Shaster riding, at the command of his enlightened Governor, to be once more the standard of his obedience.[65]

For all Hamilton's advocacy of Christianity, the supposed mildness of Hinduism is preferable to the 'unhallowed' rapacity of Islam under the Mughals. The apparent congeniality of British laws in the eyes of the

Hindu population also associates Hastings' rule with gentleness and respect for the sanctity of religion in general.

The second marker of colonial virtue is the continued ability of Britons in India to interact sympathetically with each other, irrespective of climatic factors or the corruptions of trade. While not all the Britons encountered are Orientalists, Zāārmilla travels with a select band of exemplary figures all of whom are friends of the late Captain Percy. With Grey, the raja witnesses a scene in a Calcutta coffee house, involving a destitute-looking 'young man of about seventeen or eighteen years', slumped dejectedly in a corner; on overhearing the host address the youth as Morton, Grey springs up, 'his eyes glistening with pleasure, and his manly countenance animated by the glow which warmed his bosom', and greets him as the son of his old university tutor and friend (vol. 1, p. 162). Grey furnishes young Morton (who has recently been orphaned) with papers of introduction to the East India Company, an exchange that Zāārmilla reads as a selfless act of charity and the very proof of Christian virtue he is looking for. Hamilton depicts the episode in the sentimental mode, as a sign of emotional sincerity on the part of Grey and his associates, whom she wishes to distance from the frivolous British characters portrayed elsewhere. Sympathy transmits emotion between members of the gathering: 'The tear of filial sensibility, which trembled in the eye of Morton, appeared to be infectious', Zāārmilla records, 'my friend Grey seemed afraid of it; and taking the young man by the arm, he instantly led him to the house that is now our home' (vol. 1, p. 162). Like Percy, the Orientalists are upstanding Christians, in contrast to the European women overheard shortly afterwards discussing their love affairs in public, and the young 'griffins' with their coarse sense of humour.

The second volume begins with Zāārmilla on the voyage between India and Britain, during which he develops a gradually more refined capacity for making moral judgements. He learns to discriminate between 'false' sentimentality and 'true' expressions of feeling (such as were displayed in the Calcutta coffee house), confronting the first in a novel he reads on board ship, the generically entitled *History of a Nobleman*, which he mistakes for an authentic memoir and in which only extreme states of emotion are represented. He does not understand the appeal of such a book, admitting his failure to feel sympathy for the extravagant displays of feeling shown by the various characters, something he innocently attributes to a want of sensitivity on his part as a non-European:

> Never before did my heart refuse its sympathy to human misery; but the distresses of the Lady Hariots [sic], and the Lady Charlottes,

which called forth the overflowing of compassion, in the breasts of their fair correspondents were of a nature too refined and delicate to be discernable to any save the Microscopic eye of European sensibility! (vol. 2, p. 19)

Pondering the matter further, he imagines that human nature must have changed between the time of Kalidas and Shakespeare (a comparison taken direct from Jones), who depict '*Unchanging, everlasting Nature!*', and the modern age, whose writings do not speak to his genuine inner feelings (vol. 2, p. 21). In attacking the excesses of sentimental fiction in this way, Hamilton inverts the trope of Oriental hypersensitivity derived from climate theory to present the raja as a person possessed of sound moral sense.

Kelly and Mellor both argue that Zāārmilla is 'de-orientalised' on his arrival in England while England 'orientalises' around him; but degenerate as Britain appears, there is nothing specifically Oriental about the succeeding tableaux of folly, corruption and vice.[66] Rather, as a social conservative, Hamilton objects to the irreligion and inhumanity of European modernity as a whole: as the raja's shipboard reading forewarns, England is a land wanting in true sympathy. As do many fictional Oriental spies, Zāārmilla visits the 'great, gloomy mansion' of Newgate, and is appalled by the treatment of the inmates there, becoming convinced that the biblical commandment to love thy neighbour must have been replaced by a precept condemning poverty to the harshest conceivable punishment.[67] Grey's acquaintance Sir Caprice Ardent, as great a fool as his name suggests, claims a false affinity with Eastern civilisation as he plans a building that incorporates all the classical orders superimposed on a gothic base, topped off with a Chinese pagoda. On learning that Zāārmilla is a Hindu, Ardent asks whether he can furnish him with a design for a mosque. Yet Hamilton's most sustained satire is against Ardent's philosopher friends, Puzzledorf, Vapour, Axiom and Sceptic, all devoted to various schools of systematic thought. Their experiments are shown to be irrational and inhumane. In one scene at Ardent Hall, the philosophers try to transform birds into honeybees in order to demonstrate the power of external circumstances, for which purpose they imprison 300 sparrows in a beehive; three days later, the hive is opened to reveal the results of the philosophers' experiment: 'Sight of horrors! and smell, worse than the sight! The lifeless corses [*sic*] of the three hundred half-fledged nestlings lay at the bottom of their hive, in a promiscuous heap' – a microcosm of the deadly effects of speculative theory (vol. 2, p. 164).

Sensibility itself comes to be viewed as an abstraction or default emotional setting, which operates without regard for contingency, circumstance or genuine human needs. As befits the relocation to a metropolitan setting, Hamilton's political agenda modulates from being pro-Hastings to anti-Burke, seen when Zāārmilla is buttonholed by a figure obviously intended to be Burke in a crowded coffee house. The raja learns that, as an inhabitant of a land that has been the subject of so much contention, he is now an object of great interest, a newspaper report having circulated to the effect that he has come to England 'to complain of the horrid cruelties, and unexampled oppression' of Hastings. 'A gentleman' (intended to be Burke) steps forward, and before the raja has a chance to speak launches into a speech combining allusions to his speeches at Hastings' trial with a parody of his *Reflections on the Revolution in France*:

> I hope to convince you, in spite of the reasons you have had to the contrary, that we are not a *nation* of monsters. Some virtue still remains among us, confined to me, and my honourable friends, it is true; but we, sir, are Englishmen. Englishmen, capable of blushing at the nefarious practices of delegated authority. Englishmen, who have not been completely disembowelled of our natural entrails: our hearts, and galls, and spleens, and livers, have not been forcibly torn from our bodies, and their places supplied by shawls, and lacks, and nabobships, and dewannes! We have real hearts of flesh and blood, within our bosoms. Hearts, which bleed at the recital of human misery, and feel for the woes of your unhappy country, with all the warmth of unsophisticated virtue. (vol. 2, pp. 118–19)

This is a slur on Burke's claims as an Irishman to represent Englishness, of course, but also an attack on the wider culture of sentiment, which is figured here in absurdly visceral terms. The fact that Zāārmilla looks stoically on while Burke rants thus upends Montesquieu's notion that the people of the East are excessively subject to the passions and suggests that sensibility, uncoupled from sound moral judgement, is little more than a pathological disorder: 'a paroxysm of delirium'.

Hamilton resumes her critique of sensibility as enemy of true sympathy in an episode towards the end of the novel, where she reverts to the theme of female education, as part of which she had earlier satirised the bluestocking Miss Olivia as 'a gentleman in petticoats' (vol. 2, p. 91). Yet Olivia's 'unladylike' conduct and the timidity of her sister, Miss Caroline Ardent, are shown to be far preferable to the artificially heightened sensibility of Miss Julia Ardent. Zäärmilla reports in his letter an incident that 'will serve to illustrate' his observations on their characters (vol. 2, p. 175). A runaway horse-drawn cart knocks down an elderly man who tried to bring the horses under control. The accident presents a richly pathetic scene to the sisters, and a test: 'in a moment the mangled and bleeding body was discovered lying, to all appearance, lifeless, in the track which the cart had passed' (vol. 2, p. 176).

Julia flees the scene as quickly as she can, returns to Ardent Hall and promptly falls upon the floor, 'as is customary with young ladies on such occasions', adds Zäärmilla, not yet informed enough to single out such behaviour for criticism. 'When she had fainted for a decent length of time', he goes on, 'she screamed, laughed, and cried alternately, and continued long enough in the second stage of fright, called *An Hysteric Fit*, to draw round her the greatest part of her family' (vol. 2, p. 176). The doughty Olivia, by contrast, gathers up medicinal herbs and cordials 'totally unconcerned for her sister, on whom, indeed, she seemed to dart a look of contempt'. She returns to the scene of the accident with a crowd of followers, including the raja, at her heels, to confront a spectacle that demands true sympathy of the reader:

> There, seated on the ground, we beheld the twin-sister of Olivia. Her fair arms supported the unfortunate old man, whose wounded head, reclined upon her lap. His wounds were, however, bound up. The robe of Olivia, having been torn in pieces for that purpose. And now, with a tenderness that equalled her activity, she knelt at the old man's side, and carried to his pale lips the cordials she had, with so little ceremony, snatched from her sister. (vol. 2, p. 177)

Lady Grey afterwards reproves Julia for her specious show of emotion, speaking for Hamilton when she declares that what passes for sensibility 'is but too often another word for selfishness. Believe me, that sensibility which turns with disgust from the sight of misery it has the power to relieve, is not of the right kind.' The philosophers, also present at the scene, interject that Lady Grey has spoken in accord with Hume's principle of general utility, to which she retorts, 'I have taken them ... from the doctrines and examples of Jesus Christ and his apostles' (vol. 2, pp. 178–9). The personal imitation of Christ trumps meretricious sensibility and the imposition of dehumanised systems as a measure of compassion for others, something to which the raja is tacitly alert.

The novel's intensifying evangelical tone raises the question of Zāārmilla's own receptiveness to Christianity. As he is drawn ever deeper into the network of Christian friends and associates that began with Percy, the scene transfers to the rural idyll of Violet-Dale, birthplace of one of Percy's Indian acquaintances, Mr Denbeigh. Denbeigh is visiting his parents for the first time since his sojourn in India, and his mother is taken aback by his change of complexion, once 'fair red and white' but now 'the deep brown shade, that marks the European Asiatic' – revealing him to be a nabob who has not been corrupted by India (vol. 2, p. 195). Denbeigh is unaffected by this outward transformation, and in his company the raja witnesses scenes which finally convince him that, in England, 'Christianity is not yet *entirely extinct* ... like Virtue and Wisdom, it still has some adherents, in the retired scenes of life' (p. 233). The Denbeighs are a dissenting family who say grace before meals, pray before bedtime and raise their children according to the precepts of the Bible. It is not long before that he regards the Denbeigh home as the 'Temple of domestic bliss' and assures Māāndāāra that 'the remembrances of their virtues shall be the companions of my life' (vol. 2, p. 230). Evangelical Christianity elides differences between nationalities and reconfigures the outward shows of sensibility as internally located moral good sense.

A nominal Hindu to the end of the book, Zāārmilla judges Christianity by its results and finds it to be more conducive to human happiness than any of the philosophical systems practised at Ardent Hall. His conclusions on British life, delivered in his final letter to Māāndāāra, signal a rejection of Montesquieu's theory. Adopting the resigned tone of Johnson's *Rasselas*, who discovers that things are the same everywhere, the raja maintains that Europeans are equally subject to the vicissitudes of their passions as the supposedly more excitable Asiatics:

> Thou wilt observe, that to extend our knowledge of the world, is but to become acquainted with new modes of pride, vanity, and folly. Thou wilt perceive that in Europe, as in Asia, an affected singularity often passes for superior wisdom; bold assertion for truth; and sticky fastidiousness for true delicacy of sentiment. Thou wilt see that the passions of men are every where the same; and that the variety made by the Idol of Doctor Sceptic (existing circumstances) is not in the passions themselves, but in the complexion of the objects which excite them. (vol. 2, pp. 232–3)

As a Hindu, Zāārmilla is seen throughout the novel as a competent judge of human nature despite his adherence to the tenets of his own faith, portrayed as not wholly incompatible with Hamilton's Christian ideals. *Translation of the Letters of a Hindoo Rajah* is an unusual text in that it combines an Orientalist appreciation of Hinduism (partly as a memorial to her brother's work) with a Christian moral framework. As such it stands at the end of an era. Hamilton's attitude towards India was perhaps gilded by her respect for her brother's scholarly legacy but her evangelicalism naturally inclined her away from an appreciation of Hinduism in its own right. Thus, Zāārmilla's Hinduism is aligned very closely with Hamilton's own religious opinions through the unifying operations of sympathy, regarded as a universal index of human behaviour. The raja's own 'delicacy of sentiment', clearly unaffected by the climate of his homeland, eschews the predilection for extravagant emotional displays associated with the earlier culture of sensibility in favour of a more discerning appreciation of moral judgement. As such Hamilton invites the reader to think of Zāārmilla and other Indians of his ilk as ripe for a reasoned accession to Christianity, a conversion most devoutly to be wished by British authors of a similarly evangelical disposition.

4
Gothic Sympathy and Missionary Writing

Whilst not easily categorised as an 'evangelical' herself (she was in fact Episcopalian), Hamilton conveys overtones of Christianity that align *Translation of the Letters of a Hindoo Rajah* chronologically, if not denominationally, with the Evangelical Revival that emerged in Britain in the mid to late eighteenth century.[1] This movement harked back to the 'great awakening' experienced by Methodists and other dissenting groups in the mid eighteenth century, but swiftly spread to the established Church of England, where evangelical clergy rose to prominence around the country. The Evangelical Revival has long been acknowledged as a force in early nineteenth-century culture and society, but has more recently been given its due as a prevailing influence on the culture of empire in Britain.[2] Its impact, traced over the texts covered in this chapter, centred on the growth of the missionary movement and its drive to convert Britain's Indian subjects to Christianity, a change from the religious tolerance practised under the governorship of Hastings and promulgated by Jones. Indian religion, particularly Hinduism, became less an object of scholarly curiosity and increasingly one of moral alarm and revulsion in the eyes of the assurgent evangelical lobby. Hindu beliefs, ceremonies and rites were construed in new ways that may be characterised as gothic. As with the gothic novels of the eighteenth century, this involved an interplay of sympathies and antipathies between the reader (or spectator), the perpetrators of evil and their victims. Unlike Burke's configurations of sympathy between a conscientious public and the victims of colonial misrule, however, evangelical writers portrayed the Brahmin priestly caste as authors of Indian suffering. India became a gothic setting akin to the oppressive Catholic societies of Italy, France and Spain. British sympathies were newly being marshalled to reform a religion that was widely regarded as cruel, corrupt and irrational, the diametric opposite of Protestant evangelicalism.

At the outset, it is useful to consider ways in which writing about colonial India can be regarded as 'gothic' in the first place. Patrick Brantlinger in his *Rule of Darkness: British Literature and Imperialism, 1830–1914* (1988) detected a gathering gloom in nineteenth-century writing on empire; writing of Indian Mutiny novels, Brantlinger observed 'an absolute polarisation of good and evil, innocence and guilt, justice and injustice, moral restraint and sexual depravity, civilisation and barbarism' that was directly comparable to the dynamics of the gothic mode.[3] Alexandra Warwick in her entry in *The Handbook to Gothic Literature* (1998), identified two broad strands of 'colonial gothic' in British literature: the first characterised by a domestic setting that represents 'the fear of the incursion of the foreign "other" into Britain' (the appearance of Mrs Rochester in Charlotte Brontë's *Jane Eyre* being a paradigmatic example); the second set in the colonial contact zone itself, with an experience of otherness 'manifested in attempts to control or domesticate the native peoples'.[4] A third sub-category, which Massimiliano Demata has coined in relation to William Beckford's *Vathek* (1786), is 'Oriental gothic': a mingling of fact and fiction, typified by the use of footnotes to provide an illusion of reality, which opens up 'a narrative space which discloses to the reader the dangerous proximity and closeness of the alien presence of the other'.[5] All these literary phenomena involve ways of looking at otherness in a colonial context that, consciously or unconsciously, occupy the psychological realms of the gothic. Such texts need not be novels in themselves but all share a preoccupation with fear of the unknown, the uncanny, darkness, depravity and vice. In them, the Burkean sublime is used to cloak Indian religious horror instead of British misrule, with the same proviso that the sympathetic imagination penetrates and ultimately purges such obscurity.

While it is well known that commentators in the nineteenth century took a dim view of customs such as *sati* and *thagi*, European engagement with Hinduism was not always marked by moralising disapproval.[6] By 1800, Britain could boast that of all European nations it had delved deepest into the history of world religions and discovered several new ones (Sikhism was added to the list in 1788 with the publication of Wilkins's 'Observations on the Seeks and their College' in the first volume of *Asiatick Researches*). But, in certain quarters, familiarity bred contempt. Britain's military and economic dominance of the subcontinent by the turn of the century, together with the progress in Britain of the Evangelical Revival, meant that Indian faiths increasingly came to be viewed as poor relations of Christianity. Moreover, a mounting sense of providence, manifest in Britain's pre-eminence in South Asia, led to calls for the conversion of the Indians to Christianity. If the creed that had served Britons so well were extended to Britain's Indian subjects, this argument ran, then not only would the British empire in the East become an unassailable, unified entity, but millions of heathen souls would be saved. Members of the influential evangelical group known as the Clapham Sect, which included William Wilberforce, Zachary Macaulay and (ironically) Sir William Jones's successor as President of the Asiatic Society of Bengal, John Shore, Lord Teignmouth, lobbied Parliament for the imposition of Christianity throughout British India. They sought to insert the so-called 'pious clause' into the East India Company charter, which was due for renewal in 1813. This read: 'it is the Duty of the Country to promote the Interests and the Happiness of the Native Inhabitants of the British Dominions in India and such Measures ought to be adopted as may tend to the introduction among them of useful knowledge, and of religious and moral improvement'.[7] The Company forbade missionary activity in their territory on security grounds, following the Vellore Mutiny of 1806, in which native sepoys, alarmed by rumours that they would be forcibly converted to Christianity, rose up and attacked their European officers. It even sponsored various local festivals, notably the ceremony at the temple of Juggernaut in Puri, Orissa. The years leading up to 1813 therefore saw a polarisation of views on Hinduism, with evangelical attacks matched in vigour by Orientalist ripostes. The exchange brought to light a new model of imaginative sympathy that could be applied to India in addition to the Jonesian ideal of cosmopolitan appreciation: that of horrified indignation at what was regarded as self-inflicted suffering.

Most significantly for literary depictions of India, evangelical polemic played a significant part in steering depictions of Indian religion towards gothic tropes. Consider, for example, the following passage from Teignmouth's *Considerations on the Practicability, Policy, and Obligation of Communicating to the Natives of India the Knowledge of Christianity* (1808). The marginality of Indian vice is daringly removed to create a sense of affective immediacy for the British reader:

> Were the same superstitions, or the same barbarous and licentious rites, which are now exhibited on the banks of the Ganges, to be practised on the banks of the Thames, or even the remotest part of the British islands, they would excite the strongest possible feelings

of horror, and stimulate our efforts to substitute a purer and more benign system in the place of this compound of cruelty and crime.[8]

Joshua Marshman, a Baptist missionary based in the Danish enclave of Serampore, similarly reached for the language of the macabre to describe his feelings in response to a *sati*:

> To have seen savage wolves thus tearing a human body limb from limb, would have seemed shocking, but to see relations and neighbours do this to one with whom they had familiarly conversed not an hour before, and to do it with an air of levity, was almost too much for me to bear.[9]

Others saw Hinduism as simply the most barbarous religion with which Europeans were then acquainted. William Ward, another Serampore Baptist, issued an expansive and influential work, *A View of the History, Literature and Religion of the Hindoos* (1811), in which he denounced that faith as 'the most PUERILE, IMPURE, AND BLOODY OF ANY SYSTEM OF IDOLATRY THAT WAS EVER ESTABLISHED ON EARTH'.[10] The discourse applied to Hinduism of violence, horror and transgression, in which all manner of natural laws were cast asunder, meant that following the publicity campaign mounted during the charter debate, India found itself cast as a land of religious nightmare. European imaginations ran amok there in multiple collisions of neurosis, fiction and reality. The second phase of a dialectic commenced in response to what was seen as sentimental Orientalist indulgence towards India.

Protestant antipathy towards Hinduism found a ready-made analogue in the established anti-Catholic rhetoric of the period, for the British popular imagination came to associate both religions with superstition, priestcraft and image-worship.[11] Evangelical observers connected the two as common obstacles to the propagation of the Gospel as they interpreted it. Edward Moor, author of *The Hindu Pantheon* (1810), which celebrated the 'pure' Vedanta strain of Hinduism, contemplated publishing a volume entitled *Pagan and Papal Rome: connecting those ancient and modern pagan rites, ceremonies and legends, with the fables of Hindu mythology: and showing the unchangableness of popery, and monkery and priestcraft – applicable to the present times.*[12] Claudius Buchanan, Vice-Provost of Fort William College, Calcutta, echoed Burke's fears about dormant sympathy when he cautioned in his *Christian Researches in Asia* (1811) that 'while we remain silent and unmoved spectators of the flames of the Widow's Pile, there is no hope that we shall be justly affected by the reported horrors of the Inquisition'.[13] Buchanan was referring to intelligence received from Portuguese Goa, where the inquisition was reportedly conducting brutal executions virtually under the nose of their British neighbours. Teignmouth, Marshman and Buchanan introduced a moral and aesthetic dimension into their texts that invited the reader to share their feelings and be moved to intervene in scenes of suffering. Early nineteenth-century Evangelicals inherited eighteenth-century formulations of imaginative sympathy but significantly sharpened their Protestant Christian focus. The divisions between Orientalists and Evangelicals manifested themselves in different choices of sympathetic objects when British India was discussed.

A second important development was the apparent willingness of second-generation Orientalists to repudiate the more accommodating stance of their predecessors towards Hinduism. India specialists such as Teignmouth, Charles Grant, James Forbes and Ward began to make harsher judgements about the Hindu religious ceremonies they witnessed. This may be linked in part to the growing distaste for overt displays of bodily punishment in Britain, seen in the gradual replacement of public executions with systems of imprisonment and transportation.[14] But in addition, the influence of evangelical Protestantism, together with mounting calls for missionary activity in India, led to the steady evangelisation of British Orientalism.[15] This saw the sympathetic curiosity of Jones, Halhed, Wilkins and Colebrooke being laid aside in favour of an explicitly biblical interpretation of the diverse religions of the world. Orientalist literature, a field in which, as we have seen, the authority of textual sources in explanatory notes was of paramount importance, consequently adopted a more denigrating view of Hinduism. As Governor-General of India between 1793 and 1798, Teignmouth was in a position of considerable influence in India and in Britain. Moreover, he was a founding member of the Church Missionary Society (established 1799) and subsequently of the British and Foreign Bible Society (established 1804), which, unlike the Society for the Propagation of the Gospel in Foreign Parts, also catered to dissenting groups.[16] With Grant, he represented the Indian interest within the highly politicised Clapham Sect. Grant's *Observations on the State of Society among the Asiatic Subjects of Great Britain, particularly with respect to morals* (1813) denounced the Hindus as 'a people exceedingly depraved' and argued that the diffusion of Christianity would strengthen the bond between Britain and India.[17] Teignmouth naturally benefited from the authority and experience of his proximity, as former *protégé*, to Jones, whose reputation as the most distinguished proponent of Oriental culture lived on after him. Teignmouth's widely read *Memoir of the Life, Writings and Correspondence, of Sir William Jones* (1804) took the form of an exemplary life and devoted many of its 400 pages to scouring Jones's life and work for evidence of evangelical sympathies. It also sought to tone down Jones's youthful radical Whig politics and outspoken opposition to the war in America, the biographer remarking only that 'with respect to the American war, he early adopted sentiments upon it unfavourable to the justice of the British cause'.[18]

The *Memoir* upends Jones's sympathetic view of non-Christian religions and instead presents him, thoroughly unconvincingly, as an advocate of evangelicalism. Teignmouth seized on an incident during Jones's voyage out to India in 1783, when he disputed with two Muslim clerics at Madeira, insisting that the Qur'an supports Christ's divinity because it acknowledges the miraculous nature of his virgin birth; 'a decisive proof', Teignmouth declares, 'of the belief of Sir William Jones, in the sublime doctrines of the Christian religion. Had he been an infidel, he would have smiled at the scoffs of Musselman bigotry'.[19] Jones's poem entitled 'Prayer', composed in 1782, whose first line is addressed to the 'Eternal and incomprehensible *Mind*', poses the biographer greater difficulties, but Teignmouth used it to adduce the author's ultimate acknowledgement of 'the infinite wisdom, power, and benevolence of his Creator, and of the ignorance, weakness, and depravity of human nature; sentiments which reason and experience strongly suggest, and which Revelation expressly teaches'.[20] Jones's nebulous deism eluded Teignmouth's efforts to shape it into evangelical certainty, but this did not stop him from projecting his own anti-Orientalist scorn for Hinduism onto his former mentor. In his *Considerations on the Practicability, Policy, and Obligation of Communicating to the Natives of India the Knowledge of Christianity*, Teignmouth expressed the hope that the Hindu gods, having been restored to light by Jones's researches, might just as quickly be reconsigned to oblivion: 'the power and truth of religion, which put to flight the Jupiter, Mars and Apollo of heathen superstition, may still be found of efficacy to dethrone the Indra, Cartikeia, and Surya of Hindostan'.[21]

A second conspicuous act of Orientalist apostasy was the case of James Forbes, who spent 17 years painstakingly researching the flora, fauna, languages and customs of western India only to renounce it all in his *Reflections on the Character of the Hindoos: and on the importance of converting them to Christianity: being the preface to, and conclusion of, a series of Oriental letters, which will shortly be published* (1810), which duly appeared as part of his *Oriental Memoirs* (1813).[22] In this work, which documents his years communing with Brahmins and various classes of Indian wise men, Forbes converted his scholarly credentials into a statement of evangelising intent. He distanced himself from the appreciative tradition of Jones and other first-generation Orientalist scholars and instead called for his fellow evangelicals to stand up and be counted:

> When modern philosophers, deists and sceptics of various denominations are endeavouring to undermine Christianity, and exalt paganism, it behoves every one who has acquired any real knowledge of those pagans, and who has himself been happily instructed in the truths of Christianity, to support, by any laudable means in his power, the cause of religion, purity and virtue, against priestcraft, superstition and error: – and to those advocates for Hindūism, I must, in the first instance, oppose the high authority of Sir William Jones.[23]

Jones was hardly an 'advocate for Hinduism' in the sense that Forbes suggests, but his failure to denounce its rituals and practices was taken by many evangelical commentators as tantamount to an endorsement.[24] Henceforth, accounts of Hinduism would emphasise such practices as *sati*, female infanticide and 'promiscuous' festival rites that were regarded as repugnant by increasing numbers of British observers.

Sympathisers with Hinduism such as Thomas Maurice, keeper of Oriental manuscripts at the British Museum, were increasingly discredited. Maurice's encyclopaedic *Indian Antiquities* (1800) contained the Jonesian assertion that 'the Mosaic records and Christianity, so far from being subverted by the *pretended antiquity* of the Brahmins, will derive a proud trophy from the corroborative testimony of their *genuine annals* and the congenial sentiments of their *primeval creed*'.[25] This enraged Ward, who accused Maurice of seeking to place Hinduism and Christianity on an equal footing. Ward's *View of the History, Literature and Religion of the Hindoos* turned Maurice's specialist knowledge against him in a remarkable debunking of the latter's admiration for Hindu metaphysics. The reader is invited to dwell on the absence of sympathetic sentiment among the participants of ceremonies which are very far from sublime:

> If Mr Maurice thinks there is something in Hinduism to excite the most sublime idea, let him come and join the dance before the idol; – or assist the bramhŭns in crying *Hŭree bul! Hŭree bul!* while the fire is

seizing the limbs of the young and unfortunate Hindoo widow; – or let him attend at the sacrificing of animals before the images of Kalēē and Doorga; – or come and join in the dance, stark naked, in the public street, in open day, before the image of Doorga, in the presence of thousands of spectators, young and old, male and female.[26]

According to evangelical logic, if Maurice was not willing to participate in the ritual aspects of Hinduism himself, he could not conceivably defend the precepts that underlay them.

In the evangelical imaginary, Hindu rites took on a transgressive aspect that played out in both fiction and reality. Indeed, the two spheres were essentially intertwined for the East India Company chaplain Henry Martyn, who possessed a mind seemingly primed to the gothic mode. A former Senior Wrangler at St John's College, Cambridge, Martyn 'converted' to Christianity in 1799 under the tutelage of Charles Simeon, the influential evangelical rector of Holy Trinity Church, Cambridge, who reared a generation of missionaries and had extensive links with the Clapham Sect.[27] Inspired by the pioneering example of the Serampore Baptists, he was taught Urdu by John Gilchrist in London and made no secret of his plans to translate the Bible into Indian languages, despite the ban on proselytising activity that was still in force at this time. Martyn sailed for India in 1805 and expressed in his journal his determination to gather 'an abundant harvest of souls' for Christ while in India.[28] He discomfited the ship's passengers and crew with regular sermons on the ninth Psalm, 'The wicked shall be turned into hell, and all the nations that forget God', to the point where the captain felt obliged to declare 'Mr Martyn must not damn us today, or none will come again.'[29] Martyn disapproved of Jones's secularism, writing that 'in all his plans of study, which should embrace every subject of human attention, religion bears no place'.[30] The picture of the East India Company that emerges from Martyn's journal is that of an ungodly group of European merchant-adventurers who sponsored heathen festivals while resisting efforts to import Christianity. Like Jones, he had profound misgivings about his financial dependence on the Company, but preferred to labour in Christ's vineyard rather than mine the treasure-stores of Asiatic learning.

From his first arrival off the coast of India in 1806, Martyn's diary marks a representational shift from sympathetic appreciation to gothic apprehension. Like all travellers sailing northwards to Calcutta, Martyn saw the temple of Juggernaut rear up on the coastline off the ship's port bow, dark against the setting sun. The sight sent a chill down his spine: 'Here is heathenism staring the stranger in the face on his arrival off the land', he wrote in his journal, 'the scene presented another specimen of that tremendous gloom, with which the devil has overspread the land; no house near it, we conceived no noise to be heard along the bare coast, but the hollow roar of the surf' (vol. 1, pp. 441–2). Martyn conjures up an aura of evil around the apparently deserted temple, associating the place with satanic activity. On another occasion, guided by the sound of drums and cymbals through a dark wood, Martyn confessed that 'never did sounds go through my heart with such horror in my life'. Fearful anticipation succeeded in due course to a somewhat anticlimactic revelation, as he reached a temple where a night-time ceremony was taking place:

> The people to the number of about fifty were standing on the outside, and playing the instruments. In the centre of the building was the idol, a little black ugly image, about two feet high, with a few lights burning round him. At intervals they prostrated themselves, with their foreheads to the earth.

To a Jones or a Wilkins, there would be nothing remotely unsettling or offensive about this scene, but the evangelical Martyn is affected even to the point of bodily disorder: 'I shivered at being in the neighbourhood of hell; my heart was ready to burst at the dreadful state to which the Devil had brought my poor fellow-creatures' (vol. 1, pp. 449–50). What is striking about Martyn's account, compared to the Oriental scholars of the preceding generation, is its complete absence of curiosity, let alone tolerance. He is also prey to what are entirely imagined horrors, in the manner of an Anne Radcliffe heroine or Jane Austen's characterisation of Catherine Morland in *Northanger Abbey* (1817). Unlike Catherine, who is finally able to transcend her gothic preconceptions, Martyn finds what he sees genuinely shocking. In fairness, ultimately he did not distinguish between European and Indian sinners, one day recording in his diary that he 'lay in tears interceding for the natives of this country; thinking with myself that the most despicable Soodar of India was of as much value in the sight of God as the King of Great Britain' (vol. 1, p. 457).

Another Cambridge-educated evangelical who believed in extending the Anglican Church hierarchy to India was Claudius Buchanan, Vice-Provost of Fort William College, Calcutta. His book *Colonial Ecclesiastical Establishment* (1813) outlined a plan for creating parishes and dioceses throughout Company territory, and refuted criticism that this would lead to civil unrest. Buchanan too kept a journal whilst in India, but, unlike Martyn, published it to expose the East India Company's patronage of Hindu festivals, notably the annual ceremony at the temple of Juggernaut. He brought to perfection the tendency established among earlier European eyewitnesses of the procession of viewing the scene through a biblical prism, a way of looking that Said insightfully termed a 'textual attitude'; that is, the 'fallacy' of employing works of literature to order the 'swarming, unpredictable, and problematic mess in which human beings live'.[31] Whereas Jones introduced textual references to generate sympathetic points of connection, Buchanan turned to biblical and Miltonic references to demonise the rituals he witnessed.

Evidence of this practice is found in earlier accounts of Juggernaut, including those of William Bruton and François Bernier, available to British readers in the widely read *Collection of Voyages and Travels ... from the curious and valuable LIBRARY of the late EARL OF OXFORD*, often known as 'Churchill's Collection' or 'Churchill's Travels'.[32] Bruton and Bernier also observed the phenomenon of devotees throwing themselves beneath the wheels of an enormous chariot. Bernier, who visited India in 1658 and again in 1668, wrote that 'when this hellish triumphant chariot marcheth, there are found (which is no fable) persons so foolishly credulous and superstitious as to throw themselves with their bellies under those large and heavy wheels, which bruise them to death' (vol. 2, p. 198). Bruton, harking back to his travels of 1638, declared the spectacle to be 'the mirror of all wickedness and idolatry'. He was reminded of the Moabites worshipping Baal as mentioned in the Book of Kings. When the statue of Juggernaut appeared and worshippers rushed to immolate themselves beneath it, his thoughts turned to 'the *Revelat.* and 1st verse, and likewise the 16th and 17th verses of the said chapter, in which places there is a beast, and such idolatrous worship mentioned'. He even interpreted the sandal paste on the Brahmins' foreheads as the mark of the Beast described in Revelation 16:3: 'And he causeth all, both small and great, rich and poor, free and bond, to receive a mark in their right hand, or in their foreheads' (vol. 2, p. 277).

As might be expected, these observers from the early modern period were steeped in biblical imagery. Yet a ready recourse to Scripture was also characteristic of early nineteenth-century evangelicals such as Buchanan. He visited the temple on 18 June 1806, having earlier outlined the essentials of the ceremony in his *Colonial Ecclesiastical Establishment*. On the latter occasion, recorded in his published journal in *Christian Researches in Asia* (1811), he counted over 100 human skulls littering the precincts, and recalled seeing dogs, jackals and vultures scavenging. He approached the temple on horseback in the midst of a crowd of devotees. At one point, the crush was so intense that the clergyman was nearly knocked from the saddle. At length, the chariot of Juggernaut appeared, and Buchanan recorded the following entry in his diary. The textual associations are designed to goad the reader into mounting indignation, made worse by the sensation of being powerlessly swept along in the procession:

> I have returned home from witnessing a scene which I shall never forget. At twelve o'clock of this day, being the great day of the feast, the Moloch of Hindoostan was brought out of his temple amidst the acclamations of hundreds of thousands of his followers. ...
>
> The throne of the idol was placed on a stupendous car or tower about sixty feet in height, resting on wheels which indented the ground deeply, as they turned slowly under the ponderous machine. Attached to it were six cables, of the size and length of a ship's cable, by which the people drew it along. Upon the tower were the priests and satellites of the idol, surrounding his throne. The idol is a block of wood, having a frightful visage painted black, with a distended mouth of a bloody colour. His arms are of gold, and he is dressed in gorgeous apparel. ...
>
> I went on in the procession, close by the tower of Moloch; which, as it was drawn with difficulty, grated on its many wheels harsh thunder. After a few minutes it stopped; and now the worship of the God began. – A high priest mounted the car in front of the idol, and pronounced his obscene stanzas in the ears of the people; who responded at intervals in the same strain. 'These songs', said he, 'are the delight of the God. His car can only move when he is pleased with the song'. ... A boy of about twelve years was then brought forth to attempt something yet more lascivious, if peradventure the God would move. The 'child perfected the praise' of his idol with such ardent expression and gesture, that the God was pleased, and the multitude emitting a sensual yell of delight, urged the car along. ... An aged minister of the idol then stood up, and with a long rod in his hand, which he moved with indecent action, completed the variety of this disgusting exhibition. – I felt a consciousness of doing wrong in witnessing it. I was also somewhat appalled at the magnitude and horror of the spectacle; I felt like a guilty person, on whom all eyes were fixed, and I was about to withdraw. But a scene of a different kind was about to be presented. The characteristics of Moloch's worship are obscenity and blood. We have seen the former. Now comes the blood. ... After the tower had proceeded some way, a pilgrim

announced that he was ready to offer himself a sacrifice to the idol. He laid himself down in the road before the tower as it was moving along, lying on his face, with his arms stretched forwards. The multitude passed round him, leaving the space clear, and he was crushed to death by the wheels of the chariot.[33]

The '*hissing* applause' heard on the approach to the temple evokes the Pandemonium scenes from Book 10 of Milton's *Paradise Lost*, where Satan and his fellow fallen angels metamorphose into serpents. Their only sound thereafter is 'from innumerable / A dismal universal hiss' (Book 10, ll. 507–8). Buchanan's mention of Moloch next transports the reader to the earlier Pandemonium scene, where is found the description of that god as a 'horrid King besmear'd with blood / Of human sacrifice, and parents tears' (Book 2, ll. 392–96). 'Homicide' and 'lust hard by hate' mark the 'wanton rites' of his worship, and in the scene before him, the minister witnesses acts that appear to confirm his prejudices. The Hindus were popularly believed to descend from the children of Ham, the Ammonites, and these are among the tribes condemned for idolatry throughout the Old Testament, which Bryant, Jones and others had explored. The phrase 'the child perfected the praise', presumably in this case by submitting to a sexual act, is intended to contrast with the behaviour of the children in the Temple in Jerusalem when they worshipped Jesus in defiance of the chief priests: 'And Jesus saith to them, Yea, have ye never read, Out of the mouth of babes and sucklings thou hast perfected praise?' (Matthew 21:16). Taken together, Buchanan's ironic quotations from Scripture and cross-references to *Paradise Lost* convey a powerful sense of hell on earth: one, importantly, that it was in Britain's power to redeem. The diary entry closes with Buchanan surveying what he considers a 'Golgotha' from a distant hilltop, and dreaming of a Christian establishment in India.[34]

Buchanan's accounts of Juggernaut gained currency in Britain as a vehicle of negative sentiment towards India. Southey, whose interest in the East Indies was galvanised by the missionary debate, denounced Hinduism in a series of articles for the *Quarterly* and *Annual Review*.[35] His 1815 review of James Forbes's *Oriental Memoirs* (1813), for instance, labelled the Hindu system of government a 'diabolocracy' and claimed that in Urdu the words for 'lie' and 'jest' are the same, while in Tamil there is no word for 'hope'.[36] Southey's position on the conversion of India to Christianity is worth clarifying, for while he saw Portuguese Catholicism as a threat to British interests, he nevertheless admired the zeal with which the Catholic founder of Portugal's East Indian Empire,

Albuquerque, propagated his faith. By contrast, 'if England were dispossessed of its dominion in India, the natives would retain nothing of all which we could have taught', Southey lamented in a *Quarterly Review* article published in the Spring of 1809, 'not a trace of our language would remain; and for our religion – the Hindoo would argue that we had none'.[37] Hinduism was for him, as for Buchanan, Martyn and others, a spur to sympathetically motivated intervention, yet Southey confusingly endorsed its imaginative potential in his Indian epic poem, *The Curse of Kehama* (1810).

Culture and religion were, for Southey, the twin means of imparting a moral dimension to the colonial enterprise in India and, to a large extent, redeeming what could then be construed as an initial phase of conquest and plunder. In this, he followed Burke's view that sympathetic engagement with India should foster organic bonds between the two countries. Southey, however, placed a far greater emphasis on religion as an index of national virtue, part of his well-documented drift towards cultural and political conservatism that eventually led Byron to denounce him as a 'renegado'.[38] This religiously inflected form of sympathy appears obliquely in *The Curse of Kehama*, which offsets a tale of heroism and moral virtue against an elaborate recreation of the Hindu cosmos, a combination that (as the final chapter will discuss at greater length) engendered confusion as to the author's motives among the critics. The plot follows the struggle between an Indian peasant farmer, Ladurlad, and his daughter, Kailyal, against the tyrannical raja Kehama, initiated when Ladurlad killed the raja's son for trying to rape Kailyal. The implacable Kehama pronounces a curse against Ladurlad, which protects him from death and disease but dooms him to eternal pain and lack of sleep. He is thus rendered an object of perpetual sympathy and figuratively removed from his Indian surroundings, a narrative move that serves to emphasise his inner purity. Father and daughter, after a separation, are united on Mount Meru with the aid of a friendly Glendoveer, an angelic being, and then seek the intercession of the gods to heal Ladurlad and thwart Kehama.

The poem contrasts the virtuous characters and the 'pure' religion of the Hindu gods (who occupy a Miltonic upper universe) with the worldliness and corruption of 'popular' Hinduism, which permits the evil Kehama to thrive. Southey rehearses the features of Hinduism that were most likely to be repugnant to his readers, beginning with the burning of Kehama's son's widow, which constitutes book I of *The Curse of Kehama*. Book XIV exposes Kailyal, who has been captured by devotees of 'Jaga-Naut', to the full horror of heathen inhumanity, as fanatical worshippers plan to sacrifice 'a maid of charms surpassing human thought' to the god.[39] Southey cites Buchanan's account, in addition to those of Bruton, Bernier, John Stavorinus and Johann Niekamp, as a source for his scene, in which the absence of compassion among the pilgrims is as monstrous and remorseless as the dramatic chariot of Juggernaut itself:

> Up rear'd on twenty wheels elate,
> Huge as a Ship, the Bridal Car appear'd;
> Loud creak its ponderous wheels, as through the gate
> A thousand Bramins drag the enormous load.
> There throned aloft in state,
> The Image of the seven-headed God
> Came forth from his abode; and at his side
> Sate Kailyal like a bride. ...
>
> A thousand pilgrims strain
> Arm, shoulder, breast and thigh, with might and main,
> To drag that sacred wain,
> And scarce can draw along the enormous load.
> Prone fall the frantic votaries in the road,
> And calling on the God,
> Their self-devoted bodies there they lay
> To pave his chariot-way.
> On Jaga-Naut they call,
> The ponderous Car rolls on, and crushes all.
> Through flesh and bones it ploughs its dreadful path.
> Groans rise unheard: the dying cry,
> And death and agony
> Are trodden under foot by yon mad throng,
> Who follow close, and thrust the deadly wheels along.[40]

Southey intended to offset the liberty of the individual subject and abuses perpetrated in the name of corrupt religion. Accordingly, we confront the worst aspects of religious despotism. Groans rising 'unheard' and death and agony 'trodden under foot' signify the absence of a normative, Christian sympathy. As for many other commentators, Catholicism and Hinduism were linked in Southey's mind. In his later *Book of the Church* (1824), he wrote of 'practices not less extravagant than those of the Indian Yoguees, and more loathsome' being officially sanctioned by the Church in Italy and Spain.[41]

The Hindu pantheon in *The Curse of Kehama* must be roused into a sympathetic intervention to restore justice on earth. In the earlier stages of the poem, the Glendoveer, who visits Mount Calasay in search of 'Seeva', is concerned at the god's indifference to their plight:

> There is oppression in the World below;
> Earth groans beneath the yoke; yea, in her woe,
> She asks if the Avenger's eye is blind?
> Awake, O Lord, awake!
> Too long thy vengeance sleepeth. Holy One!
> Put thou thy terrors on for mercy's sake,
> And strike the blow, in justice to mankind![42]

This can be read as a veiled evangelical clarion call to reform Indian religion (as Southey certainly wished to do) and an illustration of the ways in which interventionism, even to the point of 'vengeance', could be regarded as sympathetic in itself. *The Curse of Kehama*, however, refuses any straightforward equation with missionary politics by placing the power of redress firmly in the hands of Indian gods. Kehama, over the course of the poem, schemes to capture heaven, having accrued supernatural power through making sacrifices (a doctrine Southey explains in the poem's preface). At what seems to be his moment of triumph, the raja sips from the 'Amreeta-cup of immortality', at which point 'Seeva opened on the Accursed One / His Eye of Anger', thus condemning Kehama 'to live and burn eternally'[43] in a neat inversion of the curse against Ladurlad. Southey's India functions as a site of religious suffering and salvation, but stops short of calling for sympathetic missionary intervention, however much the plot appears to incline in that direction.

Sydney Owenson, Lady Morgan's novel *The Missionary: An Indian Tale* (1811), extols the virtues of individual sympathy as opposed to what the author calls the 'cold hand of religion' even more vigorously.[44] Both the title and publication date are significant; by 1811, the debate on missionary activity in British India was already well advanced. As in her earlier novel, *The Wild Irish Girl: A National Tale* (1806), Morgan had examined Irish national identity in the wake of the 1800 Act of Union, so she again intervened in contemporary politics under the cloak of fiction. Franklin has traced the extent to which Owenson conceived of and indeed negotiated the sale of her novel in close proximity to pro-Orientalist politicians, notably Castlereagh.[45] We can therefore reasonably expect it to rehearse certain Orientalist tropes but the author's intertwining of sympathy, religious sentiment and the passions is nevertheless of striking significance. Set in the seventeenth century, the book tells of the illicit love affair between a Portuguese Franciscan friar, Hilarion, and Luxima, a Hindu 'Brachmachira' (virgin widow), both of whom act as itinerant preacher of their respective religions.[46] The narrative steers both characters towards a sympathetic union of kindred spirits, symbolised by the confluence of two rivers where priest and prophetess behold each other face-to-face. For all its obvious regional stereotypes, the Romantic Morgan presents this encounter, charged with geo-sexual chemistry, as a sympathetic coming together of complementary opposites:

> Silently gazing, in wonder, upon each other, they stood finely opposed, the noblest specimens of the human species, as it appears in the most opposite regions of the earth; she, like the East, lovely and luxuriant; he, like the West, lofty and commanding ... she, looking like a creature formed to feel and to submit; he, like a being created to resist and to command.[47]

Hilarion and Luxima's love must contend against religious dogma imposed from within as well as without. Morgan's religious ideal, to which both characters ultimately accede, is rooted in sympathetic fellow-feeling, which is finally able to transcend differences of belief. Both the Christian and the Hindu agree on this point during one of the novel's many theological debates. Hilarion argues that 'the Christian doctrine is the doctrine of the heart, and ... full of that tender-loving mercy, which blends and unites the various selfish interests of mankind, in one great sentiment of brotherly affection and religious love!' to which Luxima replies, 'Such ... is that doctrine of mystic love, by which our true religion unites its followers to each other, and to the Source of all good' (vol. 2, pp. 27–8). Hilarion, given the tentative stage of their relationship, is obliged to reject the parallel, although he gradually relents as Morgan blends together his love and piety.

The Missionary ostensibly shows Luxima's gradual inclination towards Christianity as novice to Hilarion's preceptor, but Morgan wraps the vital question of her character's ultimate accession to Christian belief in mystery. At no point in the novel does Luxima unambiguously embrace Christianity and renounce Hinduism. Morgan treats the emerging love between Hilarion and Luxima with similar hesitancy, to the point of evasiveness. This does makes narrative sense, since the reader views the relationship principally through the lens of Hilarion's self-denial. So, at times, he is 'tempted to throw himself at her feet, and to avow the existence of that passion which he now believed, with a mingled emotion of rapture and remorse, was shared by her who had inspired it'; yet 'habits of religious restraint, even more, perhaps, than religion itself, checked the dangerous impulse' (vol. 2, pp. 55–6). Through her characters, Morgan seems to endorse the intermingling of spiritual and romantic emotion as a kind of natural religion. Hilarion, exposed at length to the temptations of Luxima's company in the middle section of the novel, wrestles with alternating feelings of pleasure and shame before 'the visitation of happiness, to a heart which had of late studiously avoided its enjoyment' (vol. 2, p. 58). Nonetheless, Hilarion makes the 'cold and severe' pronouncement that he can never love her, and at one point forces Luxima to choose between paganism and Christianity (she prevaricates). Yet Hilarion's emotional vicissitudes, exhaustively delineated by Morgan, belie his apparent sternness. When Luxima tells him a story of a hermit who fell in love with a 'vestal priestess' and drowned himself in the Ganges, Morgan writes that Hilarion's heart 'vibrated in sympathy to the tale she told' (vol. 2, p. 84). His passionate response indicates his difficulty in upholding the rule of abstinence, and the reader is encouraged to question whether it is right that he should do so.

Morgan is at pains to show that love between a Christian and a Hindu is possible, even desirable, and for a brief section of the novel the historical figure of Soleiman Shikuh is added to create a tripartite religious love triangle.[48] But sympathy only exists between Hilarion and Luxima as individuals, not as exponents of their respective creeds, which, in *The Missionary* at least, are portrayed as unfeeling and abstracted systems of thought, far removed from human nature. Catholicism and Hinduism serve as gothic cognates of each other, setting in motion parallel plots of persecution and excommunication as ministers of each pursue their errant votaries with unrelenting zeal. Luxima is apprehended and taken to a gloomy cave temple, where she is declared an outcast by her own father, the Guru of Kashmir, in a clear breach of the bond between father and daughter as well as co-religionists. Hilarion, meanwhile, is interrogated by members of the Spanish Inquisition in their Goan headquarters, described as 'the mansion of horror and superstition' (vol. 3, pp. 148–9). During one of these gruelling sessions, the now softened Hilarion pleads for a more sympathetic form of proselytising among the Indians in what, coming in 1811, can only have been read as Morgan's own contribution to the missionary debate:

> It is by a precious cultivation of their moral powers, we may hope to influence their religious belief; it is by teaching them to love us, that

we can lead them to listen to us; it is by inspiring them with respect for our virtues, that we can give them a confidence in our doctrine: but this has not always been the system adopted by European reformers, and the religion we proffer them is seldom illustrated by its influence on our own lives. (vol. 3, p. 95)

Morgan's original readers would have recognised in these comments a critique of earlier missionary enterprises, notably those of the Jesuits (who were accused of attracting Indian converts through coercion and deception) and, it would seem, the hotter brand of British evangelical reformer. Having shown how even the austere Hilarion may undergo an education of the heart, Morgan argues that by cultivating emotional connections with India, the cause of religion would actually be advanced.

Gothic comparisons between Catholicism and Hinduism become explicit at the climax of the novel, when Hilarion is condemned to death as a heretic and sentenced to burn in an *auto-da-fé*. Morgan here draws upon traditional configurations of sympathetic suffering to depict Hilarion as a stalwart victim of a brutal form of justice. The Indian crowd, gathered amidst the Spanish guards, constitute the compassionate onlookers of his fate, in whom 'nature was touched on the master-spring of emotion, and betrayed in the looks of the multitude, feelings of horror, of pity, and of admiration, which the bigoted vigilance of an inhuman zeal would in vain have sought to suppress' (vol. 3, p. 176). As the prisoner ascends the pyre, Luxima emerges from the multitude and throws herself onto the flames with a cry of '*Brahma* receive and eternally unite our spirits!' in a pointed comparison of the rite with *sati* (vol. 3, p. 179). She survives and in the ensuing fracas escapes with Hilarion, but succumbs to her injuries after a lengthy deathbed scene in which, again, sympathy for her plight is powerfully evoked. Her body is attended by her father, now reconciled with his daughter, and a 'sympathizing Pundit' (vol. 3, p. 207). After her death, Hilarion retires to the surrounding countryside as a hermit, and comes to be revered as a *genius loci* by the local population. *The Missionary* succeeds in disjoining religion, seen as gothic in both its Catholic and Hindu manifestations, and the sympathetic communion of individuals, which Morgan tends to regard as holy in itself.

Strictly speaking, *The Missionary* is neither a gothic novel nor an anti-Catholic one – that is to say, it depicts the inhumane Jesuits as the exception and not the rule of Catholic practice – yet it exhibits a vital theme commonly associated with gothic fiction: tension between the sanctity of the individual for whom we feel sympathy, and religious orthodoxy. This theme recurs throughout Charles Maturin's masterpiece of Protesant paranoia, *Melmoth the Wanderer*, published in 1820. By this date, the East India Charter debate was seven years in the past, and thus there is no reason to suppose that Maturin wished to reignite the arguments for and against the conversion of India to Christianity. Rather, his use of Hinduism, and the ceremony of Juggernaut in particular, as an archetype of misdirected religion points to the inadvertent result of the earlier controversy: India had become associated with horror and functioned in a similar way to Catholicism in the gothic novels of the late eighteenth century. Maturin's India, however, is presented as a religious worst-case scenario, a land where sympathy has died and the inhabitants have long since become brutalised in their conduct towards each other. Heathen religions such as Hinduism therefore function as more extreme versions of Catholicism in Maturin's gothic hierarchy of religious oppression.

The novel's plot concerns the Faust-like Melmoth, ancestor of the principal narrator, who entered into a Satanic pact centuries earlier, which granted him a term of immortality during which he must find a victim in a situation so bleak that they are willing to exchange fates with him. If he fails to find such a person, devils will reclaim him at the expiry of the term. Melmoth roams the world looking for scenarios of suffering. The vast majority of these are shown to be the products of the social structures and rituals of Catholic southern Europe; Maturin's family were Protestant French Huguenot emigrants who had no love for their former persecutors.[49] Yet a considerable portion of the novel is set not in Spain, Italy, Portugal or France – the heartlands of Catholic Europe – but in India. Maturin's free modulation from one locale to the other is no coincidence, for both were associated at the time with social oppression and both were pregnant with gothic possibilities. The plot layering that culminates in the 'Tale of the Indians' begins when the main narrator, young John Melmoth, rescues a Spaniard named Monçada after he is washed up on the Irish coast in a shipwreck. Monçada was one of the Wanderer's victims, who proceeds to tell John Melmoth the history of his dastardly forbear, during the course of which the extended tale is introduced. Having been enclosed in the monastery against his will, Monçada explains that he was imprisoned in the Fortress of the Inquisition, where he was tried for heresy. By a stroke of providence, the building caught fire, and in the confusion Monçada escaped. He sought refuge in an underground passageway, which it transpired was the secret entrance to the cell of an elderly cabbalistic

Jew. The Jew had in his possession an antique manuscript written in Spanish, which he asked Monçada to translate. Thus begins the 'Tale of the Indians', the story of Immalee, a maiden and child of nature, who, we are told, lived on an island near the mouth of the Hooghly River (familiar to British readers as the approach to Calcutta).

The island is initially visited by devotees of what the author describes as the 'black goddess Seeva'. Here is the first indication of Maturin's displaced anti-Catholic agenda, for the 'old devotees' mortify their flesh and tell their rosary beads, information the author claims was derived from Maurice's *Indian Antiquities* (it should be noted that Maturin's background research was of a far inferior quality to Owenson's).[50] Unreformed religion is figured as violence against the body, an act normally calculated to evince sympathy for the victims. The Protestant reader's reaction is complicated, however, by the fact that these religious devotees are inflicting wounds on themselves, 'striking sharp reeds into their arms, and tinging every bead with blood as they spoke', thus attracting a combination of sympathy for their agony and derision for their fanaticism. The discovery of Immalee, taken for a '*white* goddess', on the island initiates a form of reformation among the younger natives, who leave offerings of flowers and light paper lanterns, until 'gradually the isle lost its bad character for terror' (pp. 273–4).

Immalee is an *ingénue*, blissfully ignorant of the world beyond her island home. At this point the Wanderer approaches. He appears on the beach one day, and offers to instruct Immalee in the folly of the outside world, about which she is curious to learn. Melmoth turns the conversation to religion. 'There is only one point on which they all agree', he argues in an effective piece of satire, 'that of making their religion a torment; – the religion of some prompting them to torture themselves, and the religion of some prompting them to torture others' (p. 290). To illustrate what he means, he trains a telescope on the coast of India to reveal a veritable phantasmagoria of Eastern religious excess. Immalee sees first 'the black pagoda of Juggernaut', then a 'Turkish' mosque (erected, we are told, as part of Tipu Sultan's efforts to enforce Islam throughout his dominions) and beyond that a temple of 'Maha-Devi', 'one of the ancient goddesses of the country' (p. 291). This composite of Eastern religions, viewed through what is evidently a very powerful telescope, suits the Wanderer's purposes exactly for it displays the worst imaginable consequences of blind faith. A 'vast sandy plain' lies before the temple of Juggernaut, littered with 'the bones of a thousand skeletons, bleaching in the burning and unmoistening air'; a thousand pilgrims, 'hardly more alive, and scarce less emaciated', drag 'their charred and blackening bodies over the sands, to perish under the shadow of the temple, hopeless of ever reaching its walls'. Vultures flap overhead, while others, driven frantic in their fervour, wear their hands and knees literally through to the bone. 'Immalee withheld her breath, as if she inhaled the abominable effluvia of this mass of putrefaction, which is said to desolate the shores near the temple of Juggernaut, like a pestilence' (p. 292).

The footnote to Maurice and the phrase 'which is said' draw attention to the passage's supposed basis in reality. Maturin reminds his readers that the material is not the stuff of fantasy but actual religious practice, albeit mercifully distant. As the description of Juggernaut unfolds, it becomes clear that the principal source is Buchanan's diary, freely adapted but with several elements reproduced verbatim. The chariot itself echoes Buchanan and Southey, although here it is transformed with didactic explicitness into an emblem of heathen depravity:

> An enormous fabric, more resembling a moving palace than a triumphal car, supported the inshrined image of Juggernaut, and was dragged forward by the united strength of a thousand human bodies, priests, victims, brahmins, faqueers and all. In spite of this huge force, the impulse was so unequal, that the whole edifice rocked and tottered from time to time, and this singular union of instability and splendour, of trembling decadence and terrific glory, gave a faithful image of the meretricious exterior, and internal hollowness, of idolatrous religion. (p. 292)

As in a game of Chinese Whispers, the description of Juggernaut becomes progressively more lurid as it is transmitted from text to text. Whereas Buchanan saw one person crushed beneath the chariot wheels, Immalee sees 'multitudes' perish. Like his source, Maturin highlights biblical quotations that his original readers would have recognised. The 12-year-old boy reappears, who we are told 'perfected the praise' of the loathsome idol, 'with all the outrageous lubricities of the phallic worship' (Immalee fails to comprehend the nature of the act: we are told that 'from the slightest consciousness of the meaning of this phenomenon, her unimaginable purity protected her as with a shield'). Worshippers nearby 'cut themselves with knives and lancets in their manner', evoking the heathen prophets of Baal in the First Book of Kings (1 Kings 18:28).

These particularities confirm the debt of *Melmoth the Wanderer* to Buchanan. However, the novelist's polemical energies are not confined to Hinduism. Taking India as a free-floating signifier of spiritual corruption, Maturin picks off each sect in turn as the Wanderer endeavours to turn Immalee against religion altogether. The worship of false gods is seen to supplant compassion for other human beings, with Maturin's attack on non-Christian religions manifesting itself through his relentless focus on their physical cruelty. Thus at the temple of Maha-Devi mothers dance and sing while they hang their babies up in baskets as food for the birds, while outside the mosque 'Turks' lash out at harmless beggars as they swagger past on their way to prayers. Only 'a small obscure building overshadowed by palm-trees, and surmounted by a cross' fills Immalee with a momentary optimism (p. 297). This glimmer of (Protestant) truth recalls us to Maturin's purpose in attacking Indian religions, for he groups them along with Catholicism as unsympathetic systems that cut their worshippers off from God and their co-religionists. The parallels between faiths are strengthened when the authorial voice reminds readers that the worshippers of Juggernaut place as much faith in their exertions 'as the Catholic votarist does in the penance of St Bruno, or the ex-oculation of St Lucia, or the martyrdom of St Ursula and her eleven thousand virgins', a scorn for superstition on Maturin's part that extends to all idolatrous creeds (pp. 292–3).

Maturin further illuminated the logic of supplementing Catholicism with Indian religions in the preface to *Melmoth the Wanderer*. In his review of Maturin's earlier gothic tragedy *Bertram; or, The Castle of St Aldobrand* (1816), Coleridge denounced the work as 'jacobinical' for overturning what he regarded as reasonable moral expectations.[51] The preface to *Melmoth* accordingly voiced the author's concerns that the gothic novel as a genre was increasingly outmoded and (as Coleridge's comment shows) politically suspect. Anticipating further criticism, Maturin writes that 'a friend' had censured the section of 'The Spaniard's Tale' (i.e. the section of novel narrated by Monçada) 'as containing too much attempt at the revivification of the horrors of Radcliffe-Romance, of the persecutions of convents, and the terrors of the Inquisition'.[52] The Wanderer's speeches against religion in the main body of the novel also prompt a defensive footnote: 'the sentiments ascribed to the stranger are diametrically opposite to mine, and ... I have purposely put them into the mouth of an agent of the enemy of mankind'.[53] Given these anxieties about the enduring validity of gothic literature, it can be argued that Hinduism rejuvenated the form when its original wellsprings were drying up. Although the novels of Horace Walpole, Radcliffe and Matthew 'Monk' Lewis preserved popular anti-Catholic discourse throughout eighteenth-century Britain, by the time of *Melmoth the Wanderer*'s publication, first Jacobinism and then Napoleon Bonaparte had replaced the Roman church as spectres of continental European otherness.

Hinduism's partial occupation of the space left by Catholicism in the gothic imagination clearly exposed it to more pejorative representation, and helped to shut down the sympathetic curiosity that flourished briefly in the decades before 1800. Gothic *chiaroscuro*, and an increasingly cavalier use of documentary sources in fiction, replaced the more temperate, 'enlightened' outlook exemplified by Jones's cultural syncretism. One effect of the transition was that stronger imagery, ripe for incorporation into fiction, swept India to greater cultural prominence. Authors such as Southey and, most strikingly, Maturin exploited these extraordinary scenes and inaugurated a lasting British fascination with widow-burning and Juggernaut. Yet evangelical polemic ultimately reconfigured the sympathetic relationship between Britain and India towards one of moral superiority, with sympathy for India increasingly expressed in antipathy towards its religions. This is not to hold the gothic mode with its inherent prejudices responsible for providing a vocabulary for nineteenth-century imperialist rhetoric, but there was more than a ghostly resemblance between the imaginative imperatives of gothic writing and the ideology of nascent imperialism. Romantic period authors had to traverse India's perceived negative moral and aesthetic qualities if they were to preserve its potential for novelty and exoticism.

5
Reorientating the Orient: Sympathy, the East and Romantic Period Literary Criticism

The growth of evangelical distaste for Hindu India, with its accompanying tendency to employ the gothic mode when writing of the country, appeared to cast doubt on Orientalism as a viable literary form. The transition formed an obvious parallel to the switch from 'Orientalism' to 'Anglicism' identified by Eric Stokes in the realm of colonial government.[1] Something of the vitriol outpoured on India after 1800 is evident in James Mill's evaluation of the *Ramayana* and the *Mahabharata* in his *History of British India* (1817):

> These fictions are not only more extravagant, and unnatural, less correspondent with the physical and moral laws of the universe, but are less ingenious, more monstrous, and have less of anything that can engage the affection, awaken sympathy, or excite admiration, reverence, or terror, than the poems of any other, even the rudest people with whom our knowledge of the globe has yet brought us acquainted.[2]

Certainly Mill's position is far removed from that of Jones, who in 1772 urged Europeans to search in the literature of the East for 'a more extensive insight into the history of the human mind', and 'a new set of images and similitudes ... which future scholars might explain, and future poets might imitate', and much of the *History* is devoted to overturning Jones's generally positive view of Hindu culture.[3] Seven years earlier, Southey had seen fit to employ Hindu mythology as the basis for his own Oriental epic, *The Curse of Kehama* (1810), which was dismissed by many critics on the grounds of aesthetic and moral absurdity, and was widely remaindered. Yet in the same year that Mill made his notorious remarks, Thomas Moore published his bestselling Oriental poem,

Lalla Rookh, which sold a staggering 22,500 copies over 15 editions between 1817 and 1829 alone, fully justifying the astronomical £3000 his publisher, Thomas Longman, paid for it.[4] Moore's friend Byron's 'Turkish Tales' series (1813–16) also ranked high in the sales figures and established the poet's reputation as a literary lion. Evidently there was a right and a wrong way to compose Orientalist verse.

How then do we account for Mill's derogatory remarks, given the phenomenal popularity of Oriental topoi in literature at this time? Firstly, it must be noted that his attacks on 'India' target Hindu culture specifically. Here was a significant reversal of the sympathy towards Hinduism shown in Hamilton's *Translation of the Letters of a Hindoo Rajah*. Unlike the 'Mohammedan conquerors of India', who possessed 'an activity, a manliness, an independence', which inured them from 'weak and profligate barbarism', Mill insisted that the 'natural condition of government' among the 'passive' Hindus manifested itself in the childlike absurdity of their national epics.[5] Secondly, Mill had an ulterior motive, one that was nevertheless to have far-reaching consequences for imaginative sympathy in relation to India. According to Majeed, Mill's 'critique of a politics of imagination' was in fact a challenge to the dominant grouping at the heart of East Indian affairs which had hitherto been led by Jones; by extension, Mill was assaulting what he perceived to be the entire British *ancien régime*, 'writ large against an alien background' in India.[6] Seen in this way, Mill's objections to Sanskrit literature can be read as a displaced reaction, advanced in a spirit of strict Utilitarian correction, to what he regarded as a decadent movement in English letters. His reaction can be read in reverse as an attack on what he regarded as the irresponsible sympathy displayed towards Indian 'imaginativeness' by the likes of Jones.

Indeed the long section in Book 2 of the *History*, 'Of the Hindus', is typical of Utilitarian sallies against poetry and imaginative writing in general. The pattern for these was set in Jeremy Bentham's *La Théorie des Peines et des Recompenses* (1811, translated by Richard Smith as *The Rationale of Reward* in 1825), which sought to devalue the category of imagination altogether with its notorious assertion that 'prejudice apart, the game of push-pin is of equal value with the arts and sciences of music and poetry'. If, according to the principle of general utility, the only measure of an activity was its capacity to generate the maximum amount of pleasure for the greatest number of people, a relatively rarefied (some would say elitist) activity such as reading and writing poetry had to be judged alongside pastimes enjoyed by the majority of the population. Despite Romantic claims to the contrary, Bentham maintained, music and poetry did not occupy a realm apart: 'If the game of push-pin furnish more pleasure, it is more valuable than either'.[7] Oriental poetry had long been associated in the European mind with excessive imagination, the parent of licentious imagery and rampant hyperbole. This was characteristic of society in a primitive stage of development, redolent alike of childishness and 'unpolished' lack of restraint. Mill's choice of Sanskrit poetry as the grounds on which to pitch his ideological battle against imagination therefore made perfect sense, for he simply carried forward a centuries-old suspicion to a point where it could be regarded (in Majeed's words) as the 'threatening Eros' to Mill's preferred literary ideal of philosophic intelligence.[8]

Attitudes to sympathy in literary criticism in the Romantic period, from the belles-lettrists of the mid eighteenth century to the writings of Mill, Coleridge and Wordsworth, strongly influenced the composition of British Orientalist poetry in the decades after 1800, the high point of Romantic Orientalism. This chapter begins with a survey of opinions on Oriental literature generally, that is, the perceived qualities of imaginative writing produced in the East, and progresses to trace the critical reception of Southey's *Curse of Kehama* and Moore's *Lalla Rookh*, poems that were frequently taken as negative and positive exemplars of the Orientalist genre. It argues that during the Romantic period developments in literary criticism, and particularly those concerning imaginative sympathy, were responsible for driving Orientalist poetry into ever more Westernised forms. Strict critical parameters governed what was and was not aesthetically acceptable in poetry, chief among which was the demand that literary works engage sympathetically with the reader: a nostrum of Augustan, Romantic and even Utilitarian criticism alike. The latter may have been less influential at the level of mainstream literary production but opinions such as Mill's had especial relevance where writing on India was concerned. Since, as we have seen, literature on India was inextricably bound up with the material colonial and political spheres, Mill's *History* bore disproportionate weight on the reception of such texts in Britain, for he sharpened readers' sense of Oriental literature as absurd, fanciful and amoral.

The mechanics of imaginative sympathy in turn dictated that the contents of a poem must reflect known forms if the requisite 'interest' was to be awakened in the reader, a problem Southey acknowledged when he wrote dolefully to Walter Scott in 1810 that *Kehama* was 'too strange, too much beyond human sympathies'.[9] By contrast, Byron and his friend Moore understood early on that Orientalist poetry must combine Eastern and Western elements if it was to be exotic without relinquishing the goodwill of critics and readers. In a typically self-reflexive stanza from *Beppo: A Venetian Story* (1818), Byron describes the ideal of poetry he would write, had he 'the art of easy writing': 'How quickly would I print (the world delighting) / A Grecian, Syrian, or Assyrian tale; / And sell you, mix'd with western sentimentalism, / Some samples of the finest Orientalism'.[10] Unlike Southey, whose *Kehama* was an awkward hybrid product, Byron and Moore brought the composition of Orientalist poetry to a fine art, like alchemists conjuring poetic gold out of formerly inimical elements. This allowed them to avoid many of the pitfalls then associated with Oriental poetry proper, most conspicuous of which was the charge that Oriental poems were incapable of directing the passions towards edifying ends and gaining the sympathy of the reader.

Eighteenth-century commentators tended to regard the East as a land of imagination, a view stemming from the widely held belief that Oriental peoples were excessively subject to their passions. Rhetoricians argued that a high degree of effusiveness consequently marked Oriental poetry overall, but they could not agree on the merits of this particular quality. The Bishop of London, Robert Lowth, was an early advocate of Oriental poetry, which he defended in his *Lectures on the Sacred Poetry of the Hebrews* (1753; delivered as *Praelectiones de sacra poesi Hebraeorum*). These took the bold step of submitting the books of the Old Testament to a rigorous rhetorical analysis. He justified this procedure on the grounds that the benefits of tracing more accurately the course of this 'celestial Nile' were inestimable:

> Since then it is the purpose of sacred Poetry to form the human mind to the constant habit of true virtue and piety, and to excite the more ardent affections of the soul, in order to direct them to their proper end; whoever has a clear insight into the instruments, the machinery as it were, by which this end is effected, will certainly contribute not a little to the improvement of the critical art.[11]

From a literary point of view, Lowth investigated the little-known poetic mode known in ancient Hebrew as *mashal*. Quite unlike classical Greek and Latin metre, this figurative 'parabolic' style began as a mnemonic aid among primitive tribes and became widespread among the Oriental poets of antiquity. This proceeded according to the natural rhythms of speech, permitting a more faithful expression of the primary passions; indeed Lowth claimed that the entire Old Testament was representative of Oriental verse as a typical product of an early stage of human development.

His principal contribution to the debate on this subject was to point out that many of the criticisms levelled against Oriental poetry could equally well be applied to the Hebrew Bible: 900-year-old Methuselah's age, for example, or the 'immoderate' use of metaphor throughout the Pentateuch in general, which, viewed dispassionately, would strike readers as 'fanciful and remote'. Only the sanctity of biblical texts protected them from critical censure (vol. 1, p. 122, p. 268n). Above all, Lowth urged the need to 'read Hebrew as the Hebrews would have read it'; turns of phrase inspired by the wildness of the landscape, allusions to outmoded ways of life, and even forgotten units of measurement were all barriers to the modern reader's understanding of sacred verse (vol. 1, p. 113). This cultural relativist approach, somewhat disingenuous in reality since the majority of Lowth's readers had at least a competent grounding in biblical history, set out to legitimise Oriental poetry as a whole, taking Hebrew as its paradigm. Lowth's secondary strategy was to consider Oriental 'intemperance' as overlapping with the rhetorical and classically acceptable register of the sublime.[12] Oriental poetry was synonymous with the sublime, for

> The Orientals look upon the language of poetry as wholly distinct from that of common life ... If, therefore, it were to be reduced to the plain rule and order of reason, if every word and sentence were to be arranged with care and study, as if calculated for perspicuity alone, it would be no longer what they intended it, and to call it the language of passion would be the grossest of solecisms. (vol. 1, p. 330)

Not all rhetoricians shared Lowth's view. Hugh Blair, in his *Lectures on Rhetoric and Belles Lettres* (1783), censured the Oriental 'figured style' for its use of cumbersome phrases such as 'a spotted garment' to denote iniquity and 'the candle of the Lord shining on our head' for prosperity, an idiom he ascribed to the shortage of nouns in a primitive stage of society, and the 'Asiatic' tendency to adopt 'a Style florid and diffuse'.[13]

Jones, who had read Lowth's *Praelectiones* whilst tutor to the young Earl Spencer at Althorp House, saw Neoplatonism as the crucial link between Indian and classical European thought, an idea originating in the legend that Pythagoras had received instruction from the Brahmins. This concept is seen most clearly in Jones's essay 'On the Literature of the Hindus' (1788), where he wrote that 'wherever we direct our attention to *Hindu* literature, the notion of infinity presents itself'.[14] His essay

'On the Mystical Poetry of the Persians and Hindus' (1789) elaborated Lowth's view of figurative language as a form of sublime allegory:

> A figurative mode of expressing the fervour of devotion, or the ardent love of created spirits toward their Beneficent Creator, has prevailed from time immemorial in *Asia*; particularly among the *Persian* theists, both ancient *Húshangis* and modern *Súfis*, who seem to have borrowed it from the *Indian* philosophers of the *Védánta* school; and their doctrines are also believed to be the source of that sublime, but poetical theology, which glows and sparkles in the writings of the old *Academicks*. ... we confine this essay to a singular species of poetry, which consists almost wholly of a mystical religious allegory, though it seems, on a transient view, to contain only the sentiments of a wild and voluptuous libertinism.[15]

This bid to divest Indian poetry of its sympathy-denying strangeness was based on Jones's enthusiasm for the Vedanta strain of Hinduism, through which he could view Hinduism as an essentially monotheistic religion, here applauding the poet's 'ardent and grateful piety' whilst chiding the over-enthusiastic language in which it was framed. Oriental poetry bordered on the absurd because it dared to aspire towards the sublime, Jones argued, conjoining ideas from Lowth and Blair; without the vocabulary to express such magnificent ideas, the Hindu imagination 'has recourse to metaphors and allegories, which it sometimes extends beyond the bounds of cool reason'.[16]

After Jones's death in 1794, it fell to his colleague Charles Wilkins to maintain the 'allegorical defence' of Vedic literature, describing the Puranas in the preface to his *Grammar of the Sanskṛita Language* (1808) as 'an endless assemblage of enchanting allegory and fable ... calculated to allure the reader into the paths of Religion, Honour, and Virtue'.[17] His intervention was timely, for as the previous chapter demonstrated, evangelical attacks on Hindu religion and culture were both more widespread and more virulent after 1800. Ward baited Oriental scholars in his *View of the History, Literature and Religion of the Hindoos* by scoffing at the absurdity of kings accepting a billion gold-bedecked elephants as tribute, and denounced allegories of the union of spirit and matter in Vedic texts as plainly indecent: 'innumerable ideas are found in almost every poem, which could have become familiar to the imagination only amidst a people whose very country was a brothel'.[18] Buchanan cited the supposed licentiousness of Hindu poetry in his call for the Anglican Church hierarchy to be extended to India (his *Memoir of the Expediency of an Ecclesiastical Establishment for British India*, 1805), a move die-hard Orientalists such as Major-General Charles 'Hindoo' Stuart greeted with dismay. Stuart's riposte, *Vindication of the Hindoos from the Aspersions of the Reverend Claudius Buchanan, M.A.* (1808), attested to the upstanding character of the Hindus and defended their mythological poetry from the barbs of religiously motivated criticism:

> Whenever I look around me, in the vast region of Hindoo Mythology, I discover Piety in the garb of allegory: and I see Morality, at every turn, blended with every tale ... it appears the most complete and ample system of Moral Allegory, that the world has ever produced.[19]

The fundamentals of Hindu theology were sound, Stuart protested, echoing Jones, and the cult practices to which evangelicals objected would, given time, give way to the progress of reason, just as the Protestant religion had banished superstition in Reformation Europe: 'it was this maturity of reason, that put to flight, among ourselves, the whole host of witches and their spells: and yet, this happy revolution of the mind was not effected 'till nearly twelve centuries of Christianity'.[20]

The arguments for and against mythic allegory were concurrent with, and indeed stemmed from, the contemporary debate in the realm of mythography. Scholars discussed the notion of pagan virtue – that is, whether ancient peoples who lived before the birth of Christ might benefit from Christian salvation (Dante, of course, having consigned virtuous pagans to the first circle of hell). In religious terms, some academics believed that pre-Christian faiths should be taken seriously as repositories (however imperfect) of divine revelation. Such scholarship was partially discredited, however, when Lieutenant Francis Wilford of the Asiatic Society in Calcutta claimed to have discovered that the British druids were originally Brahmins, a theory he elaborated in an extended series of essays 'On the Sacred Isles of the West', published in *Asiatick Researches* between 1805 and 1810 (Jones too had planned to make literary capital from this apparent connection in his projected epic, *Britain Discovered*). Unfortunately, Wilford had been duped by his *pandit*, and Maurice was forced to retract material from the sixth volume of *Oriental Antiquities*, 'On the Origin of the Druids', in which he had agreed with Wilford that this circumstance helped to cement Judaeo-Christian world history.[21] The 'Brahminical fraud', as it came to be known, damaged sympathetic depictions of Brahmins inherited from Jones's day. Nonetheless, allegory theory kept Indian poetry and

Oriental literature more generally inside the all-important ambit of taste, where sympathy could rove freely.

The fullest exposition of this doctrine concerning Hinduism was produced not in Britain but in Germany, by the Romantic author Friedrich Von Schlegel in his *Über die Sprache und Weisheit der Indier* (translated as *On the Language and Philosophy of India* and published in 1808), which was widely disseminated in Britain. This echoed Jones in calling for the banishment of 'the prevailing prejudice, which keeps the study of Indian mythology entirely distinct from the Greek'.[22] Schlegel is sometimes cited as a founding father of the academic discipline of Indology, and he agreed with Jones that the inhabitants of Europe and Asia formed 'one great family' and that their language and literature should be comprehended as 'a single perfect structure'.[23] Earlier in his career, he remarked in a note to Ludwig Tiech that 'everything, everything without exception comes from India', and the essay fleshes out the proposition that Sanskrit was the *Ursprache* of most Indo-European dialects.[24] Sanskrit may not have been the language spoken in paradise, or even the original Indo-European language, Schlegel argued, but it did offer the closest approximation. He based his theory on the grammatical purity of Sanskrit as an inflecting language, which lent it a 'living germ' (a term roughly corresponding to Hegelian *Geist* or Coleridge's 'Promethean spark') far superior to the 'mere atomism' or 'agglutination' of declining languages such as Arabic and Hebrew. Sanskrit words and syllables were 'radical' both in the sense that they refer to a root and in the sense that they exist without reference to external objects, which accounted for the esoteric knowledge required by the Brahmins to read it.[25]

What this meant in practice was that '[Sanskrit] is almost entirely a philosophical or rather a religious language, and perhaps none, not even excepting the Greek, is so philosophically clear and sharply defined' (p. 457). India for Schlegel was unchanged since at least the time of Moses, whilst Hinduism was among the first religious systems to interpose between mankind and the truth, like those polytheistic religions from which Moses prudently isolated the Hebrews in the wilderness. Turning his attention to Sanskrit literature, Schlegel interpreted *Sakuntala* as a dramatisation of the loss of divine truth and the transmigration back towards God, the lost ring simultaneously representing the 'unhappy' doctrine of emanation and the human yearning for reconciliation with the deity. This was quite different from pantheism, Schlegel explained, which held all creation to be innately good and pure, rather than tragically sundered from god (pp. 469–76).

Modern critics view Schlegel's contribution to the reception of Indian poetry and culture as decidedly mixed. Inden, documenting the gradual European essentialisation of India, acknowledges the attempts of prominent German Romantics to 'take those very features of Indian civilisation which the Utilitarian-minded find wasteful, deluded, or even repulsive and criticise – ascetic practices, philosophies, cosmologies, customs, visual art forms – and find them worthy of study and perhaps even of praise'.[26] On the other hand, few besides Schlegel were more responsible for the creation of what Johannes Fabian has called the 'denial of coevalness' that has dogged Western perceptions of India in intellectual history ever since.[27] By fixing India's golden age in remotest antiquity, Schlegel arguably consigned any artefact produced since that date to cultural oblivion. Heinrich Heine's satirical essay *Die Romantische Schule* (*The Romantic School*, 1833) accused Schlegel with his brother August Wilhelm of looking back to Hinduism as 'a sort of elephantine Middle Ages' that reinforced their own Catholic beliefs.[28] Schlegel nonetheless attached great importance to Sanskrit poetry, in which 'superstitious worship of the divinely productive power in nature, and the idea of infinity attached to it' was the quintessence of its unique genius.[29] Greek, Roman, German, and medieval European poetry all formed part of this lineage from the paterfamilias Sanskrit; Indian poetry, free from subsequent accretions, afforded a closer glimpse of the divine truths lost by humanity. Adding a mythic gloss to Jones's earlier exhortation in his essay 'On the Poetry of the Eastern Nations', Schlegel argued that the devotion to Graeco-Roman culture in European curricula drew Europeans astray from 'the sole source of lofty truth', which the study of Sanskrit promised to restore:

> The study of Oriental literature, to us so completely novel in structure and ideas, will, as we penetrate more deeply into it, bring back a new idea of the Divinity, and restore that vigour to the intellect, that truth and intensity of feeling to the soul, which invests all art, science, and literature with new and glorious life.[30]

The concept of a single Indo-European family under God had the lamentable effect of casting India either (in Jones's version) as infant to Europe's intellectually more developed mentor or (in Schlegel's) as decrepit ancestor to Europe's physically more vigorous scion.

It is perhaps in this latter sense that Schwab's account of Romanticism's 'many re-creations of the past' creating in turn 'the present that propels us forward' unwittingly reiterated stereotypes of Oriental backwardness and Europe as the cradle of futurity.[31] Martin Bernal's controversial epic study *Black Athena* (1987) comments further on the predicament for Schlegel's thinking on Hindu culture after the Aryan 'germ' had migrated westwards. Denied any possibility of further development, Bernal argues that Indians were reduced to the niche status of 'exotic ancestors' before European philhellenism occluded altogether the Asian origins of its own civilisation.[32] Into this breach in Romantic Orientalism stormed Mill with his *History of British India*, touted by his son John Stuart Mill as 'the commencement of rational thinking on the subject of India'.[33] A 'critical history' in the manner of Gibbon's *Decline and Fall of the Roman Empire*, it sought to cut through the 'chaotic mass' of writing about India and attain a 'clear discernment' of historical facts, to which sympathetic Orientalist 'affection' for the country was a bar: 'a man who is duly qualified may obtain more knowledge of India in one year in his closet in England', wrote Mill with almost audible contempt, 'than he could obtain during the course of the longest life, by the use of his eyes and ears in India'.[34] He wished to institute as strict a policy of improvement for India as he had a few years earlier for his son. He saw both childhood and primitivism alike as conditions in which the imagination prevailed over rational intelligence, and saw education, rigorously administered, as the solution to both. That the *History* was in part an attack on imagination in its raw or uncultivated state is clearly seen in the section on manners in Book 2, 'Of the Hindus', where Mill wrote that 'the Hindu is a sort of sensitive plant. His imagination and passions are easily inflamed; and he has a sharpness and quickness of intellect which seems strongly connected with the sensibility of his outward frame' (vol. 1, p. 332). Quickness of intellect here does not refer to mental dexterity, rather the brevity of a juvenile attention span. Following but also upending Jones and Schlegel's arguments in favour of Hindu imaginativeness, Mill portrays Indian poetry as pre-eminently the product of an immature culture and unworthy of genuine admiration, a more discriminating emotion than mere sympathy.

The section on Hindu literature begins with general remarks on poetry's place in the history of human development. Poetry is the language of the passions, Mill begins, following the thought of Dennis, Lowth, Jones and Blair, pre-existent to the capacity to reason. The earliest forms of poetry were expressions of the primary passions, versification being the mnemonic aid necessary to preserve such outpourings prior to the invention of writing. Here Mill diverted from conventional narratives of the rise of letters, contending that whereas subsequent to this point the historians, lawmakers, philosophers and scientists of other civilisations abandoned verse and adopted prose – the language of 'philosophic intelligence' – Hindu writers obstinately refused to progress beyond poetry:

> At this first stage the literature of the Hindus has always remained ... All their compositions, with wonderfully few exceptions, are in verse. For history they have only certain narrative poems, which depart from all resemblance to truth and nature; and have evidently no further connection with fact than the use of certain names and a few remote allusions. Their laws, like those of rude nations in general, are in verse. Their sacred books, and even their books of science, are in verse; and what is more wonderful still, their very dictionaries.[35]

Majeed notes that Mill's *History* was (mistakenly) received as a 'classic in the history of philistinism', yet this passage is not an arbitrary dismissal of poetry *per se*; like Bentham's comments on the game of push-pin, Mill asserts the relative merits of one thing over another, in this case prose and verse.[36] The failure of Hindu writers to attain prose is intended to signal a people lacking in both intelligence and judgement.

Mill did not stop there in his laceration of the *Ramayana* and the *Mahabharata*; as epic poems they are 'excessively prolix and insipid' and 'trifling and childish to a degree, which those acquainted with only European poetry, can hardly conceive'. He details their literary flaws as 'inflation: metaphors perpetual, and these the most violent and strained, often the most unnatural and ridiculous; obscurity; tautology; repetition; verbosity; confusion [and] incoherence', a list that is itself guilty of many of the faults it seeks to impute. He concludes with Blair in perceiving only negative aspects of Oriental poetry, crystallised for Mill in the licentiousness of the two epics: 'All the vices which characterise the style of rude nations, and particularly those of Asia, they exhibit in perfection'.[37] He compares the *Ramayana* and the *Mahabharata* unfavourably with the epic poetry of Homer, Ossian and the British druids, who despite their scanty stock of ideas 'possessed the faculty of working powerfully on the imaginations and sympathies of their audience' (vol. 2, p. 42). This last point reveals much about Mill's expectations of good poetry, for although he personally believed that verse no longer met the needs of modern society, he acknowledged that it provided moral succour in past times before superior philosophies (such as political economy) were coined. The Indian epics did not even perform this role; their figurative and inflated style Mill saw merely as 'sterile extravagance', incapable of awakening moral feelings of any kind (vol. 2, p. 43).

The embarrassment over Wilford and the Brahminical fraud left the authenticity of many Orientalist discoveries in doubt. Mill exploited this to refute Jones's claim that Hinduism contained elements of Neoplatonism, arguing that Jones allowed the Brahmins to flatter him into thinking this was true: 'it was ... extremely natural that Sir William Jones, whose pundits had become acquainted with the ideas of European philosophers respecting the system of the universe, should hear from them that those ideas were contained in their own books: the wonder was, that without any proof he should believe them' (vol. 2, pp. 85–6). Mill's vitriol against Jones also extended to Hastings, another apologist for Hindu literature, whom he accused of seeking to sway public opinion in his favour during his trial. Altogether, Mill's assault on Indian culture and its defenders contributed to what Philip Connell has identified as a 'rapidly widening fault line within British intellectual life' between 'literature, aesthetics, and feeling' on the one hand and 'science, utility, and reason' on the other.[38] By cutting texts such as the *Ramayana* and the *Mahabharata* off from any possibility of moral or philosophic insight, Mill's ideological ally Macaulay could later deny Indian literature a place on colonial school curricula and sought to discredit it as a way of understanding the country.[39] Macaulay's dismissal of Indian history 'abounding with kings thirty feet high, and reigns thirty thousand years long' and geography 'made up of seas of treacle and seas of butter' in his 'Minute on Indian Education' (2 February 1835) reinforced the 'Anglicist' determination that henceforth writing which did not conform to recognisable European norms would be banished from the administration of British India.[40]

In the wider world of Romantic literary criticism, Oriental literature drew similar objections to imaginative writing more generally, especially where the former was felt to trespass beyond the bounds of what European commentators considered to be normative systems of morality. Whilst they obviously had very different targets in mind, Mill's disdain for the 'sterile extravagance' of Indian literature paralleled Wordsworth's objections in the 1800 preface to the *Lyrical Ballads* to the 'gross and violent stimulants' purveyed by the bulk of contemporary writers. 'German' or gothic fiction was Wordsworth's particular bugbear, which he felt shocked and jolted the passions without guiding them in any controlled direction.[41] Coleridge associated these ideas with Oriental writing directly in his 'Lectures on the Principles of Judgement, Culture, and European Literature' delivered to the London Philosophical Society in 1818. In the eleventh lecture, 'On the Arabian Nights' (3 March 1818), he accused those tales of causing 'interest without agitation'; that is, they were injurious to the growth of imagination because they were dependent on external circumstances for their effects.[42] Coleridge had dabbled with the Oriental style himself in 'Kubla Khan' (composed 1797), but we can hardly take that poem, probably composed under the narcotic stimulation of opium, as a paradigm of his morally instructive poetics. The discussions of positive and negative ideals of poetry elsewhere in his work, indeed, suggest that he regarded Oriental poetry as regressive. This is particularly the case when we take into account his ideas of East–West cultural migration developed during his year in Göttingen.[43]

In the *Biographia Literaria*, Coleridge tended to the view that arbitrary figures, 'colors [sic] of speech' and 'cold technical artifices of ornament and connection', such as are found in fanciful or fantastical verse, distract the imagination by disrupting the free flow of spontaneous moral sentiment. The problem for him was how to negotiate between a 'legitimate' expression of the passions and the spurious affectation of heightened states of emotion, what he calls 'the startling *hysteric* of weakness over-exerting itself, which bursts upon the reader in sundry odes and abstract terms'.[44] He defines the latter as a kind of poetical hysteria, displaying all the outward signs of passion yet uninformed by genuine moral sentiment. Part of the solution as he saw it was to 'desynonomize' fancy and imagination: 'two conceptions perfectly distinct [that] are confused under one and the same word', namely a flawed understanding of 'imagination' itself (pp. 55–6). The *Biographia* made the well-known distinction between fancy and the two co-existing parts of the imagination, the latter jointly defined by their potential to create *ex nihilo*, the former merely being the capacity of memory to toy with 'fixities and definities' unconstrained by time or space (p. 175).

Coleridge's eleventh lecture 'On the Arabian Nights' mentioned above demonstrates his opinion that Oriental literature displayed all the signs of composition dominated by fancy. His wider purpose was to enquire into literature's power to promote 'passive' and 'active' thought, two categories that relate to, but do not exactly correspond to, the respective notions of fancy and imagination laid down in the *Biographia*. After some stock opening remarks about the characters in Asiatic mythology being all either unnaturally large or small, and endowed with great magical power, he goes on to examine the mental process required to conceive of such fantastical beings, which he proposed was 'an exertion of the fancy in the combination and recombination of familiar objects so as to produce novel and wonderful imagery'.[45] Such texts worked by registering the *semblance* of moral ideas in the manner of a dream, thus demanding neither an act of will from the author nor engaging the sympathies of the reader and so justifying the label 'passive' thought. Coleridge concluded 'these tales cause no deep feeling of a moral kind, but an impulse of motion is communicated to the mind without excitement, and this is the reason of their being so generally read and admired'; he likened this aspect of Oriental literature to the sensationalist writings of Defoe and 'the common modern novel'.[46] Via a different route, therefore, he rejoined Wordsworth's attack on 'frantic novels' and 'deluges of idle and extravagant stories in verse', but ranked a masterpiece of Oriental literature alongside amatory fiction and 'sickly and stupid' German tragedy.

Whereas Coleridge stated his objections philosophically within a mythological schema, Wordsworth rather retrenched against exotic poetical imports from the outside, and turned to rural England for glimpses of unadorned piety. The 1800 preface, despite its *de facto* similarities to Jones's 1772 essay 'On the Arts, commonly called Imitative', made clear that the language of nature, drawn from the language and situations of 'everyday' life, was principally to be found in north-west England. The Lake District was but one locus of what Saree Makdisi has called 'Romantic anti-modernity', the 'discovery of some of the "other worlds" being surrounded and cut off by the space-time of modernisation'.[47] Marilyn Butler's reading of Wordsworth as the poet of counter-revolution, celebrating the Burkean ideology of 'hearth and home, the English plot of ground', can be usefully extended to make him also a poet of counter-exoticism.[48] His unease at the rampant cosmopolitanism of imperial London (vividly evoked in Book Seven of the *Prelude*), with its Turkish slipper merchants, Malays, Russians, rope-dancers, performing giants and dwarfs, was manifestly at odds with the syncretic Orientalism of the same period. Wordsworth here betrays a deep mistrust of consumerism, a point Tim Morton makes in *The Poetics of Spice: Romantic Consumerism and the Exotic* (2000) when he remarks that the trope of the Romantic solitary itself 'relied on some notion of surplus consumption, free time, even when this was heavily naturalised'.[49] Wordsworth's recourse to the wilderness was as much a reaction to a society steeped in the trade in luxury goods as a positive choice in its own right.

It was no coincidence that Byron and Moore, temperamentally antagonistic towards what they saw as the provincialism of the Lake School, became the foremost purveyors of Oriental subject matter in poetry. 'Stick to the East', Byron famously advised Moore in a letter of May 1813, 'the North, South, and West, have all been exhausted; but from the East, we have nothing but [Southey's] unsaleables – and these he has contrived to spoil, by adopting only their most outrageous fictions': a reference to *Kehama*'s poor reception, which, as Leask points out, set a 'negative example' of Orientalist literature from which Bryon and Moore could only benefit.[50] Southey's Indian epic, with its infelicitous epigraph, 'Curses are like young chickens, they always come to roost', was cautionary proof that writing about the East was a guarantee neither of critical nor of commercial success. Following the high profile evangelical castigation of Hinduism, that mythology represented a uniquely hazardous choice for the aspiring Oriental poet. Southey oddly disclaimed any measure of sympathetic admiration for Hinduism in his preface to *Kehama*, denouncing it as 'of all false religions ... the most monstrous in its fables, and the most fatal in its effects', an admission that raised immediately its suitability as a basis for morally acceptable poetry.[51] Critics rounded on what appeared to be his embrace of Hindu mythology and the 'inflated' Oriental style, a failure on Southey's part to offset his moral clearly enough from the crowded backcloth of Hindu imagery. If he truly believed what he states in the preface, that 'no figures can be imagined more anti-picturesque, and less poetical, than the mythological personages of the Bramins', why then (critics asked) did he strive for an authentic picture of Hinduism whose realisation would inevitably contribute to the downfall of the poem?[52] The attempt to straddle the gulf between evangelical distaste and the sympathetic Orientalist enthusiasm for Hinduism explains *Kehama*'s awkward hybridity, whose plot strains to exploit the Wordsworthian taste for rustic virtue whilst retaining a credible foothold in Oriental scholarship.[53]

Critics responding to the first edition of the poem hailed its moralistic intent but found that the possibility was obscured by the fantastic apparatus of Hindu cosmology. An unsigned review in the *Monthly Mirror* (February 1811) questioned Southey's use of exotic myth in what ought to have been a straightforward fable; *Kehama*'s plot was 'spirit-stirring', but the sheer otherness of the characters and setting made it difficult for European readers to enter into their plight: 'the pathetic has no place, for there is no room for pity, nor is it possible to shed a tear for those with whom we have nothing in common, and cannot sympathize'.[54] The centrality of imaginative sympathy in contemporary criticism is once again visible, as is the remarkably widespread resignation to cultural difference. Hindu mythology for the *Mirror*'s critic is a 'perpetual stumbling block' to sympathy, since its complexity, coupled with its focus on the supernatural and its obscure characters, meant that '*quod supra nos, nihil ad nos*' ('because it is above us, it is nothing to us'). Echoing Coleridge, Mill and Wordsworth, the critic for the *Mirror* opined that 'if Mr Southey's eccentricity had not overcome his better taste, he would have chosen his machinery, and so conducted his story, as not only to have agitated the nerves, but to have come home to the heart, and rested there'. The review ends by recommending that the poem be translated into '*Hindoostanee*' for a more favourable reception.[55] The *Critical Review* concurred with this assessment, describing the poem as 'a blaze of false enchantment, not the steady radiance of truth and nature ... if you gain the courage to look at it a second or a third time, the magic has lost its power, and you only wonder what it was that dazzled you'.[56]

John Foster, a firebrand dissenter writing in the *Eclectic Review*, went further, accusing Southey of the 'cardinal' sins of paganism and absurdity: 'to think that amidst the beams of the sun and the moon, the light of Christian religion, and the sense and philosophy of modern Europe, a genius like Mr. Southey's should be solemnly employed in a business like this!'[57] Earlier in the review, he remarked with dogged literalism that the events of *Kehama* could not have taken place since the Battle of Plassey, 'because it is impossible that such a person as Kehama should have been in India at that time, without coming into collision with Colonel Clive, who would have saved Seeva the trouble of putting him down'.[58] From Southey's point of view, the most congenial, although still ominous, appraisal came courtesy of Scott in the *Quarterly Review* (to which Southey was also a contributor). Scott confessed that despite its 'wild and extravagant tenor', the epic 'riveted our attention more powerfully than any thing [sic] which we have lately perused'; Southey had boldly departed from established principles of composition, which the article generously attributed to his fluency as a poet: 'Mr Southey resembles Alcestes, who shot merely to shew the strength of his bow, and the height to which he could send his arrow'. Ultimately, however, even Scott could 'presage nothing as to the popularity of the present poem'.[59] *Kehama* may have been praiseworthy as a poetic experiment but it was alienating as a reading experience.

It was with a view to avoiding these pitfalls that Moore carefully juxtaposed 'western sentimentalism' and 'samples of the finest Orientalism' in what would become his runaway bestseller, *Lalla Rookh*. He certainly seemed to command the confidence of his publisher, Thomas Longman, who commissioned the poem for a then unprecedented sum. Describing his initial meeting with Longman in the 1841 preface to the poem, Moore expressed his understandable satisfaction with the terms of the agreement, writing that 'there has seldom, I think, occurred any transaction in which Trade and Poesy have shone out so advantageously in each other's eyes'.[60] Indeed, his account in the preface of the composition of *Lalla Rookh* is pervaded by the language of economic production, from the description of himself as 'a slow and painstaking workman' labouring in the 'industry' of poetry, to the notion of forming 'a storehouse, as it were, of illustration purely Oriental'.[61] Seen with the benefit of hindsight (by 1841 the poem had sold over 27,000 copies), here was a work calculatedly composed to maximise the poet's financial gains and emotional appeal to his readers. Like Byron before him, Moore boasted of his ability to produce a fine read into the bargain, citing testimonies from Sir James Mackintosh, Sir William Ouseley and Mark Wilks in his favour. He used a remarkable number of textual ploys to commend the poem to the sympathies of his readers, drawing together many of the strands traced over the course of this chapter. Not least among these was his technique of leavening exotic spectacle with allusions to the moral and political concerns of the present day, making Moore's Orient not so much the hybrid that Southey's was but a highly polished alloy of topical preoccupations. This was the great prerequisite of sympathy, as Moore unabashedly acknowledged.

As he remarks in the 1841 preface, Moore's stellar reputation sprang from his *Irish Melodies* (1808–34) and it was as an Irish patriot-poet that he was principally known. Francis Jeffrey, who reviewed *Lalla Rookh* in the *Edinburgh Review* for November 1817 and who is impersonated in the poem's frame narrative by the Polonius-like chamberlain Fadladeen, referred to Moore flippantly as 'the poet in that Green Isle of the West'.[62] Two of the four inset tales comprising the poem, 'Paradise and the Peri' and 'The Fire Worshippers', refer by Moore's own admission to the struggle of Irish nationalists against English dominion. Describing the tardy progress of his initial drafts, he admitted that he found his initial subjects 'so slow in kindling my own sympathies, I began to despair of their ever touching the hearts of others', before the idea occurred to him of founding a heroic poem on the 'fierce struggle so long maintained between the Ghebers, or ancient Fire-worshippers of Persia, and their haughty Moslem masters'. This supplied the requisite personal interest that had previously been lacking, and 'the cause of tolerance was again my inspiring theme ... the spirit that had spoken in the melodies of Ireland soon found itself at home in the East'.[63] Byron emphasised this thematic connection in his dedication to Moore in *The Corsair* in 1814, effusing that 'Ireland ranks you among the firmest of her patriots' and alluded to the fact that work on *Lalla Rookh* was well underway:

> It is said among those friends, I trust truly, that you are engaged in the composition of a poem whose scene will be laid in the East; none can do those scenes so much justice. The wrongs of your own country, the magnificent and fiery spirit of her sons, the beauty and feeling of her daughters, may there be found.[64]

In his reading of the poem, Mohammed Sharafuddin erroneously states that potentially subversive messages in the text remained 'wholly implicit', something he attributes to Moore's 'political caution'.[65] More accurate is Leask's summary of the poem as 'sympathetic to the claims of an organic Irish nationalism', which captures the relatively uncontroversial nature of Moore's views, given the contemporary state of Whig politics.[66] Moore refers the reader to Voltaire's admission that his tragedy *Les Guebres* alluded to the Jansenists, adding wryly in a footnote, 'I should not be surprised if this story of the Fire-worshippers were found capable of a similar doubleness of application'.[67] Moore's Irish nationalism was an open secret at the time of the poem's publication. It had also mellowed considerably since his youthful membership in the proscribed United Irishmen organisation. As Jeffrey Vail has demonstrated, after 1799, when Moore had left Ireland for England to study law at the Middle Temple, there followed 'a period of disillusionment and painful adjustment during which he began to abandon the open radicalism that he saw fail so spectacularly in 1798 [the outbreak of the Irish Rebellion] and started moving towards an artistic strategy of moderation, disguise and concealment'.[68] Such a strategy worked both ways: not only to cloak Irish nationalism – or rather Moore's now sanitised version of it – but also to shield his Oriental poem from critical attack.

Conversely, political agitation on the subject of Ireland served to endear the work to reading audiences who might otherwise have spurned it as a confection of obscure Eastern source material. *Lalla Rookh*'s frame narrative, furthermore, contained several devices aimed at attracting the sympathy of the reader. It begins with an account of the King of Bucharia's visit to the Mughal court at Delhi, en route to Arabia for the *hajj*, based on an account taken from Alexander Dow's *History of Hindostan* (1768). During his stay, the King arranges for his son to marry the Emperor Aurangzeb's youngest daughter, Lalla Rookh ('Tulip Cheek'). The day of the princess's departure arrives and her entourage sets out for Bucharia under the supervision of the fastidious

Chamberlain of the Harem, Fadladeen. On the road, they encounter a handsome young poet by the name of Feramorz, who entertains Lalla Rookh and her ladies with a succession of verse renditions, which form the four main inset poems. Fadladeen subjects each of these to a splenetic commentary in imitation of Jeffrey, editor of the *Edinburgh Review*. The rival *British Critic* rightly identified Fadladeen as Moore's revenge 'upon his old friends, the Reviewers of the North', who had treated his previous poetic offerings harshly.[69] Besides fulfilling this Scriblerian function, Fadladeen also acts as a sympathetic bottom line for those readers left cold by Feramorz's breathless narratives, who could at least identify with the cantankerous and recognisable European man of letters.

Moore recounted in the 1841 preface how Mackintosh once asked Wilks 'whether it was true that Moore had never been in the East', to which Mackintosh answered 'never'. 'Well, that shows me', Wilks replied, 'that reading D'Herbelot is as good as riding on the back of a camel'.[70] This exchange (if true) reveals Moore's singular success in persuading contemporaries of *Lalla Rookh*'s authenticity, apparently without compromising its readability. The first of *Lalla Rookh*'s inset poems, 'The Veiled Prophet of Khorassan', is at first sight an obscure construction. The tale derives from an entry in D'Herbelot's *Bibliothèque Orientale* (1697) on the uprising against Calif Muhammad ibn Mansur al-Mahdi by Hakem ben Haschem, or Mokanna ('the veil', in Arabic), in Hegira 163 (779 AD). Moore concentrates on the figure of Azim, a 'warrior youth', who acquired a love of liberty from his Greek captors whilst imprisoned during the fighting between al-Mahdi and the Byzantine Empress Irene. Moore reorientates Islamic history to face West, as it were, rather than showing, as Sharafuddin would have it, an 'interest in Oriental revolt and tyranny for its own sake'.[71] Learning of Mokanna's revolt on his release from prison, Azim immediately enlists with the rebel cause:

> Soon as he heard an Arm Divine was rais'd
> To right the nations, and beheld, emblaz'd
> On the white flag MOKANNNA'S host unfurl'd,
> Those words of sunshine, 'Freedom to the World,'
> At once his faith, his sword, his soul obey'd
> The' inspiring summons.[72]

This premise exploits Romantic philhellenism even while it sets a geographically and historically remote episode in a European context. There are also allusions to the false promise of Jacobinism, which Moore came to repudiate. Mokanna is an impostor, whose veil, supposedly worn to protect his followers from the radiance of his celestial features, conceals a face ravaged by years of occult practices. Nigel Leask has read this discovery as 'an allegorical exposé of the "true face" of Jacobinism', which serves to distance Moore's robust patriotism from revolutionary excesses.[73]

Nor is human interest lacking in the love story between Azim and his childhood sweetheart Zelica, who has been duped into becoming Mokanna's lover during Azim's absence. When the action of the poem at length removes to the Transoxianan city of Neksheb, where al-Mahdi's army has besieged Mokanna and his adherents, the now disabused Azim has deserted to their ranks. Zelica, veiled like her former abuser, rushes out of the city only to die with keen phallic symbolism on Azim's spear-point. The reader finally takes leave of Azim in old age weeping over Zelica's grave, a motif borrowed from Southey's *Roderick: The Last of the Goths* (1814). The poignancy of this climax is lost on Fadladeen when the narrative returns to Lalla Rookh's caravanserai; he tears into Feramorz's poem with a précis modelled on the scathing style of the periodical review:

> The chief personages of the story were, ... an ill-favoured gentleman, with a veil over his face; – a young lady, whose reason went and came, according as it suited the poet's convenience to be sensible or otherwise; – and a youth in one of those hideous Bucharian bonnets, who took the aforesaid gentleman in a veil for a Divinity. 'From such materials', said [Fadladeen], 'what can be expected? – after rivalling each other in long speeches and absurdities, through some thousands of lines as indigestible as the filberts of Berdaa, our friend in the veil jumps into a tub of aquafortis; the young lady dies in a set speech, whose only recommendation is that it is her last; and the lover lives on to a good old age, for the laudable purpose of seeing her ghost, which he at last happily accomplishes, and expires' ... as to the versification, it was, to say no worse of it, execrable: it had neither the copious flow of Ferdosi, the sweetness of Hafez, nor the sententious march of Sadi; but appeared to him, in the uneasy heaviness of its movements, to have been modelled upon the gait of a very tired dromedary.[74]

Fadladeen ends his tirade only to find his audience asleep. Moore has it all ways with this complex narrative layering; the characters of his inner poems inhabit a credible cultural world, albeit one gilded with the lustre of romance, while Fadladeen's comic turns pre-empt criticism of 'Oriental exaggeration'. Doubly removed from his creation, Moore achieves an ironic detachment worthy of his friend Byron.

Further familiarising touches are found in Feramorz's second poem, 'Paradise and the Peri'. This tells of the quest of an angelic creature from Persian mythology to discover *'the Gift that is most dear to Heaven'*, through which she may enter paradise (vol. 6, p. 158). Among the objects she chooses is the last drop of blood shed by a hero fighting for his country, prompting Moore's long footnote on Eastern liberty. Here, Moore rejects the view that liberty 'is totally inapplicable to any state of things that has ever existed in the East', arguing that the 'Hindoos and Persians … fought against their Mussulman invaders with, in many cases, a bravery that deserved better success'. He praises 'that national independence, that freedom from the interference and dictation of foreigners, without which, indeed, no liberty of any kind can exist' (vol. 6, pp. 164–5n). Coming from Moore, these words cannot but have been interpreted as a call for a measure of Irish independence from Britain. Again, a little-known conflict is recast in known terms. Yet Moore benefited from the *frisson* that continued to surround colonial Ireland whilst advocating a generalised form of liberty that none but the most conservative readers could have found subversive. His nationalism is in this sense more akin to that of Morgan's novel *The Wild Irish Girl* (1806): sanitised, Whiggish and ultimately non-threatening. The remaining two gifts, the last sigh of a pair of dying lovers as they embrace by the Nile, and a penitential tear dropped by a reformed villain in Balbec, invoke high sentimental tropes and confirm Moore's intention to achieve the greatest possible emotional engagement with his readers, something he is only able to do by tapping European sensibilities.

The third and longest tale, 'The Fire-Worshippers', pursues the theme of Oriental patriotism introduced in 'Paradise and the Peri' by depicting the Zoroastrian struggle against their Arab overlords in seventh-century Iran, which, as a footnote to *Asiatic Researches* informs the reader, is the 'true general name for the empire of Persia' (vol. 6, p. 204n). The tale is prompted when Lalla Rookh and her party, nearing Bucharia, catch sight of 'the ruins of a strange and awful-looking tower, which seemed old enough to have been the temple of some religion no longer known, and which spoke the voice of desolation in the midst of all that bloom and loveliness' (vol. 6, p. 198). Feramorz, as a native of the region, explains that this picturesque antique edifice was a Zoroastrian temple built by the 'Ghebers' of pre-Islamic Persia, 'who, many hundreds of years since, had fled hither from their Arab conquerors, preferring liberty and their altars in a foreign land to the alternative of apostasy or persecution in their own', one of the poem's many allusions to colonial Ireland; Feramorz moreover adds that he 'felt a sympathy …

with the sufferings of the persecuted Ghebers, which every monument like this before them but tended more powerfully to awaken (vol. 6, pp. 199–200). The story of the persecution of the Ghebers by the Arab Emir Al-Hassan, apostrophised as a 'Hard, heartless chief, unmov'd alike / Mid eyes that weep, and swords that strike', his personal cruelty contrasting with the peaceable tenets of Islam: 'Just ALLA! what must be thy look, / When such a wretch before thee stands / Unblushing, with thy Sacred Book, – / Turning the leaves with blood-stained hands, / And wresting from its page sublime / His creed of lust, and hate, and crime' (vol. 6, pp. 203–4). The Zoroastrian resistance movement, fighting for their homeland Iran, alone kindle the spark of patriotism: 'Yet has she hearts, mid all this ill / O'er all this wreck high buoyant still / With hope and vengeance; – hearts that yet – / Like gems, in darkness, issuing rays / They've treasur'd from the sun that's set' (vol. 6, p. 206).

The Emir's daughter, Hinda, is in love with a mysterious youth, Zal, who visits her bedchamber in the Emir's palace on the cliff top. One night, Zal flings off his cloak to reveal that he is none other than the Gheber leader, Hafed, the Emir's deadliest enemy: 'Yes, EMIR! he, who scal'd that tower, / And, had he reach'd thy slumbering breast, / Had taught thee, in a Gheber's power / How safe ev'n tyrants heads may rest' (vol. 6, p. 234). The forbidden love topos recalls *Romeo and Juliet* as well as the revelation scene in Byron's 'The Bride of Abydos' (1813). Moore then interweaves the underworld scenes from Beckford's *Vathek* (1786), Satan's speech in Book I from *Paradise Lost* and the Prometheus legend to form Hafed's apostrophe when, persecuted by al-Hassan, the remaining fire-worshippers take refuge in a remote cave network:

> 'Welcome, terrific glen!' he said,
> 'Thy gloom, that Eblis' self might dread,
>   'Is Heav'n to him who flies from chains!'
> ...
> 'This home', he cried, 'at least is ours; –
> 'Here may we bleed, unmock'd by hymns
>   'Of Moslem triumph o'er our head;
> 'Here may we fall, nor leave our limbs
>   'To quiver to the Moslem's tread.
> 'Stretch'd on this rock, while vultures' beaks
> 'Are whetted on our yet warm cheeks,
> 'Here – happy that no tyrant's eye
> 'Gloats on our torments – we may die!'
> (vol. 6, p. 243)

Such intertextual echoes build a sense of cultural affinity between Moore's undeniably outlandish characters and his prospective European readership. It is difficult to read these lines as truly subversive, however much they might have resonated with the ongoing debate over the conversion of India to Christianity. Critics perceived 'The Fire-Worshippers' as concerned more with liberty and love as abstract qualities, in this sense its interest in 'Romantic rebellion', than Irish or even Indian nationalism (whatever that might have meant in 1817); indeed if anything, *Lalla Rookh* was criticised for its slightness not its latent political menace. Nonetheless, the story has a stirring conclusion. Betrayed by one of their own number, the Ghebers are attacked and overwhelmed by the emir's soldiers after a bitter struggle. With a cry of 'Now Freedom's God! I come to Thee!' Hafed throws himself onto the burning altar (a point criticised by Ouseley as profanity according to Zoroastrianism), the blaze seen by Hinda from afar who exclaims "Tis he!', as 'IRAN's hopes and hers are o'er!' (vol. 6, pp. 314–18).

The final element to Moore's strategy was to have Lalla Rookh herself fall in love with the poet, Feramorz. Sharafuddin, charmingly, reads this as the Romantic critic's response to poetry as opposed to that of 'the sterile Augustan know-it-all', represented by Fadladeen/Jeffrey.[75] When Lalla Rookh's entourage finally reaches Bucharia, Feramorz surprises the princess by declaring that he is the prince (now king, it transpires) of Bucharia himself, who had intercepted the royal party with the romantic purpose of winning his future bride's heart *incognito*. Fadladeen, who has been caustic throughout, is forced to recant his criticisms before his new master in an amusing reversal of fortune. In memory of the episode, we are told, Lalla Rookh 'never called the King by any other name than FERAMORZ'.[76]

When Jeffrey came to review the poem in November 1817, he was unconcerned that readers might be similarly seduced. Although dazzled by the 'constant succession of glittering ideas and high-strained emotions' and wearied by the rococo 'want of plainness, simplicity and repose', he had perspicacity enough to recognise that *Lalla Rookh* was composed in a poetic strain quite alien to its professed Oriental provenance: although its characters and sentiments were not exact copies of 'European nature', Jeffrey began, 'they are still less like that of any other region'; he dubbed them instead 'poetical imaginations', then, with a wanton outbreak of regionalist stereotypes, asserted that 'it is to the poetry of rational, honourable, considerate and humane Europe, that they belong – and not to the childishness, cruelty, and profligacy of Asia'; Moore's attempt to depict the East as the seat of liberty and heroic deeds exposes the poem as a fabrication, for 'so far as we have yet seen, there is no sound sense, firmness of purpose, or principled goodness, except among the natives of Europe, and their genuine descendants'.[77] Jeffrey saw this as occasion for praise, adding that Moore's 'ornaments are, for the most part, truly and exquisitely beautiful; and the general design of his pieces very elegant and ingenious' – implying that Oriental poets were themselves incapable of achieving such quality (p. 3).

It is his comments on sympathy that make Jeffrey's *Edinburgh Review* article most significant, especially in his consideration of a poem whose author 'has soared to a region beyond the comprehension of most of his readers'. This potential alienating effect has less to do with the Oriental topos in its own right, Jeffrey insists, than with Moore's vaunting subject matter:

> All his personages are so very beautiful, and brave, and agonizing – so totally wrapt up in the exaltation of their vehement emotions, and withal so lofty in rank, and so sumptuous and magnificent in all that relates to their external condition, that the herd of ordinary mortals can scarcely venture to sympathize freely with their fortunes ... the wise antient [sic] who observed, that being a man himself, he could not help but take an interest in every thing [sic] that related to man – might have confirmed his character for wisdom, by adding, that for the same reason he could take no interest in any thing [sic] else. (p. 4, 7)[78]

Jeffrey invokes Smith's neo-Stoical formula when he writes of the 'difficulty of raising our sentiments to the proper pitch', and in consequence we are 'sometimes tempted to withhold our sympathy altogether, and to seek for its objects among more familiar adventures' (p. 4). Superior poetic geniuses such as Homer, Chaucer, Ariosto, Shakespeare, Dryden and Scott educe sympathy by judicious modulations of tone and a realistically paced narrative. The tenor of these remarks is in many respects identical to the criticisms made of *The Curse of Kehama* in 1810, but where Southey's failure was perceived to lie in the impenetrability of Hindu mythology, Moore stood accused of 'excessive finery'; a more general fault that Jeffrey saw stemming from Moore's affiliation with the hedonistic Byron circle (p. 33).

Jeffrey confined his censures to 'The Veiled Prophet of Khorassan', 'The Light of the Haram' and the 'somewhat too sanguinary combat' in 'The Fire-Worshippers', and found much to praise in other parts of the poem (p. 28). The 'magnificent and most infallible chamberlain of the Haram' was a particular highlight for the critic, although he expresses surprise that his 'short, snappish remarks' were 'by no means solemn, stupid, and pompous, as was to have been expected' (p. 9). Jeffrey's silence on the decadent qualities supposedly attached to Oriental literature speaks volumes about Moore's transformation of culturally unfamiliar material. On the familiar topic of licentiousness Jeffrey does not doubt that 'many mature virgins and careful matrons may think his lucubrations on those themes too rapturous and glowing to be safely admitted among the private studies of youth', but finds the moral standard of the characters to be beyond reproach: 'all of his favourites, without exception, are dutiful, faithful, and self-denying; and no other example is ever set up for imitation' (p. 33). By concluding that *Lalla Rookh* was not an Oriental poem at all in any meaningful sense, being more a posture of style than a substantive imitation of the original, Jeffrey obviated all objections to Moore's poetic creation at a stroke.

I would, in conclusion, suggest that Jeffrey's discoveries were not coincidental. The extended metaphor of commerce in the 1841 preface suggests that Moore regarded his Eastern source material as a commodity to be marketed subsequent to the necessary re-presentation. Poetry of this class was clearly Oriental-*ist* in the sense coined by Edward Said, in that it was Eastern in provenance but appropriated and adapted by Europeans to meet European needs. But to what extent were British readers in the Romantic period ever truly exposed to Eastern literature? Without knowledge of the relevant languages, they were reliant on translations, pseudo-translations, adaptations and imitations to gain any idea of what Oriental culture was like. In many ways, poems such as *Lalla Rookh* and Byron's 'Turkish Tales' offered British readers the next best thing to direct contact with the East; genuine Orientalist scholarship was employed but rendered in a medium likely to appeal to a wide audience, who might otherwise not have read it at all. Re-orientating the Orient was thus a necessary compromise to appease European literary markets, not an arbitrary move designed to belittle other cultures, as Said suggests – admitting that non-European literatures were often harshly misrepresented as a result. Suffice to say, the British literary establishment played a major role in driving Oriental poetry into ever more Oriental-ised forms. Poets like Southey, who attempted a faithful delineation of the Hindu cosmos, felt the sting of critical censure; Byron and Moore, who read the poetic climate more accurately, reaped the benefits.

Epilogue: Orientalism under Pressure

The book comes full circle to find that sympathetic engagement with India became possible only through the medium of heavily 'Westernised' forms of representation, either through the 'costume poetry' of Jones, later reworked by Moore, or through the depiction of Indian suffering in uniquely affecting terms within European schemes of aesthetics, the discursive practice initiated by Burke. Evangelical writers appropriated this latter form of representation but adapted it so that sympathy might only be felt for the Indian victims of Brahminical or Mughal (not British) cruelty, demonising the customs and institutions of India in the process. All of this left the possibility of representing the 'real' India in Britain in doubt, for in both cases the country and the people were surrendered to the widespread acknowledgement that culturally and geographically remote entities such as the subcontinent were beyond the scope of the European imagination.

Additionally, the book has shown the various forms of pressure upon purveyors of Orientalist literature in Britain. At the theoretical level, Hume and Smith laid out what they argued were the natural confines of imaginative sympathy in their respective contributions to moral philosophy, beyond which Burke deliberately and pointedly trespassed. At the more populist level, including anti-nabob invective, journalism and reportage of the trial of Hastings, there was general agreement that domestic preoccupations always trumped colonial and international affairs. Jones brought Indian poetical forms home in neoclassical and sentimental guises in an attempt to overcome what he feared was the ingrained European predilection for Greek and Roman antiquity. Novelists and social commentators writing in or about contemporary colonial India faced pressure of a more behavioural and social kind.

The Evangelical Revival challenged Orientalists to repudiate the heathen doctrines of their subject matter and steered representations of India away from the cosmopolitanism of the eighteenth century towards more gothic imagery. And for critical and commercial reasons, authors addressing Indian topics in poetry felt compelled to produce hybrids of East and West. We must then temper an appreciation for the extent and variety of British writing on India during the years 1770–1830 with a consideration that such texts were routinely compromised by domestic strictures of taste, politics and religion. Two conclusions can be drawn from this observation. The first, and perhaps more obvious, is that a genuinely 'authentic' vision of India – be it in the realm of literature proper or Burke's parliamentary discourse – was never fully available to British readers. For all the fantastical diacritical marks that adorned Orientalist titles in a bid for accuracy, the reader of such works is continually aware of their status as translations. Like non-English poetry, they continually risk losing its original genius in transit, whatever new patina it might acquire from a skilled translator. In a literary market, even the most assiduous Orientalist scholar was required to frame their work for a European readership, which meant either Anglicising the more recondite phrases or ideas, or presenting the text in terms of a familiar European equivalent.

The second conclusion is that the corpus of texts in question developed in intimate symbiosis with the mainstream literature of the time and, as the preceding chapters have demonstrated, many of the literary developments that occurred between 1770 and 1830 (the maturation of the novel of sensibility into the novel of sentiment; the changing fortunes of the gothic mode; and the Romantic valorisation of emotional expressiveness and nationalist struggle in poetry) can also be detected in writing on India. This should come as little surprise, for as the lists of forthcoming titles in contemporary periodicals show, Orientalist texts and literature on India jostled for attention with 'non-specialist' works, and responded to the same cultural developments and market shifts; but it allows us to re-immerse texts on India and other Oriental nations, which have come to occupy an exotic niche in English studies, in the plenitude of late eighteenth and early nineteenth-century British culture.

The overarching problem faced by writers on India was that of the limited horizons of their readership or, in Burke's case, his political audience. As the introduction outlined, these limitations had both aesthetic and moral dimensions; establishing the effective outward limits of the mind was an enterprise for late seventeenth and eighteenth-century moral philosophers including Shaftesbury, Hutcheson, Hume and Smith. All acknowledged that the circumscribed boundaries of the imagination meant that equable engagement with faraway countries (that is to say, the ability to regard them exactly as one would one's native country) was nigh on impossible. Propinquity generated stronger ideas that inevitably distracted the mind from more distant objects. This discussion resurfaced in the political theory of the 1980s and 1990s. Michael J. Sandel argued that the 'limits of justice' seldom exceeded a particular society or community because justice itself is a relative, not an independent term; one society's idea of justice, nevertheless, may not equate with those of another and very differently constituted society.[1] Michael Walzer similarly concluded that despite globalisation, 'the political community is probably the closest we can come to a world of common meanings'.[2] Weighing in behind Burke, as it were, Onora O'Neill insisted that modern practices of communication and association meant the idea of such a closed community was nostalgic, and outlined principles of action that can be universally adopted in a wider call for 'transnational justice'.[3] One trembles to imagine the consequences had Burke been given access to a blog.

Burke's attempt to keep India in the public eye faced aesthetic problems that anticipated those faced by charities and lobbying organisations today. Faced with a mercurial news agenda, sustaining public interest in a faraway and obscure cause still requires a ready recourse to shock tactics and the humanisation of suffering: witness any number of charitable leaflets that feature the human face as a direct appeal to the imagination. In the literary arena, the philosopher Martha Nussbaum has given new impetus to imaginative sympathy as an ethical and moral function of literature.[4] This, I have argued, was a continuous preoccupation in British literature on India, not least (as is sometimes overlooked) because the plight of India came to be seen as on a par with the African slave trade. The colonial politics that continually broke in upon literature on India also placed sympathy at the forefront of texts, for in an age of sensibility all parties were eager to demonstrate humanitarian rectitude to their readers. British literature on India, then, came to be characterised by a struggle for authentic connection with its subject matter. The category of the exotic or 'mystic East' arose as a result of a falling short of this ideal.

A sceptical view of late eighteenth-century cosmopolitanism and Romantic Orientalism thus opens up. The simple fantasy of a despotic, sexually debauched India proved more alluring for British readers than the complexities of reality, and the imperatives of a highly competitive book market impelled authors firmly down the road to Xanadu. Similarly, in the realm of colonial and missionary reportage, lurid accounts of Indian suffering or cruelty typically prevailed over more temperate descriptions. All fed into a British imaginative conception of India as a land of extremes. The upshot for criticism of this body of writing, therefore, is that a measure of distortion in the portrayal of colonialism, India and its people was in some senses inevitable, and so ultimately the pressure on writers on India, and the Orient overall, can be located in the commercial pressures of the British book trade. These in turn related to prevalent tastes and the role of literary critics in guiding readers' appetites, who themselves articulated aesthetic formulae laid down in 'academic' moral philosophy. The story of writing on India in the years 1770–1830, in conclusion, is that of India impacting on the British imagination profoundly askance. Rather than expanding the horizons of the eighteenth-century republic of letters, as Jones had hoped, India's imaginative advent in Britain jolted and distended existing genres and tropes. Authors either glossed its essential otherness through the adoption of hybrid forms, or, like Maturin, embraced the shock of heathenism for their own reasons. The purpose of this study has not been to pass judgement on such usages, but to cast new light on how and why British literature on India emerged as a refined blend rather than a diligently preserved import.

Notes

Introduction

1. Alexander Dow, *The History of Hindostan, from the Death of Akbar, to the Complete Settlement of the Empire under Aurungzebe. To which are prefixed, I. A Dissertation on the Origin and Nature of Despotism in Hindostan. II. An Enquiry into the State of Bengal, with a Plan for Restoring that Kingdom to its Former Prosperity and Splendour*, 3 vols (London: T. Beckett and P.A. De Hondt, 1773), vol. 1, pp. xil–xl.
2. The term is from Mary Louise Pratt, *Imperial Eyes: Travel Writing and Transculturation* (London: Routledge, 1992). Pratt explores the 'strategies of representation' European colonisers employed 'to secure their innocence in the same moment as they assert European hegemony' (p. 7).
3. Jonathan Lamb, *The Evolution of Sympathy in the Long Eighteenth Century* (London: Pickering & Chatto, 2009). Lamb lists four categories of sympathy that were operative during the long eighteenth century and suggests a fifth: mechanical, social, theatrical, complete and horrid. Lamb shares with this book the premise that 'almost all contributors to this debate occupy a sceptical position' (p. 2).
4. Among the numerous existing studies on imaginative and literary engagement with India are: Sara Suleri, *The Rhetoric of English India* (Chicago: Chicago University Press, 1992); Harish Trivedi, *Colonial Transactions: English Literature and India* (Manchester: Manchester University Press, 1995); Bart Moore-Gilbert (ed.), *Writing India, 1757–1990: The Literature of British India* (Manchester: Manchester University Press, 1996); J.J. Clarke, *Oriental Enlightenment: The Encounter between Asian and Western Thought* (London: Routledge, 1997); Amal Chatterjee, *Representations of India, 1740–1840: The Creation of India in the Colonial Imagination* (London: Macmillan, 1998) and Michael J. Franklin (ed.), *Romantic Representations of British India* (London: Routledge, 2006).
5. Geoffrey Carnall, 'Thomas Campbell', in H.C.G. Matthew and Brian Harrison (eds), *Oxford Dictionary of National Biography* (Oxford: Oxford University Press, 2004), vol. 9, p. 864.
6. See William St Clair, *The Reading Nation in the Romantic Period* (Cambridge: Cambridge University Press, 2004), p. 215. See also Appendix 9, pp. 590–1.
7. Thomas Campbell, *The Pleasures of Hope; with other Poems* (Edinburgh: Mundell & Son, 1799), pp. 19, 25. Page numbers for subsequent citations are given in the text.
8. See David Arnold, 'Hunger in the Garden of Plenty: The Bengal Famine of 1770', in Alessa Johns (ed.), *Dreadful Visitations: Confronting National Catastrophe in the Age of Enlightenment* (New York: Routledge, 1999), pp. 81–111.
9. Published in *Asiatick Researches; or, Transactions of the Society, Instituted in Bengal, for Inquiring into the History and Antiquities, the Arts, Sciences, and Literature, of Asia*, 20 vols (Calcutta: Manuel Cantopher, 1788–1836), vol. 1.

10. Ros Ballaster, *Fabulous Orients: Fictions of the East in England, 1662–1785* (Oxford: Oxford University Press, 2005).
11. Shelley wrote to Peacock about the possibility of employment within the East India Company in a letter (now lost) of 1821; see Nigel Leask, *British Romantic Writers and the East: Anxieties of Empire* (Cambridge: Cambridge University Press, 1992), p. 71. Southey was considered for a legal position in India by his friend Charles Watkin Williams Wynn; see W.A. Speck, *Robert Southey: Entire Man of Letters* (New Haven: Yale University Press, 2006), pp. 87–8.
12. See P.J. Marshall, 'Taming the Exotic: The British in India in the Seventeenth and Eighteenth Centuries', in G.S. Rousseau and Roy Porter (eds), *Exoticism in the Enlightenment* (Manchester: Manchester University Press, 1990), pp. 46–65 and Nigel Leask, '"Wandering through Eblis"; Absorption and Containment in Romantic Exoticism', in Tim Fulford and Peter Kitson (eds), *Romanticism and Colonialism: Writing and Empire, 1780–1830* (Cambridge: Cambridge University Press, 1998), pp. 165–88.
13. See Julia M. Wright's commentary on the continuum of sentimentalism in *Ireland, India, and Nationalism in Nineteenth-Century Literature* (Cambridge: Cambridge University Press, 2007).
14. The historian J.R. Seeley commented that the British seemed to have 'conquered and peopled half the world' in a 'fit of absence of mind' in *The Expansion of England*, ed. John Gross (London: University of Chicago Press, 1971), p. 12. See P.J. Marshall, *Bengal: The British Bridgehead – Eastern India, 1740–1812* (Cambridge: Cambridge University Press, 1987) and C.A. Bayly, *Indian Society and the Making of the British Empire* (Cambridge: Cambridge University Press, 1988).
15. See Natasha Easton, 'Between Mimesis and Alterity: Art, Gift and Diplomacy in Colonial India', in Franklin (ed.), *Romantic Representations of British India*, pp. 84–112.
16. C.A. Bayly, *Imperial Meridian: The British Empire and the World 1780–1830* (London: Longman, 1989), p. 6.
17. Studies on British India relating to this period tend to emphasise competing political visions and disagreements about the forms colonial government should take. See most notably Eric Stokes, *The English Utilitarians and India* (New Delhi: Oxford University Press, 1959) and also Thomas R. Metcalf, *Ideologies of the Raj* (Cambridge: Cambridge University Press, 1995); Sudipta Sen, *Distant Sovereignty: National Imperialism and the Origins of British India* (London: Routledge, 2002); and Robert Travers, *Ideology and Empire in Eighteenth-Century India* (Cambridge: Cambridge University Press, 2007).
18. Mark Wilks, *Historical Sketches of the South of India, in an Attempt to Trace the History of Mysore; from the Origin of the Hindoo Government of that State, to the Extinction of the Mohammedan Dynasty in 1799*, 3 vols (London: Longman et al., 1810–17), preface, p. 15.
19. James Tod, *Annals and Antiquities of Rajast'han, or the Central and Western Rajpoot States of India*, 2 vols (London: Smith, Elder, Calkin & Budd, 1829–32).
20. Sir William Jones, *Works, with the Life of the Author*, ed. Lord Teignmouth, 13 vols (London: John Stockdale, 1807), vol. 3, p. 1.
21. See Bernard S. Cohn, *Colonialism and its Forms of Knowledge: The British in India* (Princeton, NJ: Princeton University Press, 1997) and M.J. Franklin

(ed.), *The European Discovery of India: Key Indological Sources of Romanticism*, 6 vols (London: Ganesha Publishing/ Edition Synapse, 2001).
22. Edward W. Said, *Orientalism* (London: Routledge & Kegan Paul, 1978), p. 3.
23. See Dennis Potter, 'Orientalism and its Problems', in Francis Barker, Peter Hulme, Margaret Iversen and Diana Loxley (eds), *The Politics of Theory: Conference on the Sociology of Literature: Papers* (Colchester: University of Essex, 1983) and John M. MacKenzie, *Orientalism: History, Theory and the Arts* (Manchester: Manchester University Press, 1995).
24. See Andrew Porter, *Religion versus Empire? British Protestant Missionaries and Overseas Expansion, 1700–1914* (Manchester: Manchester University Press, 2004).
25. See Uday Mehta, *Liberalism and Empire: A Study in Nineteenth-Century Liberal Thought* (London: University of Chicago Press, 1999) and Sankar Muthu, *Enlightenment against Empire* (Oxford: Princeton University Press, 2003).
26. Charles Wilkins, *The Bhăgvăt-Gēētă; or, Dialogues of Krĕĕshnă and Ărjŏŏn; in eighteen lectures; with notes* (London: C. Nourse, 1785), 'Letter to Nathaniel Smith', p. 13.
27. See Linda Colley, *Captives: Britain, Empire and the World, 1600–1850* (London: Jonathan Cape, 2002).
28. There is an extensive secondary literature on slavery and the literary culture of this period, including Carl Plasa, *Textual Politics from Slavery to Postcolonialism: Race and Identification* (London: Macmillan, 2000); Tim Morton, *The Poetics of Spice: Romantic Consumerism and the Exotic* (Cambridge: Cambridge University Press, 2000); and Brycchan Carey and Peter Kitson (eds), *Slavery and the Cultures of Abolition: Essays Marking the British Abolition Act of 1807* (Woodbridge: Boydell & Brewer, 2007). See also James Walvin's *Slaves and Slavery: The British Colonial Encounter* (Manchester: Manchester University Press, 1992) and *Black Ivory: A History of British Slavery* (London: HarperCollins, 2001).
29. S.T. Coleridge, *The Collected Works* (London: Routledge & Kegan Paul, 1969–), vol. 1 (ed. Lewis Patton and Peter Mann), p. 243.
30. Peter Hulme, *Colonial Encounters: Europe and the Native Caribbean, 1492–1797* (London: Methuen, 1986), p. 229.
31. P.J. Marshall, 'The Moral Swing to the East: British Humanitarianism, India and the West Indies', *Caribbean Societies* II, Collected Seminar Papers 34 (London: Institute of Commonwealth Studies, 1985), pp. 13–20 (p. 19).
32. Timothy Touchstone, *Tea and Sugar; or, The Nabob and the Creole; A Poem, in Two Cantos* (London: J. Ridgway, 1792), pp. 8–11.
33. Abbé Guillaume Thomas François Raynal, *Philosophical and Political History of the Settlements and Trade of the Europeans in the East and West Indies*, trans. J.O. Justamond, 8 vols (London: A. Strahan & T. Cadell, 1788), vol. 2, pp. 187–8.
34. William Hickey, *Memoirs*, ed. Alfred Spencer, 4 vols (London: Hurst & Blackett, 1913), vol. 3, pp. 343–4.
35. James Beattie, *Elements of Moral Science*, 2 vols (Edinburgh: T. Cadell, 1790–93), vol. 1, p. 180.
36. P.J. Marshall, *'A Free though Conquering People': Britain and Asia in the Eighteenth Century* (London: King's College London, 1981), p. 19.

37. Raymond Schwab, *Oriental Renaissance: Europe's Rediscovery of India and the East, 1680–1880*, trans. Gene Patterson-Black and Victor Reinking (New York: Columbia University Press, 1950), p. 18.
38. E.S. Shaffer, *'Kubla Khan' and The Fall of Jerusalem: The Mythological School in Biblical Criticism and Secular Literature* (Cambridge: Cambridge University Press, 1975).
39. Alan Richardson and Sonia Hofkosh (eds), *Romanticism, Race, and Imperial Culture, 1780–1834* (Bloomington: Indiana University Press, 1996), pp. 4–5. Amongst the works that have established the critical study of literature and empire are Saree Makdisi, *Romantic Imperialism: Universal Empire and the Culture of Modernity* (Cambridge: Cambridge University Press, 1998); Fulford and Kitson (eds), *Romanticism and Colonialism*; and Peter Kitson, *Romantic Literature, Race, and Colonial Encounter* (New York: Palgrave, 2007).
40. Leask, *British Romantic Writers and the East*, p. 9. Several critics have similarly emphasised the radical instability that empire created for the colonial and the colonised self more generally: see Parama Roy, *Indian Traffic: Identities in Question in Colonial and Postcolonial India* (London: California University Press, 1988); Ashis Nandy, *The Intimate Enemy: Loss and Recovery of Self under Colonialism* (New Delhi: Oxford University Press, 1988); Jonathan Lamb, *Preserving the Self in the South Seas* (Chicago: Chicago University Press, 2001); and Rajani Sudani, *Fair Exotics: Xenophobic Subjects in English Literature, 1720–1850* (Philadelphia: University of Pennsylvania Press, 2002).
41. See J.G.A. Pocock, *Barbarism and Religion*, vol. 4, *Barbarians, Savages and Empires* (Cambridge: Cambridge University Press, 2005).
42. Thomas Nixon, *From Passions to Emotions: The Creation of a Secular Psychological Category* (Cambridge: Cambridge University Press, 2003).
43. Horace Walpole, 'Book of Materials', 3 vols (1759–86), vol. 3, p. 41.
44. John Brewer, *The Sinews of Power: War, Money and the English State, 1688–1783* (London: Unwin Hyman, 1989).
45. Francis Hutcheson, *Essay on the Nature and Conduct of the Passions. With Illustrations on the Moral Sense* (London: S. Powell, 1728). For background on this area, see Christopher J. Berry, *Social Theory of the Scottish Enlightenment* (Edinburgh: Edinburgh University Press, 1997).
46. See, for example, John B. Radner, 'The Art of Sympathy in Eighteenth-Century Moral Thought', *Studies in Eighteenth-Century Culture* 9 (1979), pp. 189–210.
47. David Armitage, *The Ideological Origins of the British Empire* (Cambridge: Cambridge University Press, 2000), p. 11.
48. David Hume, *A Treatise of Human Nature*, ed. P.H. Nidditch and L.A. Selby-Bigge (Oxford: Clarendon Press, 1978), pp. 428–9. Page numbers for subsequent citations are given in the text.
49. Mark Salber Phillips, 'Relocating Inwardness: Historical Distance and the Transition from Enlightenment to Romantic Historiography', *PMLA* 118.3 (2003), pp. 436–49. See also Phillips, *Society and Sentiment: Genres of Historical Understanding* (Princeton, NJ: Princeton University Press, 2000), chs 1–2.
50. Adam Smith, *The Theory of Moral Sentiments*, ed. D.D. Raphael and A.L. Macfie (Oxford: Clarendon Press, 1976), p. 9. Page numbers for subsequent citations are given in the text.

51. John Mullan observes that, for Smith, sympathy is capable of arousing feelings that are analogous to those of the sufferer but not identical; see *Sentiment and Sociability: The Language of Feeling in the Eighteenth Century* (Oxford: Clarendon Press, 1988), p. 44.
52. Lynn Festa, *Sentimental Figures of Empire in Eighteenth-Century Britain and France* (Baltimore: Johns Hopkins University Press, 2006), pp. 6, 8.
53. *Ibid.*, p. 223.
54. Mary Wollstonecraft, 'Sacontalá; or, The Fatal Ring', *Analytical Review* 7 (1790), pp. 361–73 (p. 362).
55. *Ibid.*
56. *Ibid.*
57. Leask, 'Wandering through Eblis', pp. 175–6.
58. Edmund Burke, *Writing and Speeches*, ed. Paul Langford, 9 vols (Oxford: Clarendon Press, 1981), vol. 3, p. 427.
59. *Ibid.*, vol. 3, p. 403.
60. See Boyd Hilton, *The Age of Atonement: The Influence of Evangelicalism on Social and Economic Thought, 1785–1865* (Oxford: Clarendon Press, 1988).
61. See Partha Mitter, *Much Maligned Monsters: A History of European Reactions to Indian Art* (Oxford: Clarendon Press, 1977).
62. See P.J. Marshall, *The Impeachment of Warren Hastings* (Oxford: Oxford University Press, 1965).
63. Smith, *Theory of Moral Sentiments*, p. 11; David Hume, *Enquiry Concerning Human Understanding*, ed. P.H. Nidditch and L.A. Selby-Bigge (Oxford: Clarendon Press, 1975), p. 227.
64. Alexander Chalmers, *Works of the English Poets* (1810), cited in Garland Cannon, 'Sir William Jones and Literary Orientalism', in C.C. Barfoot and Theo D'haen (eds), *Oriental Prospects: Western Literature and the Lure of the East* (Amsterdam: Rodopi, 1998), p. 27.
65. Jones, *Works*, vol. 3, pp. 185–204.
66. H.E. Busteed, *Echoes from Old Calcutta: Being Chiefly Reminiscences of the Days of Warren Hastings, Francis and Impey* (London: W. Thacker, 1908).
67. See Syndy McMillan Congar (ed.), *Sensibility in Transformation: Creative Resistance to Sentiment from the Augustans to the Romantics* (London: Associated University Press, 1994).
68. E.M. Collingham, *Imperial Bodies: The Physical Experience of the Raj, c.1800–1947* (Cambridge: Polity Press, 2001), p. 7.
69. See Stephen Neill, *A History of Christianity in India 1707–1858* (Cambridge: Cambridge University Press, 1985), ch. 7, 'Government, Indians and Missions', pp. 156–85.
70. John Barrell, *The Infection of Thomas De Quincey: A Psychopathology of Imperialism* (London: Yale University Press, 1991), p. 10. The term 'self-consolidating other' is from Gayatri Chakravorty Spivak, 'The Rani of Simur', in Francis Barker, Peter Hulme, Margaret Iversen and Diana Loxley (eds), *Europe and its Others: Proceedings of the Essex Conference on the Sociology of Literature July 1984*, 2 vols (Colchester: University of Essex, 1985), vol. 1, pp. 128–51 (p. 133).
71. Henry Martyn, *Journals and Letters*, ed. S. Wilberforce, 2 vols (London: R.B. Seeley & W. Burnside, 1837), vol. 1, p. 334.

72. Homi K. Bhabha gives an ingenious analysis of the early nineteenth-century missionary movement in these terms in his article, 'Signs Taken for Wonders: Questions of Ambivalence and Authority under a Tree outside Delhi, May 1817', in *The Location of Culture* (London: Routledge, 1994), pp. 102–22. See also 'Sly Civility', pp. 93–101, on the native's 'refusal to satisfy the coloniser's narrative demand' (p. 99).
73. Pratt, *Imperial Eyes*, p. 39.

Chapter 1

1. The best factual account of Hastings' trial is Marshall's *The Impeachment of Warren Hastings*. There have also been a number of attempts to assess the wider cultural significance of the trial: see Geoffrey Carnall and Colin Nicholson (eds), *The Impeachment of Warren Hastings: Papers from the Bicentenary Commemoration* (Edinburgh: Edinburgh University Press, 1989) and Nicholas B. Dirks, *The Scandal of Empire: India and the Creation of Imperial Britain* (London: Harvard University Press, 2006).
2. See James Sayers' imitation ticket *For the Trial of Warren Ha*[-stings] (BM 7276) and James Gillray's *Impeachment Ticket* (BM 7277).
3. Frances De Bruyn, 'Edmund Burke's Gothic Romance: The Portrayal of Warren Hastings in Burke's Writings and Speeches on India', *Criticism* 29.4 (1987), pp. 415–38 (p. 425).
4. David Musselwhite, 'The Trial of Warren Hastings', in Francis Barker, Peter Hulme, Margaret Iversen and Diana Loxley (eds), *Literature, Politics and Theory: Conference Papers, 1976–84* (London: Methuen, 1986), pp. 77–103 (p. 99).
5. Suleri, *Rhetoric of English India*, pp. 68–74.
6. Thomas Hardy, *The Return of the Native*, ed. George Woodcock (London: Penguin, 1978), p. 10.
7. Burke, *Writing and Speeches*, vol. 6, p. 276. Unless otherwise specified, all quotations from Burke's speeches at the trial will be taken from this edition.
8. Dirks, *The Scandal of Empire*, p. 125.
9. O'Brien's title is a line from W.B. Yeats's poem 'The Seven Sages' (1933). F.P. Lock's biography of Burke takes a similarly 'biographical' line, seeing Irish identity and suffering at the root of many of his later political projects. For example, on his mother's family: 'the plight of aristocrats or decayed gentlefolk living in reduced circumstances always exerted a powerful emotional appeal on Burke. The Nagles first impressed this idea on his mind. He served the impoverished or dispossessed nobility of India and France chiefly through his writings and speeches'; see *Edmund Burke: Volume I, 1730–1784* (Oxford: Clarendon Press, 1998), p. 14.
10. Luke Gibbons, *Edmund Burke and Ireland: Aesthetics, Politics and the Colonial Sublime* (Cambridge: Cambridge University Press, 2003).
11. Edmund Burke, *A Philosophical Enquiry into the Origin of our Ideas of the Sublime and the Beautiful*, ed. Adam Philips (Oxford: Oxford University Press, 1990), p. 41.
12. Philip Mercer, *Sympathy and Ethics: A Study of the Relationship between Sympathy and Morality with Special Reference to Hume's* Treatise (Oxford: Clarendon Press, 1972), p. 9.

13. Burke, *Philosophical Enquiry*, p. 42. Page numbers for subsequent citations are given in the text.
14. Gibbons, *Edmund Burke and Ireland*, ch. 2, 'Philoctetes and Colonial Ireland: The Wounded Body as National Narrative', pp. 39–79.
15. See, for example, Neal Wood, 'The Aesthetic Dimensions of Burke's Political Thought', *Journal of British Studies* 4.1 (November 1964), pp. 41–64; Tom Furniss, *Edmund Burke's Aesthetic Ideology: Language, Gender, and Political Economy in Revolution* (Cambridge: Cambridge University Press, 1993) and Stephen K. White, 'Burke on Politics, Aesthetics, and the Dangers of Modernity', *Political Theory* 21.3 (August 1993), pp. 507–27.
16. See Geoffrey Carnall, 'Burke as Modern Cicero', in Carnall and Nicholson, *The Impeachment of Warren Hastings*, pp. 76–90, and H.V. Canter, 'The Impeachments of Verres and Hastings: Cicero and Burke', *Classical Journal* 9 (1914), pp. 199–211.
17. See Nicholas K. Robinson, *Edmund Burke: A Life in Caricature* (New Haven: Yale University Press, 1996).
18. Isaac Kramnick first explored questions surrounding Burke's sexuality in *The Rage of Edmund Burke: Portrait of an Ambivalent Conservative* (New York: Basic Books, 1977), making use of Burke's then recently published correspondence. Claudia Johnson briefly pursues this line of enquiry in her *Equivocal Beings: Politics, Gender and Sentimentality in the 1790s. Wollstonecraft, Radcliffe, Burney, Austen* (London: Chicago University Press, 1996).
19. Anthony Pasquin, i.e. John Williams, *Authentic Memoirs of Warren Hastings, Esq, late Governor-General of Bengal, with Strictures on the Management of his Impeachment: to which is added, an Examination into the Causes of the Alarm in the Empire* (London: J. Bew, 1793), p. 65.
20. Olivia Smith, *The Politics of Language* (Oxford: Clarendon Press, 1984), p. 38.
21. Burke, *Reflections on the Revolution in France and on the Proceedings in Certain Societies in London relative to that Event*, ed. Conor Cruise O'Brien (London: Penguin, 1969), pp. 169–70.
22. Thomas Babington Macaulay, *Critical and Historical Essays Contributed to the Edinburgh Review* (London: Longman, Green & Co., 1877), p. 643. Dr William Dodd was hanged for alleged forgery in 1777. His execution was controversial and Macaulay refers to it here as a legal *cause célèbre*.
23. Suleri, *Rhetoric of English India*, pp. 28–30.
24. Gibbons, *Edmund Burke and Ireland*, p. 6.
25. Mehta, *Liberalism and Empire*, p. 42, p. 21. See also Frederick G. Whelan, *Edmund Burke and India: Political Morality and Empire* (Pittsburgh: University of Pittsburgh Press, 1996), pp. 40–2.
26. Burke, *Writing and Speeches*, vol. 6, p. 277.
27. James Raven, *Judging New Wealth: Popular Publishing and Responses to Commerce in England, 1750–1800* (Oxford: Clarendon Press, 1992), especially ch. 11, 'Assumptive Gentry and the Threat to Stability'.
28. William Cowper, *Poetical Works* (London: William Tegg, 1858), p. 174.
29. For example, Sir Robert Raymond in Samuel Jackson Pratt's *Emma Corbett; or, The Miseries of Civil War* (1780), Admiral Harrison in Charlotte Palmer's *Female Stability; or, The History of Miss Belville*, (1780) and the eponymous Mr. Venneck in *The Indian Adventurer; or, The History of Mr. Vanneck* (1780); see Raven, *Judging New Wealth*.

30. Macaulay, *Critical and Historical Essays*, p. 535.
31. Cowper, *Poetical Works*, p. 428.
32. William Pitt, First Earl of Chatham, *Correspondence*, eds W.S. Taylor and J.H. Pringle, 4 vols (London: John Murray, 1839–40), vol. 3, p. 405.
33. See Mark Bence-Jones, *Clive of India* (London: Constable, 1974), pp. 279–90.
34. For popular representations of nabobs in the late eighteenth century, see James M. Holzman, *The Nabobs in England: A Study of the Returned Anglo-Indian, 1760–1785* (New York, 1926); Philip Lawson and Jim Phillips, '"Our Execrable Banditti": Perceptions of Nabobs in Mid-Eighteenth Century Britain', *Albion* 16.3 (1984), pp. 225–41; and Michael Edwardes, *The Nabobs at Home* (London: Constable, 1991).
35. See also M.O. Grenby, *The Anti-Jacobin Novel: British Conservatism and the French Revolution* (Cambridge: Cambridge University Press, 2001), ch. 5, 'Levellers, Nabobs and the Manners of the Great: The Novel's Defence of Hierarchy'.
36. See Lucy S. Sutherland, *The East India Company in Eighteenth-Century Politics* (Oxford: Clarendon Press, 1952), pp. 329–414 and C.H. Philips, *The East India Company 1784–1834* (Manchester: Manchester University Press, 1961), Appendix I.
37. Horace Walpole, *Correspondence*, ed. W.S. Lewis, 48 vols (New Haven: Yale University Press, 1937–83), 'To Horace Mann', 13 July 1773, vol. 23, p. 400. Lawson and Phillips provide a counterargument to this, acknowledging that while numbers of MPs representing the East India interest rose from 12 in 1761 to 27 in 1780, nabobs never constituted a 'unified and coherent lobby', nor did they display any wish to subvert the political system ('Our Execrable Banditti', p. 228).
38. Eliza Fenwick, *Secresy; or; The Ruin on the Rock*, ed. Gina Luria (London: Garland, 1974), p. 225.
39. Henry Mackenzie, *The Man of Feeling*, ed. Brian Vickers (London: Oxford University Press, 1967), p. 76.
40. Further to his ironical endorsement of Burke's position in his novel, Mackenzie expressed wariness of Burke's motives in prosecuting Hastings in his *Review of the Principal Proceedings of the Parliament of 1784*; see Henry Mackenzie, *Works*, 8 vols (Edinburgh: James Ballantyne, 1808), vol. 7.
41. Bence-Jones, *Clive of India*, pp. 242–3. Another prominent nabob on whom the character of Mite was possibly based was General Richard Smith (c. 1734–1803).
42. Samuel Foote, *The Nabob: A Comedy, in Three Acts* (London: Coleman, 1778), p. 59. Page numbers for subsequent citations are given in the text.
43. See Grenby, *The Anti-Jacobin Novel*, pp. 138–40.
44. Foote, *The Nabob*, p. 5. Page numbers for subsequent citations are given in the text.
45. Cited in Marshall's introduction to Burke, *Writings and Speeches*, vol. 5, p. 18.
46. For Burke's early involvement with Indian affairs, see Marshall, *Impeachment of Warren Hastings*, pp. 1–38 and Conor Cruise O'Brien, *The Great Melody: A Thematic Biography and Commented Anthology of Edmund Burke* (London: Chicago University Press, 1992), pp. 257–311.
47. Burke, *Writings and Speeches*, vol. 5, p. 403.

48. Burke, *Writings and Speeches*, vol. 5, p. 403.
49. Suleri, *Rhetoric of English India*, p. 30.
50. Burke, *Writings and Speeches*, vol. 3, p. 389.
51. *Ibid*.
52. Phillips, *Society and Sentiment*, p. 254.
53. Burke, *Writings and Speeches*, vol. 3, p. 402. Page numbers for subsequent citations are given in the text.
54. O'Brien, *Great Melody*, pp. 139–44.
55. James Sayers, *Galante Show*, engraving (London: T. Cornell, 6 May 1788), BM 7313.
56. James Gillray, *Camera-Obscura*, engraving (London: S.W. Fores, 9 May 1788), BM 7314. Gillray's practice was to feign Sayers's initials (J.S.F.: 'James Sayers fecit') on his satirical responses to specific works by Sayers.
57. Suleri, *Rhetoric of English India*, p. 57. *The History of the Trial of Warren Hastings, Esq.* (London: Debrett, Vernor & Hood, 1796) is a partisan account compiled from newspaper reports, although Suleri uses it as the basis of her reading. See also the pro-Hastings *The Trial of Warren Hastings, Esq., Complete from February 1788, to June 1794; with a Preface* (London: J. Owen, 1794).
58. Fanny Burney, *Diary and Letters of Madame D'Arblay (1778–1840)*, ed. Charlotte Barrett, 6 vols (London: Macmillan, 1905), vol. 3, p. 413.
59. See David Marshall, *The Figure of Theatre: Shaftesbury, Defoe, Adam Smith, and George Eliot* (New York: Columbia University Press, 1985) and *The Surprising Effects of Sympathy: Marivaux, Diderot, Rousseau and Mary Shelley* (London: Chicago University Press, 1988).
60. Burney, *Diary and Letters*, vol. 3, p. 413.
61. Marshall, introduction to Burke, *Writings and Speeches*, vol. 6, pp. 16–17.
62. Burke, *Writings and Speeches*, vol. 6, p. 346. Page numbers for subsequent citations are given in the text.
63. William Davy and Joseph White (trans.), *Institutes Political and Military written originally in the Mogul Language by the Great Timur* (Oxford: Clarendon Press, 1783). On the relativism of Hastings' administration in Bengal, see Sen, *Distant Sovereignty*, which argues that 'in the eighteenth century, and perhaps even in the early nineteenth, the self-image of British rule in India could not be fully or comfortably unfastened from the nominal regality of the Mughals. The British did not wish to be seen as an Indian power and they did not wish to assume indiscreetly the mantle of a sovereign authority in India' (introduction, p. xiii).
64. Burke, *Writings and Speeches*, vol. 6, pp. 457–8.
65. Burke, *Writings and Speeches*, vol. 7, p. 459.
66. Burke, *Philosophical Enquiry*, p. 40.
67. Burke, *Writings and Speeches*, vol. 6, p. 350.
68. Whelan produces an illuminating comparison of Burke's speeches to the late essays of Kant, notably the latter's 'Perpetual Peace' (1795); see *Edmund Burke and India*, p. 2 and 2n.
69. Burke, *Writings and Speeches*, vol. 7, p. 245.
70. E.A. Bond (ed.), *Speeches of the Managers and Counsel in the Trial of Warren Hastings*, 4 vols (London: Longman and others, 1859–61), vol. 1, pp. 593–4.
71. Burke, *Writings and Speeches*, vol. 6, p. 275.

72. Anon., *History of the Trial of Warren Hastings*, pp. 151–8; Pasquin, *Authentic Memoirs of Warren Hastings*, pp. 26–7.
73. Anon., *History of the Trial of Warren Hastings*, vol. 6, p. 421.
74. Burke, *Philosophical Enquiry*, p. 36 and Smith, *Theory of Moral Sentiments*, p. 9.
75. See Elaine Scarry, *The Body in Pain: The Making and Unmaking of the World* (Oxford: Oxford University Press, 1985) and Susan Sontag, *Regarding the Pain of Others* (London: Hamish Hamilton, 2003).
76. Sontag, *Regarding the Pain of Others*, p. 87.
77. Elizabeth Ryves, *The Hastiniad; An Historic Poem, in Three Cantos* (London: J. Debrett, 1785), p. 7.
78. Joseph Richardson, *The Rolliad, in Two Parts: Probationary Odes for the Laureatship; and Miscellanies: with Criticism and Illustrations* (London: J. Ridgway, 1795). The title alludes to the MP for Devonshire, John Rolle, a contemporary politician and buffoon figure.
79. Ralph Broome, *Letters from Simpkin the Second to his Dear Brother in Wales; Containing a Humble Description of the Trial of Warren Hastings, Esq. With Simon's Answer* (London: J. Bell, 1788), p. 12. A second series was published by John Stockdale in 1790.
80. James Sayers, *The Last Scene of the Managers Farce*, engraving (London: H. Humphrey, 8 May 1795), BM 8647.
81. Mehta, *Liberalism and Empire*, p. 170.
82. Sir Charles Lawson, *The Private Life of Warren Hastings, First Governor-General of India* (London: Swan Sonnenschein, 1895), p. 42.
83. Percival Spear, *The Nabobs: A Study in the Social Life of the English in Eighteenth-Century India* (New Delhi: Oxford University Press, 1998), p. 147.

Chapter 2

1. Sir William Jones, *Letters*, ed. Garland Cannon, 2 vols. (Oxford: Clarendon Press, 1970), 'To 2nd Earl Spencer', 4–30 August 1787, vol. 2, p. 749. Page numbers for subsequent citations are given in the text.
2. Jones repeats the paraphrase of *The Tempest*, Act 5 Scene 1 in his letter to Edmund Burke of 17 March 1782; see Jones, *Letters*, vol. 2, p. 520.
3. Sir William Jones, *Poems, consisting chiefly of translations from the Asiatick Languages. To Which are Added, Two Essays, I. On the Poetry of the Eastern Nations. II. On the Arts, commonly called Imitative* (Oxford: Clarendon Press, 1772), p. 217.
4. Said, *Orientalism*, p. 78.
5. Studies of Jones and Orientalism that broadly follow the approach inaugurated by Said include Rana Kabbani, *Imperial Fictions: Europe's Myths of Orient* (London: Macmillan, 1986); Ronald Inden, *Imagining India* (London: Hurst, 1990); Metcalf, *Ideologies of the Raj*; Cohn, *Colonialism and its Forms of Knowledge*; and Chatterjee, *Representations of India*. Studies that take a more critical view of this approach include Aijaz Ahmad, *In Theory: Classes, Nations, Literatures* (London: Verso, 1992); MacKenzie, *Orientalism: History, Theory and the Arts*; and Ibn Warraq, *Defending the West: A Critique of Edward Said's Orientalism* (London: Prometheus Books, 2007).

6. See Cohn, *Colonialism and its Forms of Knowledge*, pp. 20–1 for an analysis of Jones's appropriation of Indian law
7. Jones, *Letters*, vol. 2, p. 642, p. 615. Jones's *Dialogue* was distributed by the Society for Constitutional Information and became the subject of a sedition trial when William Shipley, Dean of St Asaph and Jones's future brother-in-law, republished it as *The Principles of Government, in a Dialogue between a Gentleman and a Farmer* in 1783. On the inconsistency in Jones's political views regarding India, see S.N. Mukherjee, *Sir William Jones: A Study in Eighteenth-Century British Attitudes to India* (Cambridge: Cambridge University Press, 1968); R.K. Kaul, *Studies in Sir William Jones: An Interpreter of Oriental Literature* (Shimla: Indian Institute of Advanced Study, 1995); and Kate Teltscher, *India Inscribed: European and British Writing on India 1600–1800* (New Delhi: Oxford University Press, 1995), pp. 193–4.
8. Jawaharlal Nehru, *The Discovery of India* (London: Meridian, 1945), p. 266.
9. A.J. Arberry, *Asiatic Jones: The Life and Influence of Sir William Jones (1746–1794)* (London: Longmans, Green & Co., 1946), p. 39.
10. David Kopf, *British Orientalism and the Bengal Renaissance: The Dynamics of Indian Modernisation 1773–1835* (Berkeley: University of California Press, 1969), pp. 24–5.
11. Garland Cannon, *The Life and Mind of Oriental Jones: Sir William Jones, the Father of Linguistics* (Cambridge: Cambridge University Press, 1990), p. 358.
12. Teltscher, *India Inscribed*, p. 192, pp. 194–5.
13. Rosane Rocher, 'Weaving Knowledge: Sir William Jones and the Indian Pandits', in Cannon and Kevin R. Brine (eds), *Objects of Enquiry: The Life, Contributions and Influences of Sir William Jones (1746–1794)* (London: New York University Press, 1995), pp. 51–79 (p. 63).
14. Said, 'Orientalism Reconsidered', in Barker *et al.* (eds), *Europe and its Others*, vol. 1, pp. 14–27 (p. 15).
15. See also Ahmad, *In Theory* and Dipesh Chakrabarty, *Provincialising Europe: Postcolonial Thought and Historical Difference* (Oxford: Princeton University Press, 2000).
16. P.J. Marshall, *The British Discovery of Hinduism in the Eighteenth Century* (Cambridge: Cambridge University Press, 1970), p. 17.
17. See M.H. Abrams, *The Mirror and the Lamp: Romantic Theory and the Critical Tradition* (New York: Oxford University Press, 1953), pp. 87–8.
18. Jerome McGann, *The Poetics of Sensibility: A Revolution in Literary Style* (Oxford: Clarendon Press, 1996), p. 128.
19. Sir William Jones, *A Grammar of the Persian Language* (London: W. & J. Richardson, 1771), preface, p. xii.
20. On the literariness of the *Grammar*, see Cannon, 'Sir William Jones and the New Pluralism over Language and Cultures', *The Yearbook of English Studies* 28 (1998), pp. 128–43 (p. 130).
21. Jones, *Poems*, preface, p. xiii.
22. Cannon, for example, has described the volume's title as 'somewhat misleading', given its assortment of translated Oriental and Italian poetry, alongside Jones's own juvenile verse compositions (*Life and Mind of Oriental Jones*, p. 48).
23. Jones, *Poems*, preface, p. vii.

24. See, for instance, his comments to Richard Wilson in 1784 'that *Jūdishteīr, Arjen, Corno*, and the other warriours of the *M'hab'harat* appear greater in my eyes than Agamemnon, Ajax, and Achilles appeared, when I first read the Iliad' (*Letters*, vol. 2, p. 652) and his remarks in the eleventh anniversary discourse 'On the Philosophy of the Asiatics' (1794).
25. Sir William Jones, *Selected Poetical and Prose Works*, ed. Michael J. Franklin (Cardiff: University of Wales Press, 1995), p. 320. Quotations will be taken from this edition where texts are available (page numbers are given in the text).
26. Zak Sitter, 'William Jones, "Eastern" Poetry, and the Problem of Imitation', *Texas Studies in Literature and Language* 50.4 (Winter 2008), pp. 385–407 (p. 402).
27. William Wordsworth, *Poetical Works*, ed. Thomas Hutchinson and Ernest de Selincourt (London: Oxford University Press, 1966), p. 735.
28. Abrams, *The Mirror and the Lamp*, p. 88.
29. Jones, *Selected Poetical and Prose Works*, p. 343. Page numbers for subsequent citations are given in the text.
30. Consider, for example, Henry Homes, Lord Kames's account of the 'common sense of mankind' in his *Elements of Criticism*, 2 vols (Edinburgh: Miller, Kincaid & Bell, 1762), where he states that 'every doubt with relation to this standard, occasioned by the practice of different nations and different times, may be cleared by appealing to the principles that ought to govern the taste of every individual' (vol. 2, pp. 497–8).
31. Sitter, 'William Jones', p. 403.
32. Jones, *Poems*, preface, p. i.
33. Jones, *Poems*, preface, pp. iii–v.
34. Leask, 'Wandering through Eblis', p. 172.
35. John Guillory, *Cultural Capital: The Problem of Literary Canon Formation* (London: University of Chicago Press, 1993), p. 87.
36. Jones, *Letters*, vol. 1, p. 24. See Garland Cannon, 'Sir William Jones and Dr Johnson's Literary Club', *Modern Philology* 63.1 (August 1965), pp. 20–37, where Cannon notes that the young Jones was valued for 'Oriental learning rather than poetry; the latter naturally being the province of Goldsmith', (p. 22).
37. Dow's translation of Ináyat Allah appeared as *Tales, Translated from the Persian of Inatullah of Delhi*, 2 vols (London: T. Becket & P.A. De Hondt, 1768). The section corresponding to Jones's 'The Palace of Fortune' is 'The Baar Danesh; or, Garden of Knowledge', vol. 2, pp. 56–103.
38. Although Dow explains that while he has adapted the English language 'in order to bend it to the Persian idiom' he has also 'retrenched many of the redundancies of [the] author' (*Tales*, vol. 1, Preface).
39. Jones, *Selected Poetical and Prose Works*, p. 37n. Page numbers for subsequent citations are given in the text.
40. This quintessential Orientalist image reappeared in Southey's *The Curse of Kehama* (London: Longman *et al.*, 1810) and Shelley's *Queen Mab* (1813). See E. Koeppel, 'Shelley's *Queen Mab* and Sir William Jones's *The Palace of Fortune*', *Englische Studien* 28 (1900), pp. 43–53. The magical Palace of Fortune itself, undoubtedly inspired the 'stately pleasure dome' of Coleridge's 'Kubla Khan':

>   on a rock of ice, by magick rais'd,
>   High in the midst a gorgeous palace blaz'd;
>   The sunbeams on the gilded portals glanc'd,

> Play'd on the spires, and on the turrets danc'd;
> To four bright gates four ivory bridges led,
> With pearls illumin'd, and with roses spread.
>
> (Jones, *Selected Poetical and Prose Works*, p. 40)

For a full range of Jones's influences on the Romantics, see Cannon, 'Sir William Jones and Literary Orientalism'.
41. Dow, *Tales*, vol. 2, pp. 75–6.
42. Jones had access to the Arabic original, courtesy of a friend in Aleppo, and also Antoine Galland's French translation, *Mille et une nuits* (1704). The latter was popularised in English through the so-called 'Grub Street' edition; the sections that correspond to 'The Seven Fountains' are Nights 57–62, *Arabian Nights Entertainments: consisting of One Thousand and One Stories told by the Sultaness of the Indies ... Translated into French from the Arabian MSS, by M. Galland, of the Royal Academy; and now done into English from the last Paris edition*, 6 vols (London: J. Osborne & T. Longman, 1725), vol. 1, pp. 95–116. See Margaret Sironval, 'The Image of Sheherazade in French and English editions of the *Thousand and One Nights*', in Yuriko Yamanaka and Tetsuo Nishio (eds), *The Arabian Nights and Orientalism: Perspectives from East and West* (London: I.B. Tauris, 2006), pp. 219–45.
43. See Ballaster, *Fabulous Orients*.
44. Horace Walpole, *Correspondence*, 'To Rev. William Mason', 25 May 1772, vol. 28, p. 36.
45. Elizabeth Montagu to James Beattie, 5 September 1772, in Jones, *Letters*, vol. 1, p. 111; Chalmers, *Works of the English Poets* (1810), vol. 18, p. 440. See Cannon, 'Sir William Jones and Literary Orientalism'.
46. Jenny Sharpe, 'The Violence of Light in the Land of Desire; or, How William Jones Discovered India', *Boundary* 2, 20.1 (Spring 1993), pp. 26–46 (p. 43).
47. Marshall, *British Discovery of Hinduism*, p. 33. Bishop James Ussher pinpointed the Creation date at 4004 BC in his *Annales veteris testamenti* (1650), although his findings built on medieval tradition; see Graham Parry, *The Trophies of Time: English Antiquarians of the Seventeenth Century* (Oxford: Oxford University Press, 1996), Patrick Wyse Jackson, *The Chronologers' Quest: The Search for the Age of the Earth* (Cambridge: Cambridge University Press, 2006) and Alan Ford, *James Ussher: Theology, History, and Politics in Early Modern Ireland and England* (Oxford: Oxford University Press, 2007).
48. See Frank E. Manuel, *The Eighteenth Century Confronts the Gods* (Cambridge, MA: Harvard University Press, 1959) and Nigel Leask, 'Mythology', in Iain McCalman (gen. ed.), *An Oxford Companion to the Romantic Age* (Oxford: Oxford University Press, 1999), pp. 338–45.
49. Jones, *Letters*, 'To Viscount Althorp', 19 August 1777, vol. 1, pp. 239–40.
50. See Mukherjee, *Sir William Jones*, pp. 95–6. Rocher alerts us to the provisional nature of Jones's thoughts on linguistic affinities during the 1770s and 1780s, claiming that 'his statement on the relationship of what were to be called the Indo-European languages was later quoted out of context, and made the charter of a new discipline', i.e. comparative linguistics (Rosane Rocher, *Orientalism, Poetry and the Millennium: The Checkered Life of Nathaniel Brassey Halhed 1751–1830* (Delhi: Motilal Banarsidass, 1983), pp. 243–4).

182 *Notes*

51. Jones, *Letters*, 'To Adam Czartoryski', 17 February 1779, vol. 1, p. 285.
52. Nathaniel Brassey Halhed, *A Grammar of the Bengal Language* (Hoogly: [Charles Wilkins], 1778), preface. Charles Wilkins hand-made the Bengali types for this pioneering book, which earned him the epithet 'Caxton of Bengal'. See Rocher, *Orientalism, Poetry and the Millennium*, p. 83.
53. Jones, *Letters*, 'To Adam Czartoryski', 17 February 1779, vol. 1, p. 285.
54. Jones, *Letters*, 'To Richard Johnson', 15 December 1783, vol. 2, p. 624.
55. Jones, *Letters*, 'To Charles Wilkins', 6 January 1784, vol. 2, p. 625 and 'To John Hyde', January 1784, vol. 2, p. 626.
56. Jones, *Letters*, 'To Warren Hastings', 22 January 1784, vol. 2, p. 627. The Members of the Society invited Hastings and his fellow members of the Supreme Council to become patrons of the society. Hastings declined but was continually supportive of the Society, notably in his dedicatory letter published in Wilkins's *Bhăgvăt-Gēētă*. The Society was renamed the Asiatic Society of Bengal following the establishment by Henry Colebrooke of the Royal Asiatic Society in London in 1823.
57. The title page of the first volume of *Asiatick Researches* bears the date 1788. The Appendix, listing society members, was not printed until 1789. Drew gives an account of how demand for copies seemed to outstrip supply. Due to the shortage of copies much of the content of the *Asiatick Researches*, including some of Jones's essays, reached the public in the form of reprints or extracts in critical reviews (John Drew, *India and the Romantic Imagination* (Delhi: Oxford University Press, 1987), p. 71).
58. See Sharpe, 'Violence of Light in the Land of Desire', p. 29, and Rocher, 'Weaving Knowledge', p. 63. Jones himself commented on the situation 'among *Europeans* resident in *India*', whereby 'every individual is a man of business in the civil or military state, and constantly occupied either in the affairs of government, in the administration of justice, in some department of revenue or commerce, or in the one of the liberal professions'; under these unpropitious circumstances, '*a change of toil*' must perforce be considered '*a species of repose*' (*Asiatick Researches* 1 (1788), introduction).
59. Inden acknowledges Jones's desire to produce a 'totalizing account of India' but considers him to have failed, the first truly 'hegemonic account' being James Mill's *History of British India* of 1817. See *Imagining India*, pp. 44–5.
60. Jones, *Works*, vol. 3, p. 319.
61. See Mitter, *Much Maligned Monsters*; and Richard H. Davis, *Lives of Indian Images* (Princeton, NJ: Princeton University Press, 1997).
62. Jones, *Works*, vol. 3, p. 320. Page numbers for subsequent citations are given in the text.
63. Marshall, *British Discovery of Hinduism*, p. 36. Jones's findings were taken up by, amongst others, William Robertson in his *An Historical Disquisition concerning the Knowledge which the Ancients had of India* (London: A. Strahan & T. Cadell, 1791) and Thomas Maurice in his *Indian Antiquities; or, Dissertations, relative to the Ancient Geographical Divisions, the Pure System of Primeval Theology, the Grand Code of Civil Laws, the Original Form of Government, the Widely-Extended Commerce, and the Various and Profound Literature, of Hindostan: compared, throughout, with the Religion, Laws, Government, and Literature, of Persia, Egypt, and Greece*, 7 vols (London: H.L. Galabin, 1800).
64. Inden, *Imagining India*, p. 42.

65. See Drew, *India and the Romantic Imagination*, p. 53. Drew takes this as evidence that, for Jones, 'an extended response to Asia was possible in terms of ideas concerning the mystical state already existent within the European tradition', i.e. Platonic philosophy (p. 67).
66. Sharada Sugirtharajah, *Imagining Hinduism: A Postcolonial Perspective* (London: Routledge, 2003), ch. 1.
67. Three volumes of this influential Indian journal were published as *The Asiatic Miscellany, consisting of Translations, Imitations, Fugitive Pieces, Original Productions, and Extracts from Curious Publications. By W. Chambers, Esq. and Sir W. Jones, Judges of the Supreme Court of Judicature, at Fort William in Bengal, and other literary gentlemen, now resident in India*, 2 vols (Calcutta: Daniel Stuart, 1785; Calcutta: William Makay, 1786) and 1 vol. (London: J. Wallis, 1787). A fourth appeared as *The New Asiatic Miscellany: Consisting of Original Essays, Translations, and Fugitive Pieces* (Calcutta: Joseph Cooper, 1789).
68. Jones, *Selected Poetical and Prose Works*, p. 81. Page numbers for subsequent citations are given in the text.
69. *The Enchanted Fruit* was reviewed in London in 1787 as part of the contents of the *Asiatic Miscellany*. The *Monthly Review* was typical in regarding it as a piece of artful gaiety: the critic John Parsons encouraged readers who have 'a taste for delicacy, as well as sprightliness and vivacity', to 'gather the fruit for themselves'. See 'The Asiatic Miscellany, Nos I. and II.', *Monthly Review* 76 (January–June 1787), pp. 480–4 (p. 482).
70. Jones, *Selected Poetical and Prose Works*, p. 154. Page numbers for subsequent citations are given in the text.
71. Bennett Zon, 'From "Very Acute and Plausible" to "Curiously Misplaced": Sir William Jones's "On the Musical Modes of the Hindus" (1792) and its Reception in Later Music Treatises', in Franklin, *Romantic Representations of British India*, pp. 197–219 (p. 204). See also Tilar J. Mazzeo's chapter 'The Strains of Empire: Shelley and the Music of India' in the same volume, pp. 180–96.
72. Jones, *Works*, vol. 4, p. 190. Jones explains that the source for the content of the essay was the '*Rágavibódha*, or '*The Doctrine of Musical Modes*', which he describes as 'the most valuable work, that I have seen, and perhaps the most valuable that exists, on the subject of *Indian* musick' (*Works*, vol. 4, p. 182).
73. Jones, *Works*, vol. 4, pp. 196–7, p. 206.
74. See Zon, 'From "Very Acute and Plausible"', p. 197.
75. Jones, *Selected Poetical and Prose Works*, p. 114. Page numbers for subsequent citations are given in the text.
76. Drew, *India and the Romantic Imagination*.
77. Jones, *Works*, vol. 4, pp. 219–20.
78. Jones, *Works*, vol. 4, p. 220.
79. Jones, *Selected Poetical and Prose Works*, p. 106. Page numbers for subsequent citations are given in the text.
80. Drew provides an account of the influence of the hymns and 'The Palace of Fortune' on the poetry of Shelley (*India and the Romantic Imagination*, pp. 266–79).
81. The play was published in Calcutta in 1789 for the benefit of insolvent debtors and subsequently in London in the following year. Both editions were anonymous, although certain clues in the preface led to the rapid association of Jones's name with the work. The two editions were *Sacontalá; or, The*

Fatal Ring; An Indian Drama by Câlidás: translated from the original Sanscrit and Prácrit (Calcutta: Joseph Cooper, 1789) and *Sacontalá; or, The Fatal Ring; An Indian Drama by Câlidás: translated from the original Sanscrit and Prácrit* (London: J. Cooper, 1790).
82. Cited in Schwab, *Oriental Renaissance*, p. 59.
83. Jones, *Letters*, vol. 2, pp. 766–68.
84. See Richard King's *Orientalism and Religion: Postcolonial Theory, India and 'The Mystic East'* (London: Routledge, 1999), which accuses Jones and other members of the Asiatic Society in Bengal of fabricating a 'mystical' version of Hinduism based upon eighteenth-century European conceptions of neo-Platonism (pp. 89–90).
85. Rocher, 'Weaving Knowledge', p. 52.
86. Jones, *Works*, vol. 3, pp. 12–13.
87. *Asiatick Researches* 1, introduction.

Chapter 3

1. Eliza Fay, *Original Letters from India (1779–1815)*, ed. E.M. Forster (London: Hogarth Press, 1925; originally 1817), p. 20.
2. See, for example, Isobel Grundy, '"The Barbarous Character We Give Them": White Women Report on Other Races', *Studies in Eighteenth-Century Culture* 22 (1992), pp. 73–86, and the entry on Fay in Virginia Blain, Patricia Clements and Isobel Grundy (eds), *The Feminist Companion to Literature in English: Women Writers from the Middle Ages to the Present* (London: B.T. Batsford, 1990), p. 360.
3. Anne Jessie Van Sant, *Eighteenth-century Sensibility and the Novel: The Senses in a Social Context* (Cambridge: Cambridge University Press, 1993), p. 15.
4. On the changes taking place in the culture of sensibility and its association with Jacobinism, see Markman Ellis, *The Politics of Sensibility: Race, Gender and Commerce in the Sentimental Novel* (Cambridge: Cambridge University Press, 1996); Janet Todd, *Sensibility: An Introduction* (London: Methuen, 1986); Mullan, *Sentiment and Sociability*; and Chris Jones, *Radical Sensibility: Literature and Ideas in the 1790s* (London: Routledge, 1993).
5. Collingham, *Imperial Bodies*, p. 3.
6. Charles-Louis de Secondat, Baron de Montesquieu, *The Spirit of the Laws*, trans. Anne M. Cohler, Basia Carolyn Miller and Harold Samuel Stone (Cambridge: Cambridge University Press, 2000), p. 234. Page numbers for subsequent citations are given in the text.
7. Montesquieu cites the original French editions of François Bernier's *Histoire de la dernière révolution des États du Gran Mogol*, 4 vols (Paris: Claude Barbin, 1670-1) and Jean-Baptiste Tavernier's *Six Voyages de J.B. Tavernier … en Turquie, en Perse et aux Indes*, 2 vols (Paris, 1676).
8. David Hume, 'Of National Characters', in *Selected Essays*, ed. Stephen Copley and Andrew Edgar (Oxford: Oxford University Press, 1996), p. 116. Page numbers for subsequent citations are given in the text.
9. Collingham, *Imperial Bodies*, p. 24.
10. *The World* 1.1 (15 October 1791), p. 3.
11. Paul Keen, *The Crisis of Literature in the 1790s: Print Culture and the Public Sphere* (Cambridge: Cambridge University Press, 1999).

12. Prints of the paintings by Thomas and William Daniell were compiled and published in Britain as *Oriental Scenery* (London: Longman et al., 1812). The phrase comes from the 1824 poem of the same name by James Atkinson; see J.P. Losty, *Calcutta, City of Palaces: A Survey of the City in the Days of the East India Company 1690–1858* (London: The British Library, 1990), p. 8.
13. William Hodges, *Travels in India, during the years 1780–1783* (London: J. Edwards, 1793), p. 16.
14. Fay, *Original Letters from India*, p. 202.
15. Hickey, *Memoirs*, vol. 2, p. 137.
16. Sir John Kaye, 'The English in India – Our Social Morality', *Calcutta Review* 2.1 (May–August 1844), pp. 290–336 (p. 300).
17. Suresh Chandra Ghosh, *The Social Condition of the British Community in Bengal 1757–1800* (Leiden: E.J. Brill, 1970), p. 61, and Thankappan Nair, *A History of the Calcutta Press: The Beginnings* (Calcutta: Firma KLM, 1987), p. 83.
18. See Busteed, *Echoes from Old Calcutta*, pp. 182–3.
19. Busteed, *Echoes from Old Calcutta*, p. 194; Kaye, 'The English in India', p. 314.
20. Nair, *History of the Calcutta Press*, pp. xiii–xv. Despite the unavailability of a daily newspaper until the arrival of the *Bengal Hircarrah* in 1795, Nair describes the arrangement whereby different newspapers were timed to appear on different days of the week, effectively providing a daily coverage (pp. 217–18).
21. Graham Shaw, *Printing in Calcutta to 1800: A Description and a Checklist of Printing in Late 18th-Century Calcutta* (London: Bibliographical Society, 1981), p. 1.
22. Jerome McGann (ed.), *The New Oxford Book of Romantic Period Verse* (Oxford: Oxford University Press, 1993), introduction, p. xxi.
23. Christopher Anstey, *The New Bath Guide; or, Memoirs of the B-----r---d Family, in a series of poetical epistles* (Cambridge: Fletcher & Hodson, 1766).
24. See the account in Shaw, *Printing in Calcutta to 1800*, pp. 48–50.
25. Emily Brittle, *The India Guide; or, Journal of a Voyage to the East Indies, in the year MDCCLXXX, in Poetical Epistle to her Mother* (Calcutta: George Gordon, 1785), p. 14.
26. Balachandra Rajan, 'Feminising the Feminine: Early Women Writers on India', in Richardson and Hofkosh, *Romanticism, Race, and Imperial Culture*, p. 155.
27. Fay, *Original Letters from India*, p. 68, Page numbers for subsequent citations are given in the text.
28. Fay gives a brief account of Ayres up to 1780: a former saddler's apprentice turned highwayman born in London, he was spared the death sentence only on condition he was transported from Britain for life. He sailed to India and resumed his criminal activities there, narrowly escaping several convictions in the Bengal Supreme Court. He fled British Bengal for Mysore in 1773, where Hyder Ali employed him as a mercenary. 'Being a thorough paced villain, he has during these seven years taken the lead in every species of barbarity ... the least punishment inflicted by him was cutting off the noses and ears of those miserable wretches, whose hard fate subjected them to his tyranny' (p. 116).
29. As a woman's captivity narrative, Fay's account is curiously underplayed in Linda Colley's otherwise extensive study of British victimhood in the earlier colonial era, *Captives*, except for a passing reference (p. 277).

30. Grundy, 'The Barbarous Character we Give Them', pp. 76–7.
31. Hodges, *Travels in India*, print facing p. 84; see Teltscher, *India Inscribed*, pp. 37–73 and Lata Mani, *Contentious Traditions: The Debate on Sati in Colonial India* (London: University of California Press, 1998).
32. James Johnson, *The Influence of Tropical Climates on European Constitutions* (London: Thomas & George Underwood, 1827; originally 1813), p. 552 and *The Oriental Voyager; or, Descriptive Sketches and Cursory Remarks, on a Voyage to India and China* (London: James Aspeme, 1807). See Dane Kennedy, 'The Perils of the Midday Sun: Climate Anxieties in the Colonial Tropics', in John M. MacKenzie (ed.), *Imperialism and the Natural World* (Manchester: Manchester University Press, 1990), pp. 118–40.
33. See Blain, 'Phebe Gibbes', in *Feminist Companion to Literature in English*, p. 420.
34. Cited in H.E.A. Cotton and John Macfarlane's edition of Phebe Gibbes, *Hartly House, Calcutta* (Calcutta: Thacker, Spink & Co., 1908), p. 293n.
35. See Felicity Nussbaum, *Torrid Zones: Maternity, Sexuality, and Empire in Eighteenth-Century English Narratives* (London: Johns Hopkins University Press, 1996) and Balachandra Rajan's reading of the novel, 'Feminising the Feminine'.
36. Phebe Gibbes, *Hartly House, Calcutta* (Dublin: William Jones, 1789), p. 1.
37. Gibbes, *Hartly House, Calcutta*, p. 192.
38. Nussbaum, *Torrid Zones*, p. 20.
39. Rajan, 'Feminising the Feminine', p. 154.
40. Franklin, 'Radically Feminising India: Phebe Gibbes' *Hartly House, Calcutta* (1789) and Sydney Owenson's *The Missionary: An Indian Tale* (1811)' in *Romantic Representations of British India*, pp. 154–79 (p. 162). See the comprehensive account of eighteenth-century interracial amatory fiction in Roxan Wheeler, *The Complexion of Race: Categories of Difference in Eighteenth-Century British Culture* (Philadelphia: Pennsylvania University Press, 2000), pp. 138–75.
41. Gibbes, *Hartly House, Calcutta*, p. 8. Page numbers for subsequent citations are given in the text.
42. Nussbaum, *Torrid Zones*, pp. 172, 182.
43. Grundy, 'The Barbarous Character We Give Them', p. 78.
44. Gibbes, *Hartly House, Calcutta*, pp. 22–4.
45. The quotation is from James Thomson, *The Seasons*, 'Summer', ll. 451–3.
46. Gibbes, *Hartly House, Calcutta*, p. 104. Page numbers for subsequent citations are given in the text.
47. Grundy, 'The Barbarous Character We Give Them', p. 80. On the image of rape in colonial discourse, see Jenny Sharpe, *Allegories of Empire: The Figure of Woman in the Colonial Text* (London: Minnesota University Press, 1993).
48. Gibbes, *Hartly House, Calcutta*, p. 292.
49. Elizabeth Hamilton, *Translation of the Letters of a Hindoo Rajah; written previous to, and during the period of his residence in England*, 2 vols. (Dublin: H. Colbert, 1797), vol. 1, preliminary dissertation, xxiv.
50. Grenby, *The Anti-Jacobin Novel*, p. 148n.
51. Susan B. Egenolf, *The Art of Political Fiction in Hamilton, Edgeworth and Owenson* (Farnham: Ashgate, 2009), p. 18.
52. Hamilton, *Translation*, vol. 1, p. x. Page numbers for subsequent citations are given in the text.

53. See Clifford Siskin, 'The Year of the System', in *1798: The Year of The Lyrical Ballads*, ed. Richard Cronin (Basingstoke: Macmillan, 1998), pp. 9–31.
54. Gary Kelly comments on the 'footnote novel' in *Women, Writing and Revolution 1790–1827* (Oxford: Clarendon Press, 1993), p. 16. There is also an extensive secondary literature on the sometimes veiled political function of novels written by women: see Patricia Meyer Spacks, *Desire and Truth: Functions of Plot in Eighteenth-Century English Novels* (London: University of Chicago Press, 1990); Catherine Craft-Fairchild, *Masquerade and Gender: Disguise and Female Identity in Eighteenth-Century Fictions by Women* (University Park, PA: Pennsylvania State University Press, 1993); and Mary Ann Schofield, *Masking and Unmasking the Female Mind: Disguising Romances in Feminine Fiction, 1713–1799* (Newark: University of Delaware Press, 1990).
55. Harriet Guest, *Small Change: Women, Learning, Patriotism, 1750–1810* (London: University of Chicago Press, 2000), p. 329; see also Claudia L. Johnson, *Jane Austen: Women, Politics and the Novel* (London: University of Chicago Press, 1988), where Johnson describes Hamilton as 'ideologically compromised' (p. 9).
56. Colley, *Captives*, p. 304.
57. Hamilton, *Translation*, vol. 1, p. 198.
58. Gary Kelly, *English Fiction of the Romantic Period 1789–1830* (London: Longman, 1989), p. 60.
59. Anne K. Mellor, 'Romantic Orientalism Begins at Home: Elizabeth Hamilton's Translations of the Letters of a Hindoo Rajah', *Studies in Romanticism* 44.2 (Summer 2005), pp. 151–64 (p. 156).
60. Hamilton, *Translation*, vol. 1, p. 135.
61. Hamilton's footnote reads: 'The benevolent reader will be happy to learn from the account of the Rajah ... that the race of peacocks has not been utterly exterminated by the cruel rapacity of the British governors of Bengal! If the misrepresentations of credulity had been always restrained to external objects, their confutation would have been an easy task. But who can follow the historian, who pretends to expose the secret workings of the human mind and pursues the victim of his prejudice [Clive] even to the throne of God!' (Hamilton, *Translation*, vol. 1, p. 135).
62. See, for example, the contesting viewpoints expressed in Sir Philip Francis's anonymous *Observations on Mr. Hastings' Narrative of his Transactions in Banares in the Year 1781* (London: J. Ridgway, 1786) and Hastings' rejoinder, *Memoirs relative to the State of Bengal* (London: John Murray, 1787). Francis was responding to Hastings' earlier *Present State of the East Indies. With Notes by the Editor* (London: John Stockdale, 1786).
63. Hamilton, *Translation*, vol. 1, pp. 127–8).
64. Bayly has written on how Hastings and his circle, of whom Charles and by extension Elizabeth Hamilton herself were very much a part, 'sought to present themselves as inheritors of the Indian polity as refounded by the Emperor Akbar'; see *Empire and Information: Intelligence Gathering and Social Communication in India, 1780–1870* (Cambridge: Cambridge University Press, 1996), p. 52.
65. Hamilton, *Translation*, vol. 1, p. 147. Page numbers for subsequent citations are given in the text.

66. Kelly, *Women, Writing and Revolution*, p. 136; see also Mellor, 'Romantic Orientalism Begins at Home'.
67. Hamilton, *Translation*, vol. 2, p. 110. Page numbers for subsequent citations are given in the text.

Chapter 4

1. See Colin Haydon, S. Taylor, and J. Walsh (eds), *The Church of England 1689–1833: From Toleration to Tractarianism* (Cambridge: Cambridge University Press, 1993) and John Kent, *Wesley and the Wesleyans: Religion in Eighteenth-Century Britain* (Cambridge: Cambridge University Press, 2002).
2. See Hilton, *The Age of Atonement*; Brian Stanley (ed.), *Christian Missions and the Enlightenment* (Cambridge: William B. Eerdmans, 2001); and Stewart J. Brown, *Providence and Empire 1815–1914* (Harlow: Pearson, 2008).
3. Patrick Brantlinger, *Rule of Darkness: British Literature and Imperialism, 1830–1914* (London: Cornell University Press, 1988), p. 200.
4. Alexandra Warwick, 'Colonial Gothic', in Marie Mulvey-Roberts (ed.), *The Handbook to Gothic Literature* (Basingstoke: Palgrave Macmillan, 1998), pp. 261–2. See also Lizabeth Paravisini-Gebert, 'Colonial and Postcolonial Gothic: The Caribbean', in Jerrold E. Hogle (ed.), *The Cambridge Companion to Gothic Fiction* (Cambridge: Cambridge University Press, 2002), pp. 229–57.
5. Massimiliano Demata, 'Discovering Eastern Horrors: Beckford, Maturin and the Discourse of Travel Literature', in William Hughes and Andrew Smith (eds), *Empire and the Gothic: The Politics of Genre* (Basingstoke: Palgrave Macmillan, 2003), p. 21.
6. On the perceptions and realities of *thagi* see Mike Dash, *Thug: The True History of India's Murderous Cult* (London: Granta, 2005) and Kim A. Wagner, *Thuggee: Banditry and the British in Early Nineteenth-Century India* (Basingstoke: Palgrave Macmillan, 2007).
7. Cited in Porter, *Religion versus Empire?*, p. 74.
8. Teignmouth, *Considerations on the Practicability, Policy, and Obligation of Communicating to the Natives of India the Knowledge of Christianity* (London: John Hatchard, 1808), p. 57.
9. Cited in William Wilberforce, *Substance of the Speeches of William Wilberforce, Esq. on the Clause in the East-India Bill for Promoting the Religious Instruction and Moral Improvement of the Natives of the British Dominion in India, on the 22nd of June, and the 1st and 12th of July, 1813* (London: John Hatchard et al., 1813), p. 49.
10. William Ward, *A View of the History, Literature and Religion of the Hindoos: Including a Minute Description of their Manners and Customs, and Translations from their Principal Works*, 4 vols (London: Baptist Missionary Society, 1811), vol. 1, p. 103.
11. See Colin Haydon, *Anti-Catholicism in Eighteenth-Century England, c. 1714–80* (Manchester: Manchester University Press, 1993) and Brian Young, '"The Lust of Empire and Religious Hate': Christianity, History and India, 1790–1820' in Stefan Collini, Richard Whatmore and Brian Young (eds), *History, Religion and Culture: British Intellectual History 1750–1950* (Cambridge: Cambridge University Press, 2000), pp. 91–111. For a consideration of anti-Catholicism

after 1800, see Susan M. Griffin, *Anti-Catholicism and Nineteenth-Century Fiction* (Cambridge: Cambridge University Press, 2004).
12. Portions of this unpublished work appeared in Moor's *Oriental Fragments* (London: Smith, Elder & Co., 1834); see Moor's own account of this putative work, p. 94.
13. Claudius Buchanan, *Christian Researches in Asia: With Notices of the Translation of the Scriptures into the Oriental Languages* (Cambridge: J. Smith, 1811), p. 155.
14. Michel Foucault, *Discipline and Punish: The Birth of the Prison* (London: Penguin, 1991).
15. See Neill, *History of Christianity in India*, pp. 133–55.
16. See Porter, *Religion versus Empire?* and Brian Stanley, *The Bible and the Flag: Protestant Missions and British Imperialism in the Nineteenth and Twentieth Centuries* (London: Apollos, 1990).
17. Charles Grant, *Observations on the State of Society among the Asiatic Subjects of Great Britain, particularly with respect to morals; and on the means of improving it – Written chiefly in the Year 1792* (London, 1813), p. 25.
18. Lord Teignmouth (John Shore), *Memoirs of the Life, Writings, and Correspondence, of Sir William Jones* (London: John Hatchard, 1804), p. 173.
19. Teignmouth, *Memoir*, p. 232.
20. Teignmouth, *Memoir*, p. 370.
21. Teignmouth, *Considerations*, p. 57.
22. James Forbes, *Oriental Memoirs*, 4 vols (London: White & Cochrane, 1813), vol. 4, pp. 276–349. See K.K. Dyson, *A Various Universe: A Study of the Memoirs and Journals of British Men and Women in the Indian Subcontinent, 1765–1856* (New Delhi: Oxford University Press, 1978).
23. Forbes, *Reflections on the Character of the Hindoos: And of the Importance of Converting them to Christianity* (London: White & Cochrane, 1810), p. 28.
24. Jones went so far as to contrast Hindu morality with Christian teaching in a letter to Spencer of 4 September 1787: 'I am no Hindu; but I hold the doctrine of the Hindus concerning a future state to be incomparably more rational, more pious, and more likely to deter men from vice, than the horrid opinions inculcated by Christians on punishments *without end*' (*Letters*, vol. 2, p. 766).
25. Maurice, *Indian Antiquities*, vol. 4, viii.
26. Ward, *View of the History, Literature and Religion of the Hindoos*, introduction, p. 100.
27. See John Sarjent, *Memoir of the Rev. Henry Martyn, B.D. Late Fellow of St John's College, Cambridge, and Chaplain to the Honourable East India Company* (London: J. Hatchard, 1819) and the more recent John R.C. Martyn, *Henry Martyn (1781–1812): Scholar and Missionary to India and Persia* (Lewiston: Edwin Mellen Press, 1999).
28. Martyn, *Journals and Letters*, vol. 1, p. 156.
29. Sarjent, *Memoir of the Rev. Henry Martyn*, p. 132. Reginald Heber, who took his passage to India in 1823, found a much greater receptivity to Christianity among the ship's company, which he ascribed to a generally improved state of morals. See his *Narrative of a Journey through the Upper Provinces of India, from Calcutta to Bombay, 1824–1825*, 3 vols (London: John Murray, 1828), 'Journal of a Voyage to India', vol. 1, xlii.

30. Martyn, *Journals and Letters*, vol. 1, p. 172. Page numbers for subsequent citations are given in the text.
31. Said, *Orientalism*, p. 93.
32. Anon., *A Collection of Voyages and Travels ... from the curious and valuable LIBRARY of the late EARL OF OXFORD*, 2 vols (London: Thomas Osbourne, 1745). Page numbers for subsequent citations are given in the text.
33. Buchanan, *Christian Researches*, pp. 24–7.
34. Buchanan, *Christian Researches*, p. 27.
35. On Southey's involvement with India, see Diego Saglia, '"Words and Things": Southey's East and the Materiality of Oriental Discourse', in Linda Pratt (ed.), *Robert Southey and the Contexts of English Romanticism* (Aldershot: Ashgate, 2006), pp. 167–86 (p. 184); Pratt, 'Southey the Literary East Indiaman', in Franklin (ed.), *Romantic Representations of British India*, pp. 131–53; and Carol Bolton, *Writing the Empire: Robert Southey and Romantic Colonialism* (London: Pickering & Chatto, 2007).
36. Robert Southey, 'Oriental Memoirs', *Quarterly Review* 12 (October 1814–May 1815), pp. 180–227 (p. 196).
37. Southey, 'Periodical Accounts Relative to the Baptist Missionary Society', *Quarterly Review* 1 (May–June 1809), pp. 193–226 (p. 210).
38. Byron referred to the denunciation of Southey in Parliament by the MP William Smith in the preface to *The Vision of Judgement* (1821) and dubbed Southey an 'epic renegade' in the dedication to *Don Juan* (1819–24); see George Gordon, Lord Byron, *Poetical Works*, ed. Frederick Page (Oxford: Oxford University Press, 1970), pp. 156, 635. On Southey's conservatism, see Geoffrey Carnall, *Robert Southey and his Age: The Development of a Conservative Mind* (Oxford: Clarendon Press, 1960) and David M. Craig, *Robert Southey and Romantic Apostasy: Political Argument in Britain, 1780–1840* (Woodridge: Boydell Press, 2007).
39. Southey, *Poetical Works 1793–1810*, gen. ed. Lynda Pratt, vol. 4, *The Curse of Kehama*, ed. Daniel Sanjiv Roberts (London: Pickering & Chatto, 2004), p. 112.
40. Southey, *The Curse of Kehama*, p. 113.
41. Southey, *The Book of the Church*, 2 vols (London: John Murray, 1824), vol. 1, p. 305.
42. Southey, *The Curse of Kehama*, p. 155.
43. Southey, *The Curse of Kehama*, p. 188.
44. Sydney Owenson, Lady Morgan, *The Missionary: An Indian Tale*, 3 vols (London: J.J. Stockdale, 1811), vol. 2, pp. 7–8.
45. See Franklin, 'Radically Feminising India', pp. 166–7.
46. A possible source of information for Morgan was Henry Colebrooke's essay 'On the Duties of a Faithful Hindu Widow', in *Asiatick Researches* 4 (1799), pp. 209–19. Colebrooke relates that 'it is held to be the duty of a widow to burn herself with her husband's corpse, but she has an alternative: "On the death of her husband to live as *Brahmachàrì*, or commit herself to the flames" VISHNU' (p. 213).
47. Morgan, *The Missionary*, vol. 1, pp. 149–50. Page numbers for subsequent citations are given in the text.
48. See Michael J. Franklin, '"Passion's Empire": Sydney Owenson's "Indian Venture", Phoenicianism, Orientalism and Binarism', *Studies in Romanticism* 44.2 (Summer 2006), pp. 181–97 for a consideration of this figure.

49. Maturin's anti-Catholicism complicates Demata's interpretation of *Melmoth the Wanderer* as a critique of English colonialism 'from an Irish perspective'; see Demata, 'Discovering Eastern Horrors', p. 30 and Joseph W. Lew, "Unprepared for Sudden Transformations": Identity and Politics in *Melmoth the Wanderer*', *Studies in the Novel* 26 (Summer 1994), pp. 173–95.
50. Charles Maturin, *Melmoth the Wanderer*, ed. Douglas Grant (Oxford: Oxford University Press, 1998), p. 273. Page numbers for subsequent citations are given in the text.
51. S.T. Coleridge, *Biographia Literaria*, ed. Nigel Leask (London: Everyman, 1997), p. 342. These comments were published in the *Courier*, 29 August and 7, 9–11 September 1816; see Charles I. Patterson, 'The Authenticity of Coleridge's Reviews of Gothic Romance', *Journal of English and Germanic Philology* 50 (1951), pp. 512–21 and Alethea Hayter, 'Coleridge, Maturin's Bertram', in Donald Sultana (ed.), *New Approaches to Coleridge: Biographical and Critical Essays* (London: Vision, 1981), pp. 17–37.
52. Maturin, *Melmoth*, p. 5.
53. Maturin, *Melmoth*, p. 303n.

Chapter 5

1. Stokes, *The English Utilitarians and India*.
2. James Mill, *The History of British India*, ed. Horace Hayman Wilson, 10 vols (London: James Madden, 1858; originally 1817), vol. 2, pp. 35–6.
3. Jones, *Poems*, p. 198. Wilson's 1858 edition of Mill's *History*, in its turn, endeavoured to fight a rearguard action against the Anglicist assertions in the original in the form of an ongoing critical commentary.
4. See St Clair, *The Reading Nation in the Romantic Period*, appendix 9, p. 619.
5. Mill, *History of British India*, vol. 2, p. 347.
6. Javed Majeed, *Ungoverned Imaginings: James Mill's The History of British India and Orientalism* (Oxford: Clarendon Press, 1992), p. 195. Mill's identification of Jones with the British *ancien régime* is highly ironic considering that both men sought East India Company patronage to support themselves financially. Unlike Jones (whose appointment came from the Crown), Mill was rewarded for his Indian scholarship with the post of Assistant Examiner of Correspondence in 1819.
7. Jeremy Bentham, *The Rationale of Reward*, ed. and trans. Richard Smith (London: J. & H.L. Hunt, 1825), p. 206.
8. Majeed, *Ungoverned Imaginings*, pp. 184–5.
9. Cited in Majeed, *Ungoverned Imaginings*, p. 85.
10. Byron, *Poetical Works*, p. 627.
11. Robert Lowth, *Lectures on the Sacred Poetry of the Hebrews*, trans. G. Gregory, 2 vols (London: J. Johnson, 1787), vol. 1, pp. 44–5. Page numbers for subsequent citations are given in the text.
12. For discussions of the sublime in a European context, see Peter De Bolla, *The Discourse of the Sublime: Readings in History, Aesthetics and the Subject* (Oxford: Blackwell, 1989); Frances Ferguson, *Solitude and the Sublime: Romanticism and the Aesthetics of Individuation* (London: Routledge, 1992); Samuel Holt Monk, *The Sublime: A Study of Critical Theories in XVIIIth-Century England* (Ann Arbor, MI: University of Michigan Press, 1960); and Thomas

Weiskel, *The Romantic Sublime: Studies in the Structure and Psychology of Transcendence* (London: Johns Hopkins University Press, 1976).
13. Hugh Blair, *Lectures on Rhetoric and Belles Lettres*, 3 vols (London, 1787), vol. 1, pp. 141–7.
14. Jones, *Works*, vol. 4, p. 112.
15. Jones, *Works*, vol. 4, pp. 211–2.
16. Jones, *Works*, vol. 4, p. 212. See the commentary in Drew, *India and the Romantic Imagination*, pp. 44–82, and Shaffer, *'Kubla Khan'*, pp. 20–22, 116–23.
17. Charles Wilkins, *A Grammar of the Sanskṛita Language* (London: W. Bulmer, 1808), preface.
18. Ward, *View of the History, Literature and Religion of the Hindoos*, vol. 4, p. 374.
19. Charles Stuart, *Vindication of the Hindoos from the Aspersions of the Reverend Claudius Buchanan, M.A. ... By a Bengal Officer* (London: R. and J. Dodwell, 1808), p. 97.
20. *Ibid.*, p. 69.
21. See Nigel Leask, 'Francis Wilford and the Colonial Construction of Hindu Geography', in Amanda Gilroy (ed.), *Romantic Geographies: Discourses of Travel, 1775–1844* (Manchester: Manchester University Press, 2000), pp. 204–22.
22. Friedrich Von Schlegel, *The Aesthetic and Miscellaneous Works*, trans. E.J. Millington (London: Bohn, 1849), p. 522.
23. Schlegel, *Aesthetic and Miscellaneous Works*, p. 526.
24. Cited in Schlegel, *Über die Sprache und Weisheit der Indier*, ed. Sebastiano Timpanaro (Amsterdam: John Benjamins B.V., 1977), p. 29.
25. Schlegel, *Aesthetic and Miscellaneous Works*, pp. 445–9. Page numbers for subsequent citations are given in the text.
26. Inden, *Imagining India*, p. 67.
27. Johannes Fabian, *Time and the Other: How Anthropology Makes its Object* (New York: Columbia University Press, 1983), p. 31. See also Robert Young, *White Mythologies: Writing History and the West* (London: Routledge, 1990), for the role of Hegelian dialectics, particularly 'The Oriental World' section of Hegel's *Philosophy of History* (1830) in bringing about 'the phenomenon of Eurocentrism' (p. 2).
28. Heinrich Heine, *Travel-Pictures: Including The Tour in the Harz, Norderney, and Book of Ideas, together with The Romantic School*, trans. Francis Storr (London: George Bell & Sons, 1887), p. 245. Despite this apparent scepticism for Hindu culture, Heine nevertheless published three sonnets inspired by *Sakuntala* in 1824.
29. Schlegel, *Aesthetic and Miscellaneous Works*, p. 499.
30. Schlegel, *Aesthetic and Miscellaneous Works*, p. 526.
31. Schwab, *Oriental Renaissance*, p. 18.
32. Martin Bernal, *Black Athena: The Afroasiatic Roots of Classical Civilisation*, 2 vols (London: Free Association Books, 1987), vol. 1, pp. 230–6.
33. Cited in Majeed, *Ungoverned Imaginings*, p. 122.
34. Mill, *History of British India*, vol. 1, xxiii.
35. Mill, *History of British India*, vol. 2, pp. 34–5.
36. Majeed, *Ungoverned Imaginings*, p. 195.

37. Mill, *History of British India*, vol. 2, pp. 35–6. Page numbers for subsequent citations are given in the text.
38. Philip Connell, *Romanticism, Economics and the Question of 'Culture'* (Cambridge: Cambridge University Press, 2001), p. 11.
39. On the complex interrelation of colonial politics and educational curricula, particularly regarding the study of English literature, see Harish Trivedi, *Colonial Transactions*, and Gauri Viswanathan, *Masks of Conquest: Literary Study and British Rule in India* (New Delhi: Oxford University Press, 1998).
40. Macaulay, 'Minute on Indian Education', cited in Barbara Harlow and Mia Carter (eds), *Imperialism and Orientalism: A Documentary Sourcebook* (Oxford: Blackwell, 1999), p. 58.
41. Wordsworth, *Poetical Works*, p. 735.
42. Coleridge, *Lectures 1809–1819 on Literature*, ed. R.A. Foakes, 2 vols, in *Collected Works of Samuel Taylor Coleridge* (London: Routledge & Kegan Paul, 1987–), vol. 2, p. 192.
43. On Coleridge's year in Germany, see Shaffer, *'Kubla Khan'*, pp. 20–3.
44. Coleridge, *Biographia Literaria*, pp. 232–3.
45. Coleridge, *Collected Works*, vol. 5b, p. 191.
46. *Ibid.*
47. Makdisi, *Romantic Imperialism*, p. 12.
48. Marilyn Butler, *Romantics, Rebels and Reactionaries: English Literature and its Background 1760–1830* (Oxford: Oxford University Press, 1981), pp. 64–8.
49. Morton, *Poetics of Spice*, p. 86. There is an extensive secondary literature on attitudes to consumerism in this period, including Neil McKendrick, John Brewer and J.H. Plumb, *The Birth of a Consumer Society: The Commercialisation of Eighteenth-Century England* (Bloomington: University of Indiana Press, 1982); Colin Campbell, *The Romantic Ethic and the Spirit of Modern Consumerism* (Oxford: Basil Blackwell, 1987); John Brewer and Roy Porter (eds), *Consumption and the World of Goods* (London: Routledge, 1992); James Walvin, *Fruits of Empire: Exotic Produce and British Taste, 1660–1800* (New York: New York University Press, 1997) and Maxine Berg and Elizabeth Eger (eds), *Luxury in the Eighteenth Century: Debates, Desires and Delectable Goods* (Basingstoke: Palgrave Macmillan, 2003).
50. Byron, *Letters and Journals*, ed. Leslie A. Marchand, 13 vols (London: John Murray, 1973–94), vol. 3, p. 101; Leask, *British Romantic Writers and the East*, p. 14.
51. Southey, *The Curse of Kehama*, preface.
52. *Ibid.*
53. Fulford writes on the persistent difficulty of Indian subject matter, despite Jones's 'relative tact'; see 'Plants, Pagodas and Penises' in Pratt (ed.), *Robert Southey and the Contexts of English Romanticism*, pp. 187–201 (p. 194).
54. Anon, 'The Curse of Kehama', *Monthly Mirror* 9 (February 1811), pp. 122–35, cited in Lionel Madden (ed.), *Robert Southey: The Critical Heritage* (London: Routledge & Kegan Paul, 1972), p. 133.
55. Madden, *Robert Southey*, pp. 133–4.
56. *Critical Review* 22 (March 1811), cited in Madden, *Robert Southey*, p. 136.
57. John Foster, 'The Curse of Kehama', *Eclectic Review* 7.1 (January–June 1811), pp. 183–205 and 334–50 (p. 205).
58. *Ibid.*, p. 186.

59. 'The Curse of Kehama', *Quarterly Review* 5 (August 1810), pp. 40–61, 54–5, 61.
60. Thomas Moore, *Poetical Works*, 10 vols (London: Longman, Orme, Brown, Green & Longmans, 1841), vol. 6, preface.
61. *Ibid.*
62. Francis Jeffrey, 'Lalla Rookh', *Edinburgh Review* 21.57 (November 1817), pp. 1–35 (p. 1).
63. Moore, *Poetical Works*, vol. 6, preface.
64. Byron, *Poetical Works*, p. 277.
65. Mohammed Sharafuddin, *Islam and Romantic Orientalism: Literary Encounters with the Orient* (London: I.B. Tauris, 1994), p. 172.
66. Leask, *British Romantic Writers and the East*, p. 113. Majeed notes that Moore, despite his nationalism, urged Irish Catholics to participate in the British constitution in his *Letter to the Roman Catholics of Dublin* (1810); see *Ungoverned Imaginings*, pp. 90–1.
67. Moore, *Poetical Works*, vol. 6, preface.
68. Jeffrey Vail, 'Thomas Moore in Ireland and America: The Growth of a Poet's Mind', *Romanticism* 10. 1 (2004), pp. 41–61 (p. 52).
69. 'Lalla Rookh', *The British Critic* 7 (January–June 1817), pp. 604–16 (p. 610).
70. Moore, *Poetical Works*, preface.
71. Sharafuddin, *Islam and Romantic Orientalism*, p. 141.
72. Moore, *Poetical Works*, vol. 6, p. 25.
73. Leask, *British Romantic Writers and the East*, p. 112.
74. Moore, *Poetical Works*, vol. 6, pp. 146–8. Page numbers for subsequent citations are given in the text.
75. Sharafuddin, *Islam and Romantic Orientalism*, p. 212.
76. Moore, *Poetical Works*, vol. 7, p. 69.
77. Jeffrey, 'Lalla Rookh', p. 2. Page numbers for subsequent citations are given in the text.
78. The reference is to Terence's aphorism, '*Homo sum: humani nil a me alienum puto*' ('I am a man: nothing that is human is foreign to me').

Epilogue

1. Michael J. Sandel, *Liberalism and the Limits of Justice* (Cambridge: Cambridge University Press, 1998).
2. Michael Walzer, *Spheres of Justice: A Defence of Pluralism and Equality* (Oxford: Martin Robertson, 1983), p. 28.
3. Onora O'Neill, 'Transnational Justice', in David Held (ed.), *Political Theory Today* (Cambridge: Polity Press, 1991).
4. Martha Nussbaum, *Poetic Justice: The Literary Imagination and Public Life* (London: Beacon, 1997).

Sources

I. Manuscript

Walpole, Horace, 'Book of Materials', 3 vols. (1759–86)

II. Primary Sources (Periodicals)

Anon., 'The Curse of Kehama', *Monthly Mirror* 9 (February 1811), 122–35
Anon., 'First Establishment of a Press in Calcutta', *Friend of India* 9.1 (26 February 1835), 1
Asiatic Miscellany, consisting of Translations, Imitations, Fugitive Pieces, Original Productions, and Extracts from Curious Publications. By W. Chambers, Esq. and Sir W. Jones, Judges of the Supreme Court of Judicature, at Fort William in Bengal, and other literary gentlemen, now resident in India, vols. 1–2 (Calcutta: Daniel Stuart, 1785; Calcutta: William Makay, 1786), vol. 3 (London: J. Wallis, 1787) and *The New Asiatic Miscellany. Consisting of Original Essays, Translations, and Fugitive Pieces* (Calcutta: Joseph Cooper, 1789)
Asiatic(k) Researches; or, Transactions of the Society, Instituted in Bengal, for Inquiring into the History and Antiquities, the Arts, Sciences, and Literature, of Asia, 20 vols (Calcutta: Manuel Cantopher, 1788–1836)
Bengal Gazette 48.1 (16–22 December 1780)
Calcutta Gazette; or, Oriental Advertiser. Published by Authority 1.2 (11 March 1784)
Foster, John, 'The Curse of Kehama', *Eclectic Review* 7.1 (January–June 1811), 183–205 and 334–50
Jeffrey, Francis, 'Lalla Rookh', *Edinburgh Review* 21.57 (November 1817), 1–35
Kaye, Sir John, 'The English in India – Our Social Morality', *Calcutta Review* 2.1 (May–August 1844), 290–336
Parsons, John, 'The Asiatic Miscellany, Nos I. and II.', *Monthly Review* 76 (January–June 1787), 480–4
Southey, Robert, 'Buchanan's Journey through Mysore, Canara, and Malabar', *Annual Review* 6 (1808), 49–61
—— 'Periodical Accounts Relative to the Baptist Missionary Society', *Quarterly Review* 1 (May–June 1809), 193–226
—— 'Oriental Memoirs', *Quarterly Review* 12 (Oct 1814–May 1815), 180–227
Town and Country Magazine; or, Universal Repository of Knowledge, Instruction, and Entertainment 8 (July 1776)
Wollstonecraft, Mary, 'Sacontalá; or, The Fatal Ring', *Analytical Review* 7 (1790), 361–73
World 1.1 (15 October 1791)

III. Primary Sources (Books)

Anon., *Arabian Nights Entertainments: consisting of One Thousand and One Stories told by the Sultaness of the Indies ... Translated into French from the Arabian MSS, by M. Galland, of the Royal Academy; and now done into English from the last Paris edition*, 6 vols (London: J. Osborne & T. Longman, 1725)

Anon., *A Collection of Voyages and Travels, Consisting of Authentic Writers in our own Tongue, which have not before been collected in English, or have been abridged in other Collections ... From the curious and valuable LIBRARY of the late EARL OF OXFORD*, 2 vols (London: Thomas Osbourne, 1745)

Anon. (ed.), *Dissertations and Miscellaneous Pieces relating to the History and Antiquities, the Arts, Sciences, and Literature of Asia. By Sir W. Jones ... and others* (Dublin: P. Byrne & W. Jones, 1793)

Anon., *The History of the Trial of Warren Hastings, Esq.* (London: Debrett, Vernor & Hood, 1796)

Anon., *The Trial of Warren Hastings, Esq., Complete from February 1788, to June 1794; with a Preface* (London: J. Owen, 1794)

Anstey, Christopher, *The New Bath Guide; or, Memoirs of the B——r--d Family, in a series of poetical epistles* (Cambridge: Fletcher & Hodson, 1766)

Beattie, James, *Elements of Moral Science*, 2 vols (Edinburgh: T. Cadell, 1790–93), vol.1, p. 180

Jeremy Bentham, *The Rationale of Reward*, ed. and trans. Richard Smith (London: J. & H.L. Hunt, 1825)

Bernier, François, *Histoire de la dernière révolution des États du Gran Mogol*, 4 vols (Paris: Claude Barbin, 1670–1)

Blair, Hugh, *Lectures on Rhetoric and Belles Lettres*, 3 vols (London: A. Strahan & T. Cadell, 1787; originally 1783)

Blake, William, *Poetry and Prose*, ed. Geoffrey Keynes (London: Nonesuch Press, 1948)

Bond, E.A. (ed.), *Speeches of the Managers and Counsel in the Trial of Warren Hastings*, 4 vols (London: Longman et al., 1859–61)

Brittle, Emily, *The India Guide; or, Journal of a Voyage to the East Indies, in the year MDCCLXXX, in Poetical Epistle to her Mother* (Calcutta: George Gordon, 1785)

Broome, Ralph, *Letters from Simpkin the Second to his Dear Brother in Wales; Containing a Humble Description of the Trial of Warren Hastings, Esq. With Simon's Answer* (London: J. Bell, 1788)

Bryant, Jacob, *A New System; or, An Analysis of Ancient Mythology: wherein an attempt is made to divest Tradition of Fable; and to reduce the Truth to its Original Purity*, 2 vols (London: T. Payne, 1774)

Buchanan, Claudius, *The Star in the East: A Sermon, preached in the parish-church of St. James, Bristol, on Sunday, Feb. 26, 1809, for the benefit of the "Society for Missions to Africa and the East"* (London: Longman, 1809)

—— *Christian Researches in Asia: with Notices of the Translation of the Scriptures into the Oriental Languages* (Cambridge: J. Smith, 1811)

—— *Colonial Ecclesiastical Establishment: being a Brief View of the State of the Colonies of Great Britain, and of her Asiatic Empire, in respect to Religious Instruction* (London: Cadell & Davies, 1813)

—— *Apology for Promoting Christianity in India: containing two letters, addressed to the Honourable East India Company, concerning the idol Juggernaut* (London: Cadell & Davies, 1813)

Burke, Edmund, *Writing and Speeches*, general ed. Paul Langford, 9 vols (Oxford: Clarendon Press, 1981)

—— *Correspondence*, ed. Thomas W. Copeland, 10 vols (Cambridge: Cambridge University Press, 1958–78)

—— *A Philosophical Enquiry into the Origin of our Ideas of the Sublime and the Beautiful*, ed. Adam Philips (Oxford: Oxford University Press, 1990)

—— *Reflections on the Revolution in France and on the Proceedings in Certain Societies in London relative to that Event*, ed. Conor Cruise O'Brien (London: Penguin, 1969)

Burney, Fanny, *Diary and Letters of Madame D'Arblay (1778–1840)*, ed. Charlotte Barrett, 6 vols (London: Macmillan, 1905)

Byron, Lord (George Gordon), *Poetical Works*, ed. Frederick Page, rev. John Jump (Oxford: Oxford University Press, 1970)

—— *Letters and Journals*, ed. Leslie A. Marchand, 13 vols (London: John Murray, 1973–94)

Campbell, Thomas, *The Pleasures of Hope; with other Poems* (Edinburgh: Mundell & Son, 1799)

Coleridge, Samuel Taylor, *The Collected Works*, ed. Kathleen Coburn and Bart Winer, 16 vols (London: Routledge & Kegan Paul, 1969–)

—— *Collected Letters*, ed. Earl Leslie Griggs, 6 vols (Oxford: Oxford University Press, 2000)

—— *Biographia Literaria*, ed. Nigel Leask (London: Everyman, 1997)

Colman, George, 'the elder', *Dramatick Works*, 4 vols (London: T. Beckett, 1778)

Cowper, William, *Poetical Works* (London: William Tegg, 1858)

Daniell, Thomas and William Daniell, *A Picturesque Voyage to India; by the Way of China* (London: Longman et al., 1810)

—— *Oriental Scenery* (London: Longman et al., 1812)

Davy, William and Joseph White (trans.) *Institutes Political and Military written originally in the Mogul Language by the Great Timur* (Oxford: Clarendon Press, 1783)

Dow, Alexander, *Tales, Translated from the Persian of Inatullah of Delhi*, 2 vols (London: T. Becket & P.A. De Hondt, 1768)

—— *The History of Hindostan, from the Death of Akbar, to the Complete Settlement of the Empire under Aurungzebe. To which are prefixed, I. A Dissertation on the Origin and Nature of Despotism in Hindostan. II. An Enquiry into the State of Bengal; with a Plan for Restoring that Kingdom to its former Prosperity and Splendour*, 3 vols (London: T. Beckett & P.A. De Hondt, 1773)

Fay, Eliza, *Original Letters from India (1779–1815)*, ed. E.M. Forster (London: Hogarth Press, 1925)

Fenwick, Eliza, *Secresy; or, The Ruin on the Rock*, ed. Gina Luria (London: Garland, 1974),

Ferguson, Adam, *An Essay on the History of Civil Society*, ed. Fania Oz Salzberger (Cambridge: Cambridge University Press, 1995)

Foote, Samuel, *The Nabob: A Comedy, in Three Acts* (London: Coleman, 1778)

Forbes, James, *Reflections on the Character of the Hindoos: and of the Importance of Converting them to Christianity* (London: White & Cochrane, 1810)
—— *Oriental Memoirs*, 4 vols (London: White & Cochrane, 1813)
Francis, Sir Philip, *Observations on Mr. Hastings' Narrative of his Transactions in Banares in the Year 1781* (London: J. Ridgway, 1786)
Gerard, Alexander, *An Essay on Taste* (London: A. Millar, 1759)
Gibbes, Phebe, *Hartly House, Calcutta* (Dublin: William Jones, 1789)
—— *Hartly House, Calcutta*, ed. H.E.A. Cotton and John Macfarlane (Calcutta: Thacker, Spink & Co., 1908)
Gibbon, Edward, *The History of the Decline and Fall of the Roman Empire*, ed. David Womersley, 3 vols (London: Penguin, 1994)
Gladwin, Francis (trans.), *Ayeen Akbery; or, The Institutes of the Emperor Akber*, 2 vols (London: G. Auld, 1800)
Goldsmith, Oliver, *Works*, ed. Peter Cunningham, 4 vols (London: John Murray, 1854)
Grant, Charles, *Observations on the State of Society among the Asiatic Subjects of Great Britain, particularly with respect to Morals; and on the Means on Improving it. – Written chiefly in the Year 1792* (London, 1813)
Halhed, Nathaniel, *A Grammar of the Bengal Language* (Hoogly: [Charles Wilkins] 1778)
Hamilton, Charles, *An Historical Relation of the Origin, Progress, and Final Dissolution of the Government of the Rohilla Afghans in the Northern Provinces of Hindostan* (London, 1787)
—— *The Hedàya; or, Guide: A Commentary on the Mussulman Laws: translated by order of the Governor General and council of Bengal by Charles Hamilton*, 4 vols (London: T. Bensley, 1791)
Hamilton, Elizabeth, *Translation of the Letters of a Hindoo Rajah; written previous to, and during the period of his residence in England*, 2 vols (Dublin: H. Colbert, 1797)
—— *Letters on the Elementary Principles of Education*, 2 vols (Alexandria: Cottom & Stewart, 1803; originally *Letters on Education*, 1801)
Hardy, Thomas, *The Return of the Native*, ed. George Woodcock (London: Penguin, 1978; originally 1878)
Hastings, Warren, *The Present State of the East Indies. With Notes by the Editor* (London: John Stockdale, 1786)
—— *Memoirs relative to the State of Bengal* (London: John Murray, 1787)
Hazlitt, William, *The Spirit of the Age: or Contemporary Portraits* (London: Henry Colburn, 1825)
Heber, Reginald, *Narrative of a Journey through the Upper Provinces of India, from Calcutta to Bombay, 1824–1825*, 3 vols (London: John Murray, 1828)
Hegel, G.W.F., *Lectures on the Philosophy of History*, ed. C.J. Friedrich, trans. J. Sibree (New York: Dover, 1956)
Heine, Heinrich, *Travel-Pictures: including The Tour in the Harz, Norderney, and Book of Ideas, together with The Romantic School*, trans. Francis Storr (London: George Bell & Sons, 1887)
Hickey, William, *Memoirs*, ed. Alfred Spencer, 4 vols (London: Hurst & Blackett, 1913)
Hodges, William, *Travels in India, during the years 1780–1783* (London: J. Edwards, 1793)

Hume, David, *A Treatise of Human Nature*, ed. P.H. Nidditch and L.A. Selby-Bigge (Oxford: Clarendon Press, 1978)
—— *Enquiry Concerning Human Understanding*, ed. P.H. Nidditch and L.A. Selby-Bigge (Oxford: Clarendon Press, 1975)
—— *Selected Essays*, ed. Stephen Copley and Andrew Edgar (Oxford: Oxford University Press, 1996)
Hutcheson, Francis, *Essay on the Nature and Conduct of the Passions. With Illustrations on the Moral Sense* (London: S. Powell, 1728)
Jones, Sir William, *Works, with the Life of the Author*, ed. John Shore, Lord Teignmouth, 13 vols (London: John Stockdale, 1807)
—— *Selected Poetical and Prose Works*, ed. Michael J. Franklin (Cardiff: University of Wales Press, 1995)
—— *Letters*, ed. Garland Cannon, 2 vols (Oxford: Clarendon Press, 1970)
—— *Histoire de Nader Shah connu sous le nom de Thahmas Kuli Khan, Empreur de Perse, traduite d'un manuscript Persan* (London: P. Elmsly, 1770)
—— *A Grammar of the Persian Language* (London: W. and J. Richardson, 1771)
—— *Poems, consisting chiefly of translations from the Asiatick Languages. To Which are Added, Two Essays, I. On the Poetry of the Eastern Nations. II. On the Arts, commonly called Imitative* (Oxford: Clarendon Press, 1772)
Jones, Sir William, *Sacontalá; or, The Fatal Ring; An Indian Drama by Cálidás: translated from the original Sanscrit and Prácrit* (Calcutta: Joseph Cooper, 1789)
Johnson, James, *The Oriental Voyager; or, Descriptive Sketches and Cursory Remarks, on a Voyage to India and China* (London: James Aspeme, 1807)
—— *The Influence of Tropical Climates on European Constitutions* (London: Thomas & George Underwood, 1827)
Kames, Lord (Henry Home), *Elements of Criticism*, 2 vols (Edinburgh: Millar, Kincaid & Bell, 1762)
—— *Sketches on the History of Man*, 2 vols (Edinburgh: W. Creech, 1774)
Lewis, M.G., *Rivers; or, the East Indian: A Comedy in Five Acts* (Dublin: P. Wogan et al., 1800)
Lowell, Thomas Jackson, *India: Land of the Black Pagoda* (London: Hutchinson, 1931)
Lowth, Robert, *Lectures on the Sacred Poetry of the Hebrews*, trans. G. Gregory, 2 vols (London: J. Johnson, 1787)
Lyttelton, Lord George, *Letters from a Persian in England, to his Friend in Ispahan* (London: J. Millan, 1735)
Macaulay, Thomas Babington, *Critical and Historical Essays Contributed to the Edinburgh Review* (London: Longman, Green & Co., 1877)
Mackenzie, Henry, *The Man of Feeling*, ed. Brian Vickers (London: Oxford University Press, 1967)
Martyn, Henry, *Journals and Letters*, ed. S. Wilberforce, 2 vols (London: R.B. Seeley & W. Burnside, 1837)
Marx, Karl and Friedrich Engels, *Articles on Britain* (Moscow: Progress, 1971)
Maturin, Charles, *Melmoth the Wanderer*, ed. Douglas Grant, intro. Chris Baldick (Oxford: Oxford University Press, 1998)
Maurice, Thomas, *Indian Antiquities; or, Dissertations, relative to the Ancient Geographical Divisions, the Pure System of Primeval Theology, the Grand Code of Civil Laws, the Original Form of Government, the Widely-Extended Commerce, and the Various and Profound Literature, of Hindostan: compared, throughout, with the*

Religion, Laws, Government, and Literature, of Persia, Egypt, and Greece, 7 vols (London: H.L. Galabin, 1800)
McGann, Jerome (ed.), *The New Oxford Book of Romantic Period Verse* (Oxford: Oxford University Press, 1993)
Mill, James, *The History of British India*, ed. Horace Hayman Wilson, 10 vols (London: James Madden, 1858)
Montesquieu, Charles-Louis de Secondat, Baron de, *Persian Letters*, ed. and trans. C.J. Betts (London: Penguin, 1977)
—— *The Spirit of the Laws*, trans. Anne M. Cohler, Basia Carolyn Miller and Harold Samuel Stone (Cambridge: Cambridge University Press, 2000)
Moor, Edward, *The Hindu Pantheon* (London: J. Johnson, 1810)
—— *Hindu Infanticide: An Account of the Measures Adopted for Suppressing the Practice of the Systematic Murder by their Parents of Female Infants* (London: J. Johnson, 1811)
—— *Oriental Fragments* (London: Smith & Elder, 1834)
Moore, Thomas, *Poetical Works*, 10 vols (London: Longman, Orme, Brown, Green & Longmans, 1841)
Morgan, Lady (Sydney Owenson), *The Missionary: An Indian Tale*, 3 vols (London: J.J. Stockdale, 1811)
—— *Luxima, The Prophetess: A Tale of India* (London: Charles Westerton, 1859)
Orme, Robert, *A History of the Military Transactions of the British Nation in Indostan, from the Year MDCCXLV*, 3 vols (London: John Nourse, 1773; originally 1768)
Pasquin, Anthony, i.e. John Williams, *Authentic Memoirs of Warren Hastings, Esq, late Governor-General of Bengal, with Strictures on the Management of his Impeachment: to which is added, an Examination into the Causes of the Alarm in the Empire* (London: J. Bew, 1793)
Payne Knight, Richard, *An Analytical Inquiry into the Principles of Taste* (London: C. Mercier, 1805)
—— *An Inquiry into the Symbolic Language of Ancient Art and Mythology* (London: A.J. Valpy, 1818)
Pitt, William, 'the elder', First Earl of Chatham, *Correspondence*, ed. W.S. Taylor and J.H. Pringle, 4 vols (London: John Murray, 1839–40)
Raynal, Abbé Guillaume Thomas François et al., *Philosophical and Political History of the Settlements and Trade of the Europeans in the East and West Indies*, trans. J.O. Justamond, 8 vols (London: A. Strahan & T. Cadell, 1788)
Richardson, Joseph, *The Rolliad, in Two Parts: Probationary Odes for the Laureatship; and Miscellanies: with Criticism and Illustrations* (London: J. Ridgway, 1795)
Robertson, William, *An Historical Disquisition concerning the Knowledge which the Ancients had of India* (London: A. Strahan & T. Cadell, 1791)
[Rudd, Margaret], *The Belle Widows: with Characteristic Sketches of Real Personages and Living Characters. A Novel, inscribed to the Beau Monde*, 2 vols (London: J. Kerby, 1789)
Ryves, Elizabeth, *The Hastiniad; An Historic Poem, in Three Cantos* (London: J. Debrett, 1785)
Sarjent, John, *Memoir of the Rev. Henry Martyn, B.D. Late Fellow of St John's College, Cambridge, and Chaplain to the Honourable East India Company* (London: J. Hatchard, 1819)
Schlegel, Friedrich Von, *The Aesthetic and Miscellaneous Works*, trans. E.J. Millington (London: Bohn, 1849)

—— *Über die Sprache und die Weisheit der Indier*, ed. Sebastiano Timpanaro (Amsterdam: John Benjamins B.V., 1977)
Shelley, Percy Bysshe, *A Philosophical View of Reform*, ed. T.W. Rolleston (London: Oxford University Press, 1920)
Sherwood, Mary Martha, *The Indian Pilgrim; or, The Progress of the Pilgrim Nazareenee from the City of the Wrath of God to the City of Mount Zion. Delivered under the Similitude of a Dream* (London: Houlston & Wright, 1858)
Smith, Adam, *The Theory of Moral Sentiments*, ed. D.D. Raphael and A.L. Macfie (Oxford: Clarendon Press, 1976)
Southey, Robert and Richard Duppa, *Letters from England: by Don Manuel Alavarez Espriella. Translated from the Spanish*, ed. Jack Simmons (London: Cresset Press, 1951)
Southey, Robert, *Poetical Works 1793–1810*, ed. Lynda Pratt, 5 vols (London: Pickering & Chatto, 2004)
—— *The Curse of Kehama* (London: Longman et al., 1810)
—— *The Book of the Church*, 2 vols (London: John Murray, 1824)
—— *Essays, Moral and Political*, 2 vols (London: John Murray, 1832)
Stevens, George Alexander, *Songs, Comic and Satyrical* (London, 1788)
Stockdale, J.J. (ed.), *The History of the Inquisitions; including the Secret Transactions of those Horrific Tribunals* (London: J.J. Stockdale, 1810)
Stuart, Charles, *Vindication of the Hindoos from the Aspersions of the Reverend Claudius Buchanan, M.A. ... By a Bengal Officer* (London: R. and J. Dodwell, 1808)
Tavernier, Jean-Baptiste, *Six Voyages de J.B. Tavernier ... en Turquie, en Perse at aux Indes*, 2 vols (Paris, 1676)
Teignmouth, Lord (John Shore), *Memoirs of the Life, Writings, and Correspondence, of Sir William Jones* (London: John Hatchard, 1804)
—— *Considerations on the Practicability, Policy, and Obligation of Communicating to the Natives of India the Knowledge of Christianity* (London: John Hatchard, 1808)
Tickell, Richard, *Songs, Duos, Trios, Choruses, &c. in the Comic Opera of the Carnival of Venice* (London, 1781)
Touchstone, Timothy, *Tea and Sugar; or, The Nabob and the Creole; A Poem, in Two Cantos* (London: J. Ridgway, 1792)
Tod, James, *Annals and Antiquities of Rajast'han, or the Central and Western Rajpoot States of India*, 2 vols (London: Smith, Elder, Calkin & Budd, 1829–32)
Volney, Constantin François, *The Ruins: or, A Survey of the Revolutions of Empires* (London: J. Johnson, 1792)
Walpole, Horace, *Correspondence*, ed. W.S. Lewis, 48 vols (New Haven: Yale University Press, 1937–83)
—— *A Letter from Xo Ho, a Chinese Philosopher at London, to his Friend Lien Chi at Peking* (London: N. Middleton, 1757)
Ward, William, *A View of the History, Literature and Religion of the Hindoos; including a Minute Description of their Manners and Customs, and Translations from their Principal Works*, 4 vols (London: Baptist Missionary Society, 1811)
Wilberforce, William, *Substance of the Speeches of William Wilberforce, Esq. on the Clause in the East-India Bill for Promoting the Religious Instruction and Moral Improvement of the Natives of the British Dominion in India, on the 22nd of June, and the 1st and 12th of July, 1813* (London: John Hatchard et al., 1813)

Wilkins, Charles, *The Bhăgvăt-Gēētă; or, Dialogues of Krĕĕshnă and Ărjŏŏn; in eighteen lectures; with notes* (London: C. Nourse, 1785)
—— *A Grammar of the Sanskrĭta Language* (London: W. Bulmer, 1808)
Wilks, Mark, *Historical Sketches of the South of India, in an Attempt to Trace the History of Mysore; from the Origin of the Hindoo Government of that State, to the Extinction of the Mohammedan Dynasty in 1799*, 3 vols (London: Longman et al., 1810–17)
Wordsworth, William, *Poetical Works*, ed. Thomas Hutchinson and Ernest de Selincourt (London: Oxford University Press, 1966).

IV. Secondary Sources (Articles)

Cannon, Garland, 'Sir William Jones and Edmund Burke', *Modern Philology* 54 (1957), 165–86
—— 'Sir William Jones and Dr Johnson's Literary Club', *Modern Philology* 63.1 (1965), 20–37
—— 'Sir William Jones and the New Pluralism over Language and Cultures', *The Yearbook of English Studies* 28 (1998), 128–43
Canter, H.V., 'The Impeachments of Verres and Hastings: Cicero and Burke', *Classical Journal* 9 (1914), 199–211
De Bruyn, Frances, 'Edmund Burke's Gothic Romance: The Portrayal of Warren Hastings in Burke's Writings and Speeches on India', *Criticism* 29.4 (1987), 415–438
Franklin, Michael J., '"Passion's Empire" Sydney Owenson's "Indian Venture", Phoenicianism, Orientalism and Binarism', *Studies in Romanticism* 44.2 (Summer 2006), 181–97
Grundy, Isobel, "The Barbarous Character we Give Them': White Women Report on Other Races', *Studies in Eighteenth-Century Culture* 22 (1992), 73–86
Koeppel, E., 'Shelley's *Queen Mab* and Sir William Jones's *The Palace of Fortune*', *Englische Studien* 28 (1900), 43–53
Lawson, Philip and Jim Phillips, "Our Execrable Banditti': Perceptions of Nabobs in Mid-Eighteenth Century Britain', *Albion* 16.3 (1984), 225–41
Lew, Joseph W., "Unprepared for Sudden Transformations": Identity and Politics in *Melmoth the Wanderer*', *Studies in the Novel* 26 (Summer 1994), 173–95
Marshall, P.J., 'The Moral Swing to the East: British Humanitarianism, India and the West Indies', *Caribbean Societies* II, Collected Seminar Papers 34 (London: Institute of Commonwealth Studies, 1985), 13–20
Mellor, Anne K., 'Romantic Orientalism Begins at Home: Elizabeth Hamilton's *Translation of the Letters of a Hindoo Rajah*', *Studies in Romanticism* 44.2 (Summer 2005), 151–64
Patterson, Charles I., 'The Authenticity of Coleridge's Reviews of Gothic Romance', *Journal of English and Germanic Philology* 50 (1951), 512–21
Phillips, Mark Salber, 'Relocating Inwardness: Historical Distance and the Transition from Enlightenment to Romantic Historiography', *PMLA* 118.3 (2003), 436–49
Radner, John B., 'The Art of Sympathy in Eighteenth-Century Moral Thought', *Studies in Eighteenth-Century Culture* 9 (1979), 189–210

Sitter, Zak, 'William Jones, "Eastern" Poetry, and the Problem of Imitation', *Texas Studies in Literature and Language* 50.4 (Winter 2008), 385–407
Sharpe, Jenny, 'The Violence of Light in the Land of Desire; or, How William Jones Discovered India', *Boundary 2*, 20.1 (Spring 1993), 26–46
Vail, Jeffrey, 'Thomas Moore in Ireland and America: the Growth of a Poet's Mind', *Romanticism* 10.1 (2004), 41–61
White, Stephen K., 'Burke on Politics, Aesthetics, and the Dangers of Modernity', *Political Theory* 21.3 (August 1993), 507–27
Wood, Neal, 'The Aesthetic Dimensions of Burke's Political Thought', *Journal of British Studies* 4.1 (November 1964), 41–64

V. Secondary Sources (Books)

Abrams, M.H., *The Mirror and the Lamp: Romantic Theory and the Critical Tradition* (New York: Oxford University Press, 1953)
Ahmad, Aijaz, *In Theory: Classes, Nations, Literatures* (London: Verso, 1992)
Arberry, A.J., *Asiatic Jones: The Life and Influence of Sir William Jones (1746–1794), Pioneer of Indian Studies* (London: Longmans, Green & Co., 1946)
Armitage, David, *The Ideological Origins of the British Empire* (Cambridge: Cambridge University Press, 2000)
Baldwin, Anna and Sarah Hutton, *Platonism and the English Imagination* (Cambridge: Cambridge University Press, 1994)
Ballaster, Ros, *Fabulous Orients: Fictions of the East in England, 1662–1785* (Oxford: Oxford University Press, 2005)
Ballhatchet, Kenneth and John Harrison (eds), *East India Company Studies: Papers Presented to Professor Cyril Philips* (Hong Kong: Asian Research Service, 1986)
Barfoot, C.C. and Theo D'haen (eds), *Oriental Prospects: Western Literature and the Lure of the East* (Amsterdam: Rodopi, 1998)
Barker, Francis, Peter Hulme, Margaret Iversen and Diana Loxley (eds), *The Politics of Theory: Conference on the Sociology of Literature: Papers* (Colchester: University of Essex, 1983)
—— *Europe and its Others: Proceedings of the Essex Conference on the Sociology of Literature July 1984*, 2 vols (Colchester: University of Essex, 1985)
—— *Literature, Politics and Theory: Conference Papers, 1976–84* (London: Methuen, 1986)
Barrell, John, *The Infection of Thomas De Quincey: A Psychopathology of Imperialism* (London: Yale University Press, 1991)
Bayly, C.A., *Indian Society and the Making of the British Empire* (Cambridge: Cambridge University Press, 1988)
—— *Imperial Meridian: The British Empire and the World 1780–1830* (London: Longman, 1989)
—— *Empire and Information: Intelligence Gathering and Social Communication in India, 1780–1870* (Cambridge: Cambridge University Press, 1996)
—— *The Birth of the Modern World 1780–1914: Global Connections and Comparisons* (Oxford: Blackwell, 2004)
Bence-Jones, Mark, *Clive of India* (London: Constable, 1974)
Benjamin, Walter, *Illuminations*, ed. Hannah Arendt, trans. Harry Zohn (New York: Shocken Books, 1969)

Berg, Maxine and Elizabeth Eger (eds), *Luxury in the Eighteenth Century: Debates, Desires and Delectable Goods* (Basingstoke: Palgrave Macmillan, 2003)
Bernal, Martin, *Black Athena: The Afroasiatic Roots of Classical Civilisation*, 2 vols (London: Free Association Books, 1987)
Berry, Christopher J., *Social Theory of the Scottish Enlightenment* (Edinburgh: Edinburgh University Press, 1997)
Bhabha, Homi K., *The Location of Culture* (London: Routledge, 1994)
Blain, Virginia, Patricia Clements and Isobel Grundy (eds), *The Feminist Companion to Literature in English: Women Writers from the Middle Ages to the Present* (London: B.T. Batsford, 1990)
Bolton, Carol, *Writing the Empire: Robert Southey and Romantic Colonialism* (London: Pickering & Chatto, 2007)
Bourdieu, Pierre, *Distinction: A Social Critique of the Judgement of Taste* (London: Routledge & Kegan Paul, 1986)
Brantlinger, Patrick, *Rule of Darkness: British Literature and Imperialism, 1830–1914* (London: Cornell University Press, 1988)
Breckenridge, Carol A. and Peter van der Veer (eds), *Orientalism and the Postcolonial Predicament: Perspectives on South Asia* (Philadelphia: University of Pennsylvania Press, 1993)
Brewer, John, *The Sinews of Power: War, Money and the English State, 1688–1783* (London: Unwin Hyman, 1989)
Brewer, John and Roy Porter (eds), *Consumption and the World of Goods* (London: Routledge, 1992)
Bromwich, David, *On Empire, Liberty and Reform: Speeches and Letters: Edmund Burke* (New Haven: Yale University Press, 2000)
Brown, Stewart J. (ed.), *William Robertson and the Expansion of Empire* (Cambridge: Cambridge University Press, 1997)
—— *Providence and Empire 1815–1914* (Harlow: Pearson, 2008)
Busteed, H.E., *Echoes from Old Calcutta: Being Chiefly Reminiscences of the Days of Warren Hastings, Francis and Impey* (London: W. Thacker, 1908)
Butler, Marilyn, *Romantics, Rebels and Reactionaries: English Literature and its Background 1760–1830* (Oxford: Oxford University Press, 1981)
Campbell, Colin, *The Romantic Ethic and the Spirit of Modern Consumerism* (Oxford: Basil Blackwell, 1987)
Cannon, Garland, *The Life and Mind of Oriental Jones. Sir William Jones, the Father of Modern Linguistics* (Cambridge: Cambridge University Press, 1990)
Cannon, Garland and Kevin R. Brine (eds), *Objects of Enquiry: The Life, Contributions, and Influences of Sir William Jones (1746–1794)* (London: New York University Press, 1995)
Carey, Brycchan and Peter Kitson, *Slavery and the Cultures of Abolition: Essays Marking the British Abolition Act of 1807* (Woodbridge: Boydell & Brewer, 2007)
Carnall, Geoffrey, *Robert Southey and his Age: The Development of a Conservative Mind* (Oxford: Clarendon Press, 1960)
Carnall, Geoffrey and Colin Nicholson (eds), *The Impeachment of Warren Hastings: Papers from the Bicentenary Commemoration* (Edinburgh: Edinburgh University Press, 1989)
Chakrabarty, Dipesh, *Provincialising Europe: Postcolonial Thought and Historical Difference* (Oxford: Princeton University Press, 2000)

Chakravarty, Gautam, *The Indian Mutiny and the British Imagination* (Cambridge: Cambridge University Press, 2005)
Chatterjee, Amal, *Representations of India, 1740–1840: The Creation of India in the Colonial Imagination* (London: Macmillan, 1998)
Clarke, J.J., *Oriental Enlightenment: The Encounter between Asian and Western Thought* (London: Routledge, 1997)
Clery, E.J. and Robert Miles (eds), *Gothic Documents: A Sourcebook, 1700–1820* (Manchester: Manchester University Press, 2000)
Cohn, Bernard S., *Colonialism and its Forms of Knowledge: The British in India* (Princeton, NJ: Princeton University Press, 1997)
Colley, Linda, *Britons: Forging the Nation, 1707–1837* (London: Pimlico, 2003)
—— *Captives: Britain, Empire and the World, 1600–1850* (London: Jonathan Cape, 2002)
Collingham, E.M., *Imperial Bodies: The Physical Experience of the Raj, c.1800–1947* (Cambridge: Polity Press, 2001)
Collini, Stefan, Richard Whatmore and Brian Young (eds), *History, Religion and Culture: British Intellectual History 1750–1950* (Cambridge: Cambridge University Press, 2000)
Connell, Philip, *Romanticism, Economics and the Question of 'Culture'* (Oxford: Oxford University Press, 2001)
Congar, Syndy McMillan (ed.), *Sensibility in Transformation: Creative Resistance to Sentiment from the Augustans to the Romantics* (London: Associated University Press, 1994)
Craft-Fairchild, Catherine, *Masquerade and Gender: Disguise and Female Identity in Eighteenth-Century Fictions by Women* (University Park, PA: Pennsylvania State University Press, 1993)
Craig, David M., *Robert Southey and Romantic Apostasy: Political Argument in Britain, 1780–1840* (Woodridge: Boydell Press, 2007)
Cronin, Richard (ed.), *1798: The Year of the Lyrical Ballads* (Basingstoke: Macmillan, 1998)
Dalrymple, William, *White Mughals: Love and Betrayal in Eighteenth-Century India* (London: HarperCollins, 2002)
Dash, Mike, *Thug: The True History of India's Murderous Cult* (London: Granta, 2005)
Davis, Richard H., *Lives of Indian Images* (Princeton, NJ: Princeton University Press, 1997)
De Bolla, Peter, *The Discourse of the Sublime: Readings in History, Aesthetics and the Subject* (Oxford: Blackwell, 1989)
Dirks, Nicholas B., *The Scandal of Empire: India and the Creation of Imperial Britain* (London: Harvard University Press, 2006)
Drew, John, *India and the Romantic Imagination* (Delhi: Oxford University Press, 1987)
Dyson, K.K., *A Various Universe: A Study of the Journals of the Memoirs and Journals of British Men and Women in the Indian Subcontinent, 1765–1856* (New Delhi: Oxford University Press, 1978)
Edwardes, Michael, *The Nabobs at Home* (London: Constable, 1991)
Egenolf, Susan B., *The Art of Political Fiction in Hamilton, Edgeworth and Owenson* (Farnham: Ashgate, 2009)

Ellis, Markman, *The Politics of Sensibility: Race, Gender and Commerce in the Sentimental Novel* (Cambridge: Cambridge University Press, 1996)
Fabian, Johannes, *Time and the Other: How Anthropology Makes its Object* (New York: Columbia University Press, 1983)
Ferguson, Frances, *Solitude and the Sublime: Romanticism and the Aesthetics of Individuation* (London: Routledge, 1992)
Festa, Lynn, *Sentimental Figures of Empire in Eighteenth-Century Britain and France* (Baltimore, MD: Johns Hopkins University Press, 2006)
Ford, Alan, *James Ussher: Theology, History, and Politics in Early Modern Ireland and England* (Oxford: Oxford University Press, 2007)
Foucault, Michel, *Discipline and Punish: The Birth of the Prison* (London: Penguin, 1991)
Franklin, Michael J. (ed.), *The European Discovery of India: Key Indological Sources of Romanticism*, 6 vols (London: Ganesha Publishing/Edition Synapse, 2001)
—— (ed.) *Romantic Representations of British India* (London: Routledge, 2006)
Fulford, Tim and Peter Kitson (eds), *Romanticism and Colonialism: Writing and Empire, 1780–1830* (Cambridge: Cambridge University Press, 1998)
Furniss, Tom, *Edmund Burke's Aesthetic Ideology: Language, Gender, and Political Economy in Revolution* (Cambridge: Cambridge University Press, 1993)
George, M.D. (ed.), *Catalogue of Personal and Political Satires in the British Museum*, 12 vols (London: British Museum, 1870–1949)
Ghosh, Suresh Chandra, *The Social Condition of the British Community in Bengal 1757–1800* (Leiden: E.J. Brill, 1970)
Gibbons, Luke, *Edmund Burke and Ireland: Aesthetics, Politics and the Colonial Sublime* (Cambridge: Cambridge University Press, 2003)
Gilroy, Amanda (ed.), *Romantic Geographies: Discourses of Travel, 1775–1844* (Manchester: Manchester University Press, 2000)
Grenby, M.O., *The Anti-Jacobin Novel: British Conservatism and the French Revolution* (Cambridge: Cambridge University Press, 2001)
Griffin, Susan M., *Anti-Catholicism and Nineteenth-Century Fiction* (Cambridge: Cambridge University Press, 2004)
Guest, Harriet, *Small Change: Women, Learning, Patriotism, 1750–1810* (London: University of Chicago Press, 2000)
Guillory, John, *Cultural Capital: The Problem of Literary Canon Formation* (London: University of Chicago Press, 1993)
Hall, Catherine (ed.), *Cultures of Empire: Colonizers in Britain and the Empire in the Nineteenth and Twentieth Centuries. A Reader* (Manchester: Manchester University Press, 2000)
Harlow, Barbara and Mia Carter (eds), *Imperialism and Orientalism: A Documentary Sourcebook* (Oxford: Blackwell, 1999)
Haydon, Colin, *Anti-Catholicism in Eighteenth-Century England, c.1714–80* (Manchester: Manchester University Press, 1993)
Haydon, Colin, S. Taylor, and J. Walsh (eds), *The Church of England 1689–1833: From Toleration to Tractarianism* (Cambridge: Cambridge University Press, 1993)
Held, David (ed.), *Political Theory Today* (Cambridge: Polity Press, 1991)
Hilton, Boyd, *The Age of Atonement: The Influence of Evangelicalism on Social and Economic Thought, 1785–1865* (Oxford: Clarendon Press, 1988)
Hogle, Jerrold E. (ed.), *The Cambridge Companion to Gothic Fiction* (Cambridge: Cambridge University Press, 2002)

Holzman, James M., *The Nabobs in England: A Study of the Returned Anglo-Indian, 1760–1785* (New York, 1926)
Hughes, William and Andrew Smith (eds), *Empire and the Gothic: The Politics of Genre* (Basingstoke: Palgrave Macmillan, 2003)
Hulme, Peter, *Colonial Encounters: Europe and the Native Caribbean, 1492–1797* (London: Methuen, 1986)
Inden, Ronald, *Imagining India* (London: Hurst, 2000)
Johns, Alessa (ed.), *Dreadful Visitations: Confronting National Catastrophe in the Age of Enlightenment* (New York: Routledge, 1999)
Johnson, Claudia L., *Jane Austen: Women, Politics and the Novel* (London: University of Chicago Press, 1988)
—— *Equivocal Beings: Politics, Gender and Sentimentality in the 1790s. Wollstonecraft, Radcliffe, Burney, Austen* (London: Chicago University Press, 1996)
Jones, Chris, *Radical Sensibility: Literature and Ideas in the 1790s* (London: Routledge, 1993)
Kabbani, Rana, *Imperial Fictions: Europe's Myths of Orient* (London: Macmillan, 1986)
Kaul, R.K., *Studies in Sir William Jones: An Interpreter of Oriental Literature* (Shimla: Indian Institute of Advanced Study, 1995)
Keay, John, *India Discovered: The Recovery of a Lost Civilisation* (London: HarperCollins, 2001)
Keen, Paul, *The Crisis of Literature in the 1790s: Print Culture and the Public Sphere* (Cambridge: Cambridge University Press, 1999)
Kelly, Gary, *English Fiction of the Romantic Period 1789–1830* (London: Longman, 1989)
—— *Women, Writing and Revolution 1790–1827* (Oxford: Clarendon Press, 1993)
Kent, John, *Wesley and the Wesleyans: Religion in Eighteenth-Century Britain* (Cambridge: Cambridge University Press, 2002)
Kilgour, Maggie, *The Rise of the Gothic Novel* (London: Routledge, 1995)
King, Richard, *Orientalism and Religion: Postcolonial Theory, India and 'The Mystic East'* (London: Routledge, 1999)
Kitson, Peter, *Romantic Literature, Race, and Colonial Encounter* (New York: Palgrave, 2007)
Kramnick, Isaac, *The Rage of Edmund Burke: Portrait of an Ambivalent Conservative* (New York: Basic Books, 1977)
Kopf, David, *British Orientalism and the Bengal Renaissance: The Dynamics of Indian Modernisation 1773–1835* (Berkeley and Los Angeles: University of California Press, 1969)
Lamb, Jonathan, *Preserving the Self in the South Seas* (Chicago: Chicago University Press, 2001)
—— *The Evolution of Sympathy in the Long Eighteenth Century* (London: Pickering & Chatto, 2009)
Lawson, Sir Charles, *The Private Life of Warren Hastings, First Governor-General of India* (London: Swan Sonnenschein, 1895)
Leask, Nigel, *The Politics of Imagination in Coleridge's Critical Thought* (London: Macmillan, 1992)
—— *British Romantic Writers and the East: Anxieties of Empire* (Cambridge: Cambridge University Press, 1992)

—— *Curiosity and the Aesthetics of Travel Writing: 'From an Antique Land'* (Oxford: Oxford University Press, 2002)
Lock, F.P., *Edmund Burke: Volume I, 1730–1784* and *Volume II, 1784–97* (Oxford: Clarendon Press, 1998, 2006)
Losty, J.P., *Calcutta, City of Palaces: A Survey of the City in the Days of the East India Company 1690–1858* (London: The British Library, 1990)
MacKenzie, John M. (ed.), *Imperialism and the Natural World* (Manchester: Manchester University Press, 1990)
—— *Orientalism: History, Theory and the Arts* (Manchester: Manchester University Press, 1995)
Madden, Lionel (ed.), *Robert Southey: The Critical Heritage* (London: Routledge & Kegan Paul, 1972)
Majeed, Javed, *Ungoverned Imaginings: James Mill's The History of British India and Orientalism* (Oxford: Clarendon Press, 1992)
Makdisi, Saree, *Romantic Imperialism: Universal Empire and the Culture of Modernity* (Cambridge: Cambridge University Press, 1998)
Mani, Lata, *Contentious Traditions: The Debate on Sati in Colonial India* (London: University of California Press, 1998)
Manuel, Frank E., *The Eighteenth Century Confronts the Gods* (Cambridge, MA: Harvard University Press, 1959)
Marshall, David, *The Figure of Theatre: Shaftesbury, Defoe, Adam Smith, and George Eliot* (New York: Columbia University Press, 1985)
—— *The Surprising Effects of Sympathy: Marivaux, Diderot, Rousseau and Mary Shelley* (London: Chicago University Press, 1988)
Marshall, P.J., *The Impeachment of Warren Hastings* (Oxford: Oxford University Press, 1965)
—— *The British Discovery of Hinduism* (Cambridge: Cambridge University Press, 1970)
—— *'A Free though Conquering People': Britain and Asia in the Eighteenth Century* (London: King's College London, 1981)
—— *Bengal: The British Bridgehead – Eastern India, 1740–1828* (Cambridge: Cambridge University Press, 1987)
Marshall, P.J. and Glyndwr Williams, *The Great Map of Mankind: British Perceptions of the World in the Age of Enlightenment* (London: Dent, 1982)
Martyn, John R.C., *Henry Martyn (1781–1812): Scholar and Missionary to India and Persia* (Lewiston: Edwin Mellen Press, 1999)
Matthew, H.C.G. and Brian Harrison (eds), *Oxford Dictionary of National Biography* (Oxford: Oxford University Press, 2004)
McCalman, Iain (gen. ed.), *An Oxford Companion to the Romantic Age* (Oxford: Oxford University Press, 1999)
McGann, Jerome, *The Poetics of Sensibility: A Revolution in Literary Style* (Oxford: Clarendon Press, 1996)
—— (ed.), *The New Oxford Book of Romantic Period Verse* (Oxford: Oxford University Press, 1993)
McKendrick, Neil, John Brewer and J.H. Plumb, *The Birth of a Consumer Society: The Commercialisation of Eighteenth-Century England* (Bloomington: University of Indiana Press, 1982)
Mehta, Uday Singh, *Liberalism and Empire: A Study in Nineteenth-Century British Liberal Thought* (London: University of Chicago Press, 1999)

Mercer, Philip, *Sympathy and Ethics: A Study of the Relationship between Sympathy and Morality with Special Reference to Hume's* Treatise (Oxford: Clarendon Press, 1972)
Metcalf, Thomas R., *Ideologies of the Raj* (Cambridge: Cambridge University Press, 1995)
Miles, Robert, *Gothic Writing 1750–1820: A Genealogy* (London: Routledge, 1993)
Mitter, Partha, *Much Maligned Monsters: A History of European Responses to Indian Art* (Chicago: Chicago University Press, 1992)
Monk, Samuel Holt, *The Sublime: A Study of Critical Theories in XVIIIth-Century England* (Ann Arbor, MI: University of Michigan Press, 1960)
Moore-Gilbert, Bart (ed.), *Writing India 1757–1990: The Literature of British India* (Manchester: Manchester University Press, 1996)
Morton, Tim, *The Poetics of Spice: Romantic Consumerism and the Exotic* (Cambridge: Cambridge University Press, 2000)
Mukherjee, S.N., *Sir William Jones: A Study in Eighteenth-Century British Attitudes to India* (Cambridge: Cambridge University Press, 1968)
Mullan, John, *Sentiment and Sociability: The Language of Feeling in the Eighteenth Century* (Oxford: Clarendon Press, 1988)
Mulvey-Roberts, Marie (ed.), *The Handbook to Gothic Literature* (Basingstoke: Palgrave Macmillan, 1998)
Muthu, Sankar, *Enlightenment against Empire* (Oxford: Princeton University Press, 2003)
Nair, P. Thankappan, *A History of the Calcutta Press: The Beginnings* (Calcutta: Firma KLM, 1987)
Nandy, Ashis, *The Intimate Enemy: Loss and Recovery of Self under Colonialism* (New Delhi: Oxford University Press, 1988)
Nehru, Jawaharlal, *The Discovery of India* (London: Meridian, 1945)
Neill, Stephen, *A History of Christianity in India 1707–1858* (Cambridge: Cambridge University Press, 1985)
Nixon, Thomas, *From Passions to Emotions: The Creation of a Secular Psychological Category* (Cambridge: Cambridge University Press, 2003)
Norman, Edward, *Anti-Catholicism in Victorian England* (London: Allen & Unwin, 1968)
Nussbaum, Felicity, *Torrid Zones: Maternity, Sexuality, and Empire in Eighteenth-Century English Narratives* (London: Johns Hopkins University Press, 1996)
Nussbaum, Martha, *Poetic Justice: The Literary Imagination and Public Life* (London: Beacon, 1997)
O'Brien, Conor Cruise, *The Great Melody: A Thematic Biography and Commented Anthology of Edmund Burke* (London: Chicago University Press, 1992)
O'Brien, Karen, *Narratives of Enlightenment: Cosmopolitan History from Voltaire to Gibbon* (Cambridge: Cambridge University Press, 1997)
Parry, Graham, *The Trophies of Time: English Antiquarians of the Seventeenth Century* (Oxford: Oxford University Press, 1996)
Philips, C.H., *The East India Company 1784–1834* (Manchester University Press, 1961)
Phillips, Mark Salber, *Society and Sentiment: Genres of Historical Understanding* (Princeton, NJ: Princeton University Press, 2000)
Plasa, Carl, *Textual Politics from Slavery to Postcolonialism: Race and Identification* (London: Macmillan, 2000)

Pocock, J.G.A., *Barbarism and Religion*, 4 vols (Cambridge: Cambridge University Press, 1999–2005)
Porter, Andrew, *Religion versus Empire? British Protestant Missionaries and Overseas Expansion, 1700–1914* (Manchester: Manchester University Press, 2004)
Pratt, Lynda (ed.), *Robert Southey and the Contexts of English Romanticism* (Aldershot: Ashgate, 2006)
Pratt, Mary Louise, *Imperial Eyes: Travel Writing and the Transculturation* (London: Routledge, 1992)
Prickett, Stephen, *Romanticism and Religion: The Tradition of Coleridge and Wordsworth in the Victorian Church* (Cambridge: Cambridge University Press, 1976)
Punter, David, *The Literature of Terror: A History of Gothic Fictions from 1765 to the Present Day* (London: Longmans, 1980)
Raven, James, *Judging New Wealth: Popular Publishing and Responses to Commerce in England, 1750–1800* (Oxford: Clarendon Press, 1992)
Raven, James and Antonia Forster, *The English Novel 1770–1829: A Bibliographical Survey of the Fiction Published in the British Isles*, 2 vols (Oxford: Oxford University Press, 2000)
Richardson, Alan, and Sonia Hofkosh (eds), *Romanticism, Race, and Imperial Culture, 1780–1834* (Bloomington: Indiana University Press, 1996)
Robinson, Nicholas K., *Edmund Burke: A Life in Caricature* (New Haven: Yale University Press, 1996)
Rocher, Rosane, *Orientalism, Poetry and the Millennium: The Checkered Life of Nathaniel Brassey Halhed 1751–1830* (Delhi: Motilal Banarsidass, 1983)
Roger Lewis, William (ed.), *The Oxford History of the British Empire*, 5 vols (Oxford: Oxford University Press, 1998–99)
Rousseau, G.S. and Roy Porter (eds), *Exoticism in the Enlightenment* (Manchester: Manchester University Press, 1990)
Roy, Parama, *Indian Traffic: Identities in Question in Colonial and Postcolonial India* (London: California University Press, 1988)
Ryan, Robert, *The Romantic Reformation: Religious Politics in English Literature, 1789–1824* (Cambridge: Cambridge University Press, 1997)
Said, Edward W., *Orientalism* (London: Penguin, 1995 [1978])
—— *Culture and Imperialism* (London: Chatto & Windus, 1993)
Sandel, Michael J., *Liberalism and the Limits of Justice* (Cambridge: Cambridge University Press, 1998)
Scarry, Elaine, *The Body in Pain: The Making and Unmaking of the World* (Oxford: Oxford University Press, 1985)
Schofield, Mary Ann, *Masking and Unmasking the Female Mind: Disguising Romances in Feminine Fiction, 1713–1799* (Newark: University of Delaware Press, 1990)
Schwab, Raymond, *Oriental Renaissance: Europe's Rediscovery of India and the East, 1680–1880*, trans. Gene Patterson-Black and Victor Reinking (New York: Columbia University Press, 1984)
Sedgwick, Eve Kosofsky, *The Coherence of Gothic Conventions* (London: Methuen, 1996)
Seeley, J.R., *The Expansion of England*, ed. John Gross (London: University of Chicago Press, 1971)
Semmell, Bernard, *The Rise of Free Trade Imperialism: Classical Political Economy, the Empire of Free Trade and Imperialism 1750–1850* (Cambridge: Cambridge University Press, 1970)

Sen, Sudipta, *Distant Sovereignty: National Imperialism and the Origins of British India* (London: Routledge, 2002)
Shaffer, Elinor, *'Kubla Khan' and The Fall of Jerusalem: The Mythological School in Biblical Criticism and Secular Literature* (Cambridge: Cambridge University Press, 1975)
Sharafuddin, Mohammed, *Islam and Romantic Orientalism: Literary Encounters with the Orient* (London: I.B. Tauris, 1994)
Sharpe, Jenny, *Allegories of Empire: The Figure of Woman in the Colonial Text* (London: Minnesota University Press, 1993)
Shaw, Graham, *Printing in Calcutta to 1800: A Description and a Checklist of Printing in late 18th-century Calcutta* (London: Bibliographical Society, 1981)
Smith, Olivia, *The Politics of Language* (Oxford: Clarendon Press, 1984)
Sontag, Susan, *Regarding the Pain of Others* (London: Hamish Hamilton, 2003)
Spacks, Patricia Meyer, *Desire and Truth: Functions of Plot in Eighteenth-Century English Novels* (London: University of Chicago Press, 1990)
Spear, Percival, *The Nabobs: A Study in the Social Life of the English in Eighteenth-Century India* (New Delhi: Oxford University Press, 1998)
Spear, Percival and Romila Tharpur, *A History of India*, 2 vols (London: Penguin, 1965–66)
Speck, W.A., *Robert Southey: Entire Man of Letters* (New Haven: Yale University Press, 2006)
Spivak, Gayatri Chakravorty, *In Other Worlds: Essays in Cultural Politics* (London: Routledge, 1987)
Stanley, Brian, *The Bible and the Flag: Protestant Missions and British Imperialism in the Nineteenth and Twentieth Centuries* (London: Apollos, 1990)
—— (ed.) *Christian Missions and the Enlightenment* (Cambridge: William B. Eerdmans, 2001)
St Clair, William, *The Reading Nation in the Romantic Period* (Cambridge: Cambridge University Press, 2004)
Stokes, Eric, *The English Utilitarians and India* (New Delhi: Oxford University Press, 1989)
Sudani, Rajana, *Fair Exotics: Xenophobic Subjects in English Literature, 1720–1850* (Philadelphia: University of Pennsylvania Press, 2002)
Sugirtharajah, Sharada, *Imagining Hinduism: A Postcolonial Perspective* (London: Routledge, 2003)
Suleri, Sara, *The Rhetoric of English India* (London: Chicago University Press, 1992)
Sultana, Donald (ed.), *New Approaches to Coleridge: Biographical and Critical Essays* (London: Vision, 1981)
Sutherland, Lucy S., *The East India Company in Eighteenth-Century Politics* (Oxford: Clarendon Press, 1952)
Teltscher, Kate, *India Inscribed: European and British Writing on India 1600–1800* (New Delhi: Oxford University Press, 1995)
Todd, Janet, *Sensibility: An Introduction* (London: Methuen, 1986).
Travers, Robert, *Ideology and Empire in Eighteenth-Century India* (Cambridge: Cambridge University Press, 2007)
Trivedi, Harish, *Colonial Transactions: English Literature and India* (Manchester: Manchester University Press, 1995)
Van Sant, Anne Jessie, *Eighteenth-century Sensibility and the Novel: The Senses in a Social Context* (Cambridge: Cambridge University Press, 1993)

Viswanathan, Gauri, *Masks of Conquest: Literary Study and British Rule in India* (New Delhi: Oxford University Press, 1998)
Wagner, Kim A., *Thuggee: Banditry and the British in Early Nineteenth-Century India* (Basingstoke, Palgrave Macmillan, 2007)
Waldron, Jeremy (ed.), *'Nonsense Upon Stilts': Bentham, Burke and Marx on the Rights of Man* (London: Methuen, 1987)
Walvin, James, *Slaves and Slavery: The British Colonial Encounter* (Manchester: Manchester University Press, 1992)
—— *Fruits of Empire: Exotic Produce and British Taste, 1660–1800* (New York: New York University Press, 1997)
—— *Black Ivory: A History of British Slavery* (London: HarperCollins, 2002)
Walzer, Michael, *Spheres of Justice: A Defence of Pluralism and Equality* (Oxford: Martin Robertson, 1983)
Warraq, Ibn, *Defending the West: A Critique of Edward Said's* Orientalism (London: Prometheus Books, 2007)
Watt, James, *Contesting the Gothic: Fiction, Genre and Cultural Conflict, 1764–1832* (Cambridge: Cambridge University Press, 1999)
Weiskel, Thomas, *The Romantic Sublime: Studies in the Structure and Psychology of Transcendence* (London: Johns Hopkins University Press, 1976)
Wheeler, Roxan, *The Complexion of Race: Categories of Difference in Eighteenth-Century British Culture* (Philadelphia: Pennsylvania University Press, 2000)
Whelan, Frederick G., *Edmund Burke and India: Political Morality and Empire* (Pittsburgh: University of Pittsburgh Press, 1996)
Wilson, Kathleen, *The Sense of the People: Politics, Culture and Imperialism in England, 1715–1785* (Cambridge: Cambridge University Press, 1998)
—— (ed.) *A New Imperial History: Culture, Identity, and Modernity in Britain and the Empire, 1660–1840* (Cambridge: Cambridge University Press, 2004)
Wright, Julia M. *Ireland, India, and Nationalism in Nineteenth-Century Literature* (Cambridge: Cambridge University Press, 2007)
Wyse Jackson, Patrick, *The Chronologers' Quest: The Search for the Age of the Earth* (Cambridge: Cambridge University Press, 2006)
Yamanaka, Yuriko, and Tetsuo Nishio (eds), *The Arabian Nights and Orientalism: Perspectives from East and West* (London: I.B. Tauris, 2006)
Young, Robert J.C., *White Mythologies: Writing History and the West* (London: Routledge, 1990)
—— *Postcolonialism: An Historical Introduction* (Oxford: Blackwell, 2001)

Index

Akbar, (Mughal Emperor), 110
Alam II, Shah (Mughal Emperor), 7
Ali, Hyder, 98, 99
Anstey, Christopher, 96
Arabian Nights Entertainments, 24, 66–67, 152–153
Asiatic(k) Researches (1788–1833), 9, 70, 72, 86, 95
Asiatic Society of Bengal, 9, 22, 56, 70, 85, 119, 146
Aurangzeb (Mughal Emperor), 157
Austen, Jane, 87, 125

Barry, James, 30–31
Beattie, James, 13
Beckford, William, 118, 161
Bentham, Jeremy, 141–142, 150
Bernier, François, 91, 126
Blair, Hugh, 144
Bombay, 8, 13
Bonaparte, Napoleon, 13, 139
'Brittle, Emily', 96–97
Brontë, Charlotte, 118
Broome, Ralph, 52
Bruton, William, 126
Bryant, Jacob, 68–69, 128
Buchanan, Claudius, 23, 120–121, 125–128, 130, 137, 145
Burke, Edmund, 25, 68, 117, 165–167
  British India, speeches on, 20–21, 32, 33, 38–43, 63
  Hastings, Warren, trial of, 43–51, 54
  life, 32–33
  Philosophical Enquiry (1757), 20, 27, 29–30, 49, 54
  Reflections, 31–32, 113
  rhetoric, 27, 31, 32, 41, 43
  satire against, 31, 43, 50, 51–54, 113
Burke, William, 28
Burney, Charles, 77
Burney, Fanny, 27, 45–46
Busteed, H.E., 23, 96

Byron, George Gordon (Lord), 24, 141, 142–143, 153–154, 156–157, 159, 161, 163–164

Calcutta, 9, 12, 15, 22–23, 52, 56, 70, 75, 89, 92–97, 98, 101–103, 107, 110–11, 120, 124, 136
  'Black Hole' of, 10
Campbell, Thomas
  Pleasures of Hope (1799), 3–6, 7
Catholicism, 117, 120–121, 128–129, 130, 133–136, 138–139, 148
Chalmers, Alexander, 22, 67
Christianity, 67–68, 72, 89, 106, 108, 110, 114–6, 117, 119, 121–124, 126, 128, 132–133, 136, 146, 162
  see also Catholicism
  see also evangelicalism
Clapham Sect, 11, 21, 23–24, 119, 121, 124
climate, 15, 22–23, 61–62, 86, 87–93, 97–101, 104–6, 110, 112, 116
Clive, Robert, 12, 35, 36, 109, 155
Colebrooke, Henry, 121
Coleridge, Samuel Taylor, 7, 10, 13, 138, 142, 147, 151–153, 155
Cornwallis, Lord, 8, 13, 55
Cowper, William, 34
Czartoryski, Adam, 69

Daniell, Thomas and William Daniell, 93
Daula, Siraj-ud, 93
despotism, 1, 4, 6, 8, 38, 46–47, 58, 61, 91, 109, 130, 167
Diderot, Denis, 12
Dow, Alexander, 1, 65, 157

East India Company, 1, 6–7, 15, 20–21, 24, 26, 28, 38, 41, 60, 88, 101, 108, 111, 124
  Charter of 1813, 21, 119

East India Company – *continued*
  criticism of, 5, 11, 20–21, 29, 34, 39, 126
  diwani (1765), granted over Bengal, Bihar and Orissa, 7
  evangelicalism, 8, 11, 21, 23–25, 107, 115–116, 117–126, 131, 134, 139, 140, 145–146, 154, 165–166
  exoticism, 3, 6–7, 14, 19, 24, 35, 42, 139, 142, 149, 153–154, 156, 166–167

Famine, Bengal (1769–70), 1, 12–13, 75–76
Fay, Eliza, 23
  Original Letters (1779–1815), 87, 97–101
Fazl, Abu'l, 110
Fenwick, Eliza, 36
Foote, Samuel
  Nabob, the (1772), 37–38
Forbes, James, 121–123, 128
Forster, E.M., 87
Foster, John, 155
Francis, Sir Philip, 28, 52
French Revolution, 3, 26, 89
  see also Jacobinism

Gibbes, Phebe, 23, 101
  Hartly House, Calcutta (1789), 101–5
Gibbon, Edward, 14, 35–36, 57, 149
Gilchrist, John, 124
Gillray, James, 43, 46, 89
Gladwin, Francis, 70, 73, 96
Goethe, Johann Wolfgang von, 83
Goldsmith, Oliver, 65, 109
gothic mode, 23–24, 27, 50, 112, 117–119, 124–125, 133–135, 138–139, 140, 151, 166
Grant, Charles, 11, 121
Gray, Thomas, 65

Halhed, Nathaniel Brassey, 9, 69
Hamilton, Charles, 9, 89, 105, 107
Hamilton, Elizabeth, 105, 108, 117
  Translation of the Letters of a Hindoo Rajah (1789), 6, 31, 89, 105–116, 117, 141
Hardy, Thomas, 28

Hastings, Warren
  accusations against, 28, 46–47, 47–48, 50
  Governor-General of India, as, 8, 54, 93, 95, 96, 106, 109, 113
  patronage, 10, 55
  trial of, 1, 21–22, 26, 43–46, 52, 54, 165
heathenism, 21, 24, 79, 119, 122, 124–125, 129, 135, 137, 166, 168
Heine, Heinrich, 148
Hickey, William, 11–12, 93
Hicky, James, 95–96
Hinduism, 6, 21, 70–75, 76–77, 79, 80, 82, 85, 103, 106, 110–111, 116, 117–120, 121–126, 128–130, 132–135, 138–139, 141, 145, 147–148, 151, 154
Hodges, William, 93, 99
Hume, David, 3, 16–17, 89, 113, 165, 167
Hutcheson, Francis, 15, 167

India
  conversion to Christianity, 119–121, 129, 131, 135, 162
  cultural difference, 10, 15, 19–20, 39, 41–42, 72, 100, 115, 132, 148, 154, 165
  distance from Britain, 2, 14–15, 20, 25–26, 39, 41–43, 48, 119
  moral condition of, 11, 23–24, 93–95, 113, 118–121, 139–140, 146, 151, 154
  proximity to, 56–57, 70
  political reform, 8
  see also climate
  westernised representations of, 10, 25, 64, 74, 85, 142, 156, 165
Islam, 47, 61, 63, 67, 106, 110, 136, 158, 161

Jacobinism, 23, 89, 107, 138, 158–159
Jeffrey, Francis, 156, 158, 162–164
Johnson, James, 100–101
Johnson, Richard, 70
Johnson, Samuel, 6, 65, 115
Jones, Anna Maria, 68

Jones, Sir William, 9, 22, 55, 56–86, 117, 121–122, 128, 140, 144–145, 146, 148, 151, 153, 165, 168
   'Hindu Hymns', 22, 70, 75–82
   Poems (1772), 60–67
   Sacontalá (1789), 10, 19, 57, 82–85
   theory of monoculturalism, 70–72, 78, 86
Juggernaut, 23–24, 119, 124, 126–128, 130, 135–139

Kalidasa, 10, 57, 82, 112
Kames, Henry Home (Lord), 14, 63
Kaye, Sir John, 93, 95, 96

Lewis, Matthew, 138
Lowth, Bishop Robert, 63, 143–145
Lyttelton, George (Lord), 109

Macaulay, Thomas Babington, 32, 35, 151
Mackenzie, Henry, 36–37
Madras, 8, 100
Marana, Giovanni Paulo, 109
Marshman, Joshua, 120, 121
Martyn, Henry, 24, 124–126, 129
Maturin, Charles, 135, 168
   Melmoth the Wanderer (1820), 135–139
Maurice, Thomas, 123–124, 136–137, 146
Mill, James, 6, 140–141, 142, 155
   History of British India (1817), 24, 140, 142, 149–151
Mill, John Stuart, 6, 149
Milton, John, 81, 126, 128, 129, 161
missionaries, 9, 21, 23, 24, 96, 117–121, 124, 128, 131, 133–134, 168
Montagu, Elizabeth, 67
Montesquieu, Charles de Secondat, Baron de, 88–91, 92, 98, 100, 109, 113, 115
Moor, Edward, 120
Moore, Thomas, 140, 142–143, 153, 157–158, 164, 165
   Lalla Rookh (1817), 24, 140, 142, 155–164
Mysore, 8, 99

Nandakumar, Raja, 28
nabobs, 7, 8, 11–12, 21, 23, 26, 34–36, 39, 52, 54, 88, 89, 102, 113, 115, 165
   see also Foote, *The Nabob*
Nehru, Jawaharlal, 58

Orientalism, 3–7, 9, 12, 19, 22, 25, 55, 56, 58–59, 68, 70, 75, 88, 105–108, 110–111, 121, 140, 142–143, 149, 153, 165
   Romantic Orientalism, 13–14, 142, 148–149, 167
   see also Said, Edward
Owenson, Sydney (Lady Morgan), 131, 136, 160
   Missionary, The (1811), 131–134

'Pasquin, Anthony', a.k.a John Williams, 31, 50
Peacock, Thomas Love, 6
Pitt, 'diamond', Thomas, 35
Pitt 'the elder', William, 35
Pitt 'the younger', William, 36

Radcliffe, Anne, 125, 138
Raynal, Abbé Guillaume Thomas François, 12
Richardson, Joseph, 52
Ryves, Elizabeth, 52

Said, Edward, 9, 57–58, 59, 74, 85, 126, 164
sati, 23, 99–100, 103–4, 108, 118, 120–121, 123, 134, 139
Sayers, James, 43, 52–53
Schlegel, Friedrich von, 147–148, 149
Schwab, Raymond, 13, 58, 148
Scott, Walter, 142
sensibility, 2, 3, 13, 20, 22–23, 43, 46, 86–90, 96–98, 101, 104, 106, 109, 112–16, 149, 166, 176
Serampore (Baptists), 76, 120, 124
Shakespeare, William, 66, 112
Shelley, Percy Bysshe (Lord), 7
Sheridan, Richard Brinsley, 27, 44, 50
Shikuh, Soleiman, 133
Sikhism, 118
Simeon, Charles, 124

slavery, 4, 10–11, 13, 91, 106, 108, 167
Smith, Adam, 30–31, 39, 51, 163, 165, 167
  Theory of Moral Sentiments (1759), 17–18
Southey, Robert, 7, 9, 109, 128–131, 137, 139, 140, 154, 159, 163–164
  Curse of Kehama, The (1810), 24, 109, 129–131, 140, 142–143, 154–156, 163
Spencer, Earl (formerly Viscount Althorp), 56, 69, 83, 144
Stuart, Charles 'Hindu', 146
Sultan, Tipu, 136
sympathy
  barriers to, 14, 15, 16–18, 42–43, 48, 51, 70, 92
  British subjects, for, 10, 106, 108
  colonial subjects, for, 9, 12–13, 23, 29, 34, 51, 54, 75–76, 79, 106–107, 111, 121
  evolution of, 2–3, 7, 14–16, 142
  interiority of, 62–63, 64, 84, 99
  literary criticism, in, 142, 153–155
  music and, 76–78, 83
  religion and, 115–116, 132–134, 139, 165
  Scottish Enlightenment, and, 2, 10, 14–15, 167
  slavery, for victims of, 10
  sympathetic revenge, 49–50
  threat to selfhood, 19
  'total' sympathy, 80–82, 85
sublime, the, 14, 22, 29–34, 48–51, 61, 67, 75, 80, 82, 85, 118, 123, 144–145

Tavernier, Jean-Baptiste, 91
Teignmouth, Lord (John Shore), 23, 56, 119, 121, 122
thagi, 118
Thomson, James, 104
Tickell, Richard, 52
Tod, James, 8
'Touchstone, Timothy', 11–12

Utilitarianism, 141–142

Vellore mutiny, 119
Volney, Constantin François de Chasseboeuf, comte de, 68
Voltaire (François-Marie Arouet), 61, 68, 157

Walpole, Horace, 14–15, 36, 67, 109
Ward, William, 120, 145
Wedgwood, Josiah, 10
Wilberforce, William, 11, 23, 119
Wilford, Francis, 146, 151
Wilkins, Charles, 10, 70, 118, 121, 125, 145
Wilks, Mark, 8, 156, 158
Wollstonecraft, Mary, 19–20, 100
Wordsworth, William, 63, 81, 151–152, 155